AN EX IN THE PUZZLE

A CROSSWORD PUZZLE COZY MYSTERY

LOUISE FOSTER

An Ex in the Puzzle; A Crossword Puzzle Cozy Mystery

DISCLAIMER:

Only a few of the clues from the chapters made it into either the crossword puzzle at the end of the book or the one on my web-site. So, readers still have the fun of solving the crossword puzzles on their own. Enjoy!

ACKNOWLEDGMENTS

There are so many people who have helped me make this book a reality:

Cindy Kirk and Chery Griffin, two of the first writers I met on my journey. Both of whom helped make me a better writer and helped make this book a reality.

My editor, Mary-Theresa Hussey, who kept me in line and my story on track.

Lee Hyat, who created my wonderful book covers.

Debbie Manber Kupfer, who used her skill and talent to create the crossword puzzles in this book and on my website.

Keith Jones for setting up my website.

Thank you all so much!! You made the journey much easier.

This book is dedicated to my family.
Thank you for believing in me, especially during the times
when I doubted
my dreams would ever come true.
I don't know where I would be without you.
I love you all.

I'M TRACY BELDEN

I'm Tracy Belden. Creating crossword puzzles is my passion, but it doesn't pay the rent. Being a part-time PI does.

My current case is about a missing woman. The chief suspect is her husband, my ex. It's only three days into the case. Early still, and there's no proof that she's dead or that my ex-husband killed her.

To be honest, I'm not that concerned with clearing his name.

What's important... is solving the puzzle.

1

14 Across; 9 Letters;
Clue: Not eager.
Answer: Reluctant

"Didja find the body?" Marcus, my eleven-year-old Korean foster son, thumped his backpack onto a kitchen chair without breaking eye contact. He walked over and planted himself between me and the coffee pot. He knew the danger. He just didn't care. He's a crime junkie.

He'd asked me the same question Monday through Wednesday. The three days I'd been on the case.

Tracy Rae Belden's my name. Five-nine. Short, straight brown hair. A moderately slim form that owes nothing to self-restraint. It's also no secret I hit thirty-five last week.

I wanted to tell my boy-child I wasn't looking for a body, especially not a possibly dead female. However, with the promise of coffee within sight, I ignored his ghoulish question. I pivoted around him and walked to the small kitchen of our loft apartment. Grabbing a mug, I poured myself a cup of ambrosia.

Stuck in a car for the past ten hours on an overnight stakeout, I had avoided drinking too much liquid, especially caffeine. Suffice it to say I considered it within my parental rights to drink my pumpkin flavored coffee before answering him. One sip of the scalding liquid sent a jolt racing through every nerve in my body and brought a smile to my lips.

"Speaking of bodies..." Mrs. Colchester, my seventy-plus landlady, looked up from cooking scrambled eggs long enough to wave my spatula at me. "I've something to say on that, ducks."

I inhaled the aroma of my coffee and tried not to listen.

Mrs. C's British accent was a perfect complement to her newly acquired air of an English ex-patriot. Her mop of white curls and a short, plump figure were the icing on the cake.

I wasn't sure how long the accent would last since it was all of four weeks old. Every time I asked about the change, she acted as though *I* were the crazy one.

Right after the accent made an appearance, she decided I needed a maid and announced she would fill the position. The woman has been letting herself into my apartment Monday through Friday for the past month. She never lifts a finger to clean, but neither do I, and it's my apartment.

Fortunately—or not—she also watches Marcus when I'm gone. I'd planned to ask a woman down the street. However, since Mrs. C was on the job, I decided to go with the flow and have her stay overnight.

The older woman continued speaking without

waiting for a response. "Me cousin works with a man who says he saw a woman's body in a gully by the new development, a mile or so from the estate. He agreed to talk with you."

"I don't want to talk to anyone about a body." I wanted to sit in my apartment and drink coffee until I stumbled to bed. "Have him call the tip line."

"I knew she was dead." Marcus slammed a bowl and a box of cereal on the table. "Her husband set a booby trap to kill her during the party so he'd have an alibi. Our science class is going to work out how today."

After making a mental note to do a background check on the science teacher, I turned to Mrs. C. Her announcement had jolted me awake faster than the caffeine. "Yesterday your theory was that she ran off."

"And I'm holding to it." Mrs. C stabbed the air with the spatula hard enough to send a chunk of egg flying across the kitchen like an angry bird with a death wish. "But it wouldn't hurt for you to talk to the man."

"T.R. will get the goods." Marcus dribbled milk on his shirt as he pointed a spoon at me. "I'll go with you."

I put my head in my hands and wondered if I'd survive the conversation much less the investigation. The fate of Mrs. Randolph McKiernan, the former Ms. Cassie Reed of Black Oaks, Kansas, has absorbed the entire city of Langsdale, Nevada, since the wealthy woman disappeared Saturday night.

She'd run upstairs during a gala she and her husband were hosting at their home and never came back. No one had seen or heard from her since. No ransom demands. No calls. Nada.

Her disappearance was like a mystery play had come to town. Was she dead? Had she gone hiking in the desert? Had she run off with a lover? Pick a theory. Everyone had one. Most included a trip to Las Vegas, a bright lure three hours south of Langsdale.

I imagine the woman in the South of France, living large with a huge chunk of her hubby's money. After a second, longer sip of coffee, I smacked my mug on the table. I only hope she cleaned him out.

Why do I care?

The missing woman is wifey-number-two.

I was wifey-number-one.

Fifteen years ago, with my usual impeccable sense of timing and luck, I divorced my deadbeat spouse eighteen months before a stock tip earned him a fortune. He has a mega-mansion on the outskirts of the city. I live in a downtown apartment and work three jobs.

After wifey-number-two went missing, a PI buddy I do research for asked if I'd help with surveillance. Since I'd just gotten my PI License, and stakeouts pay more than shuffling paper, I agreed. My second job, when I'm not watching ex-husbands whose second wives have disappeared, is mailing items sold via infomercials.

In whatever spare time I have left, I create crossword puzzles and sell them to several on-line sites. The pay barely keeps me in flavored coffee, but it's my first love and by far the most entertaining.

A rare moment of silence had me hoping that the body disposal debate had ended.

With a plate of scrambled eggs in hand, Mrs. C hustled to her usual chair at the kitchen table. Her ever-present pink slippers slapped a quick a rhythm on the tile.

Marcus eyed me from across the table. Undersized for eleven, he had golden skin and straight black hair that made his Korean ancestry a no-brainer. That was all anyone knew for sure. He had christened himself Marcus during years of surviving on the streets.

He'd caught my attention a little over three years ago when he tried to steal my wallet. Though I'd kept my money, the cheeky grin he tossed me when he got away sent hooks into my heart. Since I couldn't get him off my mind, I decided to track him down.

Several weeks later, I'd felt as if I'd hunted a wily jungle animal to its lair. The trail ended in the children's section of the local library. We bonded over books. Science Fiction. Suspense. Mysteries. Especially mysteries. Trixie Belden mysteries. She's a distant cousin of mine. At least, that's what I told Marcus.

We compared notes, discussed clues, and found plot flaws.

Since a hysterectomy due to borderline cancer cells a few years earlier had ended my chance of conceiving, I never expected to be a mother, but life surprised me. While I was weaseling my way under his defenses with my lame story of being related to a fictional teenage sleuth from the fifties, he snuck into my heart. Now I can't imagine my life without him.

The hoops involved in getting him into the system with me as his foster mom were annoying, vexing, irritating, and worth every second. My next goal is to adopt him, but bureaucracy is moving with its usual glacial speed. In the meantime, I count myself lucky to have him, even if he does drive me crazy.

Hoping for peace, I sat back and closed my eyes. Three quick hard knocks jerked me awake.

Marcus bolted across the floor and flung the door open before I could blink. "Hey, Rabi."

"Mornin', bro." Rabi dropped his bag by the wall.

Jack Rabi has picked up my packages for five years. A black man with skin so dry it looks almost ashen, he has slightly more meat on his tall frame than a cadaver. His shoulder-length black hair is always perfectly waved and glistens as if it's been oiled. Within a week of moving in, Marcus knew Rabi's entire life history, especially his twenty-two years in Special Ops.

The following week, Rabi began stopping by before Marcus left for school.

"T.R.'s got a lead on the McKiernan case." Marcus's excitement all but bounced off the walls. "A guy spotted the body. She and I are gonna check it out."

"I've told you I'm only watching the husband, not investigating a crime." I pushed away from the table. "And I never agreed to go body hunting."

"I'll grab the brew." Rabi snagged a mug from the cupboard, then stretched out a long arm and lifted the pot off the warming pad.

I sat back with a sigh. After the debate about body disposal, Rabi's quiet calm was a balm on my nerves. I flashed him a grateful smile and wrapped my hands around the fresh, hot cup.

"Marcus." I spoke in a sharp tone to grab my son's attention. "I do research. I'm only watching Randy McKiernan because Crawford is shorthanded."

The higher pay for surveillance was actually the bottom line, but I saw no need to bring up anything so crass as money.

Marcus shook his head at Rabi to make sure the man didn't buy my mundane explanation.

"Why doesn't your guy call the cops?" I asked Mrs. C,

hoping to put an end to this madness. "Have him phone the tip line they set up."

"The gent doesn't trust bobbies. He believes the calls will be traced." Mrs. C gave me a knowing wink. "Bit of a dustup years ago."

"We have to question him, T.R." A hint of desperation shadowed Marcus's dark eyes. He bumped his bowl, sloshing milk over the side. "If he doesn't call the cops, her body may never be found. Besides, the police might not follow up in time. They have thousands of tips."

A report of a corpse would certainly get the attention of the authorities. As to my boy's estimate on the volume of tipsters, his figure was only slightly exaggerated. It seemed wifey-number-two had made an appearance in every city from Seattle to Tijuana on her way to the South of France.

Marcus's midnight black eyes pleaded with me to accept Mrs. C's request. I had the impression my first case in the field meant more to him than merely a boy's idea of adventure, but a body in a gully? "The women disappeared from the second floor of her home. How could the murderer have gotten her body out of the house?"

"A hidden passage." Mrs. C sounded as if the answer was obvious. "Some of the mansions are built on silver mines. The gully originates at the base of the hill where the house sits."

I fought a laugh. "The place is a mansion, not a monastery from the Middle Ages."

My peripheral vision caught movement. I glanced at Rabi and found him nodding. "You, too?"

"Heard stories years ago," he admitted. "Old-timers talked about secret passages built during Prohibition."

I stifled a groan. Prohibition, mining, and ghosts

guarding buried treasure are a few pieces of the past that have been resurrected and built up to color the town's history. The city government will do anything to pull in outside money.

Langsdale is a resort town built on tourist dollars. In addition to casinos, there are hotels for every level of the spending public. Eclectic eateries with master chefs sit next to art galleries of every description and price bracket. With spas and mineral resorts, the town has built a reputation of being both sophisticated and artsy with a laid-back air.

A three-hour drive or a short plane ride to our local airport makes us far enough away from Vegas to be seen as a getaway. Corporate retreats are another mainstay of the local economy.

The city has developed a number of attractions. A food and wine festival, sponsored by the local wineries, has become an international draw. A jazz competition and a world-renowned golf course, designed for arid conditions, have managed to appeal to a new segment of tourists.

The resident population tops out at twenty-two thousand, but the mostly year-round stream of tourists pushes the usual total much higher.

Mrs. C gave a self-satisfied nod at Rabi's confirmation. "If the poor woman's body is in that gully, you'll have to move quickly to find it."

Marcus inched forward on his chair. "Why?"

"They're making way for a new development, aren't they?" Mrs. C said. "The cloudburst two days ago interrupted the construction company's schedule for clearing the site, but they're bound to be at it again, and soon. The rubble and sand that will be pushed into that gully will bury her body beyond recovery."

"If her body's there." I took another sip of coffee, absently noting the spicy flavor. My body and I both wanted to dismiss this nonsense and head to bed. I looked for flaws. "The police would have found the passageway by now."

"It's hidden," Mrs. C reminded me patiently. "They've been checking the grounds and investigating leads. Not that they won't find it eventually."

But not before tons of rock filled the gully. Though her words were carefully neutral, I heard her unspoken warning. Unfortunately, I found myself agreeing.

Marcus's expression had grown studious, as it did when he was unraveling a word problem in math, his favorite subject. "If the killer buried the body in a shallow grave, the cloudburst might have been enough to uncover it."

I met his gaze. "This story can't be true."

"Absolutely not." He agreed a tad too quickly, then he shrugged. "But Crawford's paying you to work the case. Wouldn't it be your duty to check it out?"

I gave him a mock glare. "Pulling the duty card is a low blow."

A triumphant grin creased his face. "You do it to me all the time."

"Fine," I said in an aggrieved tone. "First, I need to sleep. I'll meet the man this afternoon. If he's not a kook, I'll head out as soon as possible. This late in September, those hills get dark pretty early. I won't return by the time Annie drops you off after school. Mrs. C, can he stay with you?"

Annie was a high schooler on the next block. She took Marcus to and from school every day.

The older woman nodded. "Certainly."

Marcus's quick intake of breath held a note of alarm.

I looked into his wide eyes. "What?"

He scrunched up his face. "Annie called. She's not going to school today. She can't drop me off or pick me up."

"Why didn't you tell me sooner?"

Marcus bought time by chewing his soggy cereal far longer than necessary. His wide-eyed gaze would've done a Mississippi gambler proud. "We had to discuss the case. Rabi can drive me."

"We impose on him too much." Keeping my fifteen-year-old Buick running is an art form. As a result, Rabi's delivery truck has saved us more often than I can count.

"I don't mind." Rabi chuckled deep in his throat. "Marcus can ride shotgun."

Marcus hissed between his teeth as he mouthed an all but silent "Yes". Arriving at school escorted by the lean black man would only enhance Marcus's reign as king rat.

"Are you sure?" I knew Rabi enjoyed the company, but I still felt indebted. At his nod, I came up with a quick payment. "I'll make you cookies."

"T.R., don't." Marcus grimaced. "Last time we couldn't even save the cookie sheet."

Okay, so I'm no more Betty Crocker than I am a Merry Maid. That's why I stick to puzzles. Crossword. Jigsaw. Sudoku. You name it. I can solve it.

I glanced at the newspaper. I only buy it for the cross-word puzzle, a throwback to the years I worked them with my father. There was no point filling in even the first empty squares.

Well, maybe I could answer a few quick clues.

Marcus caught the direction of my gaze. His smirk had a know-it-all air. "I know what you're thinking."

My mock glare at his sing-song tone didn't faze him. It rarely did.

"You're telling yourself you'll only answer a couple of clues," he said. "But we all know that once you start a puzzle you can't stop until you have all the answers."

Silently admitting he was right, I tore my gaze away from my morning ritual. Crawford better appreciate my dedication. Maybe he'd give me hazard pay. With that in mind, I concentrated on my coffee. If this was going to be my last contact with civilization, I might as well enjoy it.

By the time I caught up on several hours of sleep, then traced the road into the hills, it would be late afternoon at best, and that was if I didn't get lost.

Did I mention directions aren't my forte either?

What's a six-word recipe for disaster?

Me in the wilderness after sundown.

2

---

25 Down; 4 Letters;
Clue: What a person ought to do.
Answer: Duty

E vening shadows had begun to lengthen by the time the car closed in on Nowhere Lane somewhere in the Nevada desert. Thankfully I wasn't alone. I also wasn't driving.

Eager to focus on something other than the quest, my gaze slid to where Kevin Tanner, my long-time best friend, sat behind the wheel. His cobalt blue eyes, framed by thick black hair, burned with excitement. At twenty-eight, with a body hardened by construction work, he's a natural for a muscleman calendar.

Lately, Kevin had made noises about taking our relationship to the next step. But, harboring my share of reservations, I'd kept matters firmly in the status quo.

The car hit another rock and I bounced off the ceiling. Drops of my chocolate raspberry coffee slopped over its lid. Cinching my seatbelt tighter, I flung the map aside. "This deer path isn't on any map. Are you sure you took the right turn?"

Kevin's eyes hardened to sapphires. Like most men, he doesn't take the whole 'you're lost' issue with good grace. Unlike most men, he has an unerring sense of direction. "I'm not the one who drove into the middle of a gang fight while trying to get their injured friend to a hospital."

"One little mistake." Some people are so touchy. Was it my fault he'd agreed to help me on an early job for Crawford? Or that my contact had just killed his partner? Admittedly, I may have pointed out a few incriminating details, but who knew he'd shoot Kevin? I retrieved the map. It didn't actually help, but holding it made me feel better. "You survived. Plus, the cops gave us an escort to the ER."

He shot me a withering look before turning his attention back to the path masquerading as a road. Normally law-abiding to a fault, speeding is his only outlet for breaking the law. "How anyone gets lost on the Vegas strip is beyond me. The place has more lights than Times Square."

"Yeah. Yeah. Yeah." I flapped my hand at him, then tried to figure out which squiggly line was us. The GPS had become hysterical after the first turn into the woods.

Kevin never listened to it anyway. He has the driving skills of a professional racer and the instincts of a homing pigeon. He couldn't get lost if he tried. He hadn't referred to the GPS or the written directions since we'd started.

I'd been poring over both, and I was still clueless. The

only way I know east is if I'm facing sunrise on a clear day. "I'm glad you called when you got off work early."

"The road buckled." Kevin looked at me with a suspicious glint in his eyes. "Lucky for you."

"They can't prove a thing." I raised my hands as a token of innocence. "But it worked out for me. Thanks for coming. I'm sure you could have found something better to do with your free time."

His brow wrinkled as if giving the idea serious thought. "Better than sleuthing with you in the desert? Nah, I love your little adventures."

I studied his handsome profile. "If that's true, you need to get out more, find drinking buddies, flirt with barmaids, and not spend all your time with Marcus and me. How are you ever going to have children of your own?"

Which we both knew wasn't going to happen with me. One more reason to keep him at arm's length.

"Blood relations are overrated." Kevin's expression melted from amused to serious. "I'd rather spend time with someone who feeds her landlady and shares coffee with her delivery guy. Not to mention taking an orphan off the street. All for no payoff. You amaze me, Belden."

The atmosphere was getting way too touchy feely for me. Fortunately, the rear tires chose that moment to swing off the road. I screamed like a four-year-old on a roller-coaster. By the time I got a death grip on my seatbelt, the car was on solid ground. I exhaled and wiped my brow. "I'd never have survived this trip on my own."

"You'd have been lost at the first turn." Kevin chuckled deep in his throat. When the car slewed sideways once again, he righted it instantly. "Tell me again why you didn't call the police when the guy laid this crazy story on you?"

Happy to focus on the case, I tried to pierce the gloom outside, but scraggly pines and steep, rocky outcrops created an ever-shifting pattern of shadows filled with dark shapes. "I'm not going to call the tip line with a secondhand story about a body. No one would believe such a crazy tale."

"Except other crazies." Kevin crested a hill and drove onto a stretch of road overshadowed by an occasional branch. "Which makes us perfect for the job."

"Once we prove this guy is a wacko, we can go home." After another turn, patterns of light played hide-and-seek in the underbrush. It was hard to tell what was solid. "I'm holding onto my South of France theory."

"You're only saying that because if she's dead and you didn't do it, odds are Randy's behind it."

I turned away from those gorgeous blue eyes that saw right through me. We'd woven through each other's lives for ten years, ever since a scam his con-artist family arranged had ended in murder. That was when he decided to end his career as a grifter. Closer than friends, we were all but family. As usual, his guess was spot on.

Though Randy's chronic gambling and allergy to work had ruined our marriage, he was my first love. I had left the hills of Kentucky with him.

"I can't believe he's a killer." I frowned as the rest of Kevin's words burned through my maudlin mood. "What do you mean if I didn't do it?"

He shrugged as if the matter were inconsequential. "Crawford called me right before I phoned you."

My sense of unease vaulted into the stratosphere. "Why call you? I'm the one who works for him."

A smooth stretch allowed Kevin to drive with only two fingers. A line of white rocks along the roadside reflected the golden glow of the dying sun. From Kevin's laid-back attitude, we might have been on Main Street. "Crawford thought it best you hear the news from me."

I eyed him impatiently. "And the news would be... what?"

"A few years ago, Randy added you as beneficiary on a million-dollar life insurance policy." Kevin delivered this bombshell in a smooth tone.

My mind froze; however, a quick shake set the marbles rolling again. "Wifey-number-two would be his beneficiary."

"Tracy Rae Belden is listed by name." Kevin cast me a quick sideways glance. "The police are planning to speak with you about it."

My mental marbles careened around randomly. I stared at a string of cottonwoods then took a gulp of coffee. "Even if she's dead, the insurance doesn't give me a motive to kill her. If I'd known about the money, I'd have offed him."

Kevin's lips curled up in a smug smile. "That attitude is why Crawford didn't want the cops to spring this on you."

I clicked my tongue. "I can lie as well as the next person."

His snort of disbelief was followed by a pitying look.

"Compared to you I may be an amateur, but most people aren't raised to be a con artist."

"We all have our talents." From his easy tone, no one would guess how much he hated scamming people. Since breaking with his family, he sometimes went too far the other way by being brutally honest.

However, that's another story. I now had my own problems. "Why would Randy name me as his beneficiary?"

"To set you up?"

I frowned in puzzlement.

"Get with it, Tracy." All hint of teasing disappeared. His eyes could have sparked flint and his voice held a touch of steel. "The police think you killed the current Mrs. M to ride the merry-go-round with Randy again or you plan to take them both out so wifey-number-two wouldn't contest your payoff."

A run-down Vegas trailer park danced in my mind. After Randy spent the last year of our marriage gambling away every penny I earned, I'd dreamed of killing him. "I almost boiled him away."

Kevin grimaced. "Not the cooking pot dream again. I heard that once and I still can't look at a bowl of stew."

"If I didn't murder him fifteen years ago, I'm not going to kill him now." I shook away the memories. "The police can't be taking this seriously."

A dying ray of sunlight lit Kevin's somber expression. "Consider it from their point of view. Wifey-number-two got mega-millions. What do you have?"

"I'm not missing."

"True," he admitted. "But cops are a suspicious lot, and you make a convenient suspect."

"I'd appreciate it if you don't write that on any bathroom walls." Hiding behind the quip bought me time to think. "What about Randy as a suspect?"

"He's already rich." Kevin's glance revealed the worry his glib tone had hidden. "You should have stayed behind. I can handle this alone."

I finally understood why he'd called me today, then

tried to insist on coming by himself. "You think it'll look bad if I discover the body?"

A muscle in his jaw jumped. "It won't look good."

"Relax." I forced a cheerful note into my voice. "She's not in the gully. She's in the South of France."

"You're right." He swept a hand through the air. "Mrs. Colchester's story was a set-up. I planned the whole thing so you and I could get lost in the woods. How's it working?"

He lowered his voice to a sexy purr and eyed me with a look that could have melted the icecaps.

Something inside of me moved toward him like steel toward a magnet. It's not like I don't like the guy. He's one of the best people I know.

However, I'm thirty-five, rapidly approaching cougar territory.

Nonetheless, I gave myself two seconds to get lost in those dazzling eyes before turning to face front. Not that I wasn't tempted. Not that I didn't love him –- as a friend.

Affairs fizzle. Lovers come and go. Friends like Kevin are rare. Why sacrifice our friendship for the elusive promise of true love?

"I'm a keeper, Belden. Someday you'll realize that."

Obviously, me side-stepping his advances hadn't destroyed his ego.

The car slowed to a stop.

I held in a sigh. I couldn't believe Kevin would push the subject now.

"My plan worked." A note of wonder echoed in his voice. "We're lost."

"We can't be. You're my wilderness warrior." I'd been too distracted to notice the rubble of dirt and uprooted trees blocking our path. "Where did that come from?"

"'Only God can make a tree.'" Despite the flippant response, Kevin's voice held a thread of worry.

Poor soul, he's probably never been lost. For me it's a common occurrence. I grabbed the map. I now had a motive for proving wifey-number-two wasn't laying in the bottom of a sandy ditch.

"The guy mentioned an old survey marker on one side of the road." Kevin peered into the shadowy trees as if he could pierce the failing light through sheer determination. "We didn't pass it."

I re-read the directions for the nth time, then leaned forward. Finally, my eyes found faint tracks leading under the barricade. I traced a stretch of bark to one side where clumps of dirt clung to vine-covered roots. "The developers must have bulldozed the trees when they leveled the area. The path is blocked with debris."

"There's the marker." Kevin pointed to an unnaturally square outline almost hidden in the underbrush. His shoulders relaxed. He turned off the motor and stepped outside.

I followed with flashlight in hand. The gloom made me grateful I'd taken it when Marcus pushed it on me.

Detectives need flashlights, he'd told me.

"The path continues for thirty yards." Kevin rounded the car. "Then we turn right and go around the bend."

The moment of truth closed in like a Venus flytrap. I wasn't ready. Unfortunately, there was nowhere else to go. I swung the flashlight from side to side. "Left? Or right?"

We went left to avoid the treacherous hole left by the roots. After enduring branches tearing my skin and pine needles grabbing my hair, I'd rather have scaled the Grand Canyon.

"Pfaugh." I pulled free of one last, clinging vine and

ran my fingers through my hair. A clump of leaves had hitched a ride, but I dumped them. I promised myself a hot bath as a reward for what I fervently hoped was a wild-goose chase.

Kevin crashed free right behind me. Blood dripped from a scratch on his cheek, and green streaks marred his shirt.

I pointed the flashlight at him. "Whose idea was this?"

"Don't talk to me." He brushed a small branch off his T-shirt then his mock irritation evaporated. "We have to make tracks before the sun goes down."

I turned the flashlight off to conserve the batteries. Enough light filtered through to see without it.

Ten minutes later the dirt path turned to gravel as it descended to what may have been a riverbed in prehistoric times. Pebbles, sticks, and tumbleweeds had built up in the lowest level of the gully. A cool breeze made me wish for a jacket. I rubbed my hands over the goosebumps on my arms.

"Stay here." Kevin's jacket enfolded me in a reassuring warmth. The weight settled around me as the familiar scent of his cologne teased my nostrils. His hands brushed my shoulders before he stepped away. "I'll check it out."

Shrugging into the jacket, I shook off the temptation to accept his chivalrous offer. "I got us into this. I'll see it through."

I steeled my nerves and walked forward, grateful for Kevin's presence. Gravel crunched beneath our feet. As we rounded the bend, the sun faded behind the hills. The dark clumps of reeds tossed by the wind looked black and eerie on the gravel.

My stomach tightened. I turned on the flashlight and swung it back and forth. Relief filled me every time a dark shape turned out to be a clump of leaves or a branch pointing at the night sky.

Kevin turned the corner and disappeared. I followed, stepping close to the edge of the gully. My light flashed on a pile of bigger sticks, but I saw nothing out of the ordinary.

Kevin searched farther ahead of me.

I glanced at him wordlessly.

He shook his head.

My shoulders unknotted. Maybe she *was* in France.

A soft trill sounded as the night wind wound through the scrub and the cactuses. As I rounded a bend too fast, my foot slipped on the overturned rocks and uneven ground. I quickly righted myself.

Up ahead, Kevin eyed a pile of boulders and sticks that had formed a slope next to an artificially flat plateau. Sand, the omnipresent face of the desert, had cascaded over the surface of the mound and worked its way through the crevices. Dark shadows indicated the gully lay immediately beyond the base of the mound.

I stepped onto a thick tree and tested the strength of the construction. It gave a little but held. I ventured farther out. A sour smell filled my nostrils. I swung the flashlight toward a bundle of grass caught in the roots.

The tunnel of light shivered as the dark knot turned into long strands of black curly hair. A loud gasp almost unstrung my taunt nerves. Then I realized I was making the noise.

Footsteps sounded behind me. A warm velvet brush of fingers sent a scream crawling up my throat until I recognized Kevin's touch. His strong hands and familiar warmth made it easier to lower the flashlight.

I told myself the strands were a wig or moss until I saw the bloated white fingers wrapped in the branches and a red silk jacket rippling in the wind.

Bile rose up my throat. I couldn't feel the flashlight. Then the sword of light tilted skyward.

I leaped off the log, only to lose my footing on the upturned earth. For a second, I teetered on the edge. Horror gripped me at the thought of sharing a makeshift grave with the corpse.

After fighting frantically to regain my balance, I bolted into the darkness.

3

_____

33 Across; 7 Letters;
Clue: Someone the police believe may be guilty of a crime
Answer: Suspect

S*he'd been dead since the party.*
That's what the cops and forensic people whispered.

I sat on the hood of my car in a wooded clearing and hugged my knees to my chest as I watched the crime scene team troop around. My Wednesday morning coffee klatch with Mrs. C, Rabi, and Marcus seemed a distant memory, but it had only been twelve hours ago, seven-thirty this morning.

Strobe lights on the cop cars painted the woods a lurid red and blue. The glow of floodlights added to the eerie atmosphere.

I shrugged off the morbid thoughts and concentrated on the cool air nipping my cheeks and rustling the leaves.

I love autumn. Spending the evening in the desert would have been fun—if not for the body and the homicide team.

Personally, I'd have rationalized tomorrow morning would have been soon enough to work the scene, but not them. They had procedures, and they followed them.

Dark of night. Blocked road. Sandy gully. Nothing was going to keep them from the dead body. Nobody got a break. And no one complained. Not even some muttering under their breath.

Okay, there was a little of that, but I was hungry, and tired, and I wanted to go home. I was only here because an eleven-year-old guilted me into coming. Now, look at me. At least I hadn't tossed my lunch. Though I did drop the flashlight. Seeing the pale skin half-buried...

I swallowed hard and decided to focus on something else. Like how lucky I was Kevin had come along. I snuggled deeper into his jacket, comforted by the familiar scent clinging to the leather. For a moment I let myself wonder which of us would be more surprised if I took him up on one of his dinner invitations.

A cold rush of wind on my neck drew me out of my fantasies. I eyed the dark trail, wondering if my bud had gotten lost. He'd offered to show the cops to the body and I hadn't seen him since.

"Okay. Sure." The sound of his voice and the crackle of twigs pulled my attention front and center.

I slid off the car, eager to escape. However, the warning look in Kevin's eyes sent worry dancing a jig up my spine.

Carol Brennan, the plainclothes detective beside him, stopped in front of me. She had ten years on me and exuded an aura of competence. "Ms. Belden, thank you for waiting."

Like I had a choice? My car was surrounded by cops and Kevin had the keys in his pocket. Not to mention it was pitch black and I didn't know where to find the highway.

I bit my tongue and smiled politely.

"I have some questions." She eyed me with a puzzled expression. "You were married to Mr. McKiernan. Correct?"

As if she didn't know.

"I divorced him fifteen years ago." Almost half-a-life-time. I tried to imbue my tone with the right measure of indifference.

A frown marred her forehead. "You two must have split right before he made his fortune. Tough break. I'd have been pretty upset."

Kevin's 'leaving me behind' idea suddenly seemed like the right decision. But, not to panic, she had to cover the basics. After all, I did know Randy. If I were in her shoes, I'd be suspicious of me. I took a deep breath and jumped into the fray. "It was a long time ago. I have my own life now."

"Surely you contacted him when he moved to Langsdale? What? Nine years ago?" she prompted. "An e-mail? A text? Maybe a call for old time's sake?"

"Not even a postcard," I assured her. "I read in the papers he moved here from Vegas due to a real estate investment, but, for me, he's ancient history."

"I know how exes can be." She scratched a line in her notepad. "Tell me about this anonymous tip."

I'd told her when she arrived. However, the police like to get the facts confirmed so I went over it again.

A new frown marred her forehead. "You gave up your entire afternoon to check out a tip from someone you'd never met?"

Her skeptical tone spiked my blood pressure again, but I hadn't spent middle school talking my way out of detention for nothing. I plastered on a sincere expression.

"I met the man this morning." I reminded her. "He was certain of his facts, but he didn't intend to follow up. The private investigator I work for is paid to investigate this case, so here I am."

Her expression changed to one of concern. "I hope this stranger won't be hard to find. So many of these anonymous calls turn out to come from people responsible for the crime."

"Good thing this guy's the real deal," I said. "You have his name and number. He'll confirm the story."

I hoped. The guy had been as wary of becoming involved as Mrs. C had warned. If he decided to make himself scarce, it wouldn't help my cause.

"Does this man know your ex-husband?"

I shrugged. "I couldn't say. I haven't talked to Randy in over fifteen years and this morning was the first I ever spoke with the other man."

"Would you have any objections to my checking your phone records?" Brennan asked.

I swallowed the panic inching up my throat. What was my problem? I'd lied my way out of the principal's office in high school over a broken state basketball trophy, and I was guilty then. This time I was innocent.

Besides, I was pretty sure they didn't need my permission to dig into my affairs. "You're welcome to look at my phone calls."

She waved a hand of dismissal. "It's standard procedure."

I acted as if I believed her, as if my gut wasn't tied up in knots. Good thing I was innocent of everything except coming on a body-hunting expedition.

Brennan's hawk-like gaze made the police technicians around us fade into the background. "Why didn't you call the police and report this information?"

Good question. Too bad my reasons included being browbeaten by an eleven-year-old Sherlock Holmes wannabe.

"The story was secondhand. It sounded too farfetched to take seriously." Which was true. I met Brennan's eyes with a straightforward gaze. "The media says the police are flooded with sightings of Randy's wife both dead and alive. Since Crawford's paying me to work the case, I figured the least I could do was confirm this sighting was fraudulent."

And look where doing the least I could do had landed me.

That explanation sounded lame even to me. Brennan's disbelieving gaze did nothing to build my confidence. Still, I kept my expression neutral and struggled to look honest.

She studied me for a long moment. "So, you drove into the woods and conveniently walked to the exact location of the body."

Okay. I did not like the way this conversation was going. For one thing, driving through these woods and trudging around in the dark was hardly what I'd call convenient. "The man gave very clear directions. He was obviously right. The body was in the gully."

A glimmer of emotion sparked in her eyes. However,

she refused to concede even one minor point. "Lucky coincidence your boyfriend was able to accompany you, but I'm sure Mr. Tanner would do anything for you."

Like kill wifey-number-two?

"Absolutely not." The insinuation in her tone kicked my protective instincts into high gear. I didn't need the detective's look of satisfaction or Kevin rolling his eyes to know I'd made a mistake.

I wanted to tell him I was a good liar. It was the truth that was making me stumble.

"What I mean is Kevin and I aren't dating." My babbling only reinforced what I already knew—my world would be a better place if my brain was quicker than my mouth. My earlier speculations about Kevin and my relationship only added to my foot-in-mouth problem. "He isn't my boyfriend."

Stop. Talking.

I finally wrested back control of my lips and clamped my jaw shut.

Brennan slapped her notebook shut. Her eyes studied the oversize leather jacket hanging on me then she shot a sideways glance to Kevin. "You two are just friends?"

In today's parlance, 'just friends' has come to mean: yes, we're having a relationship and don't want to admit it.

I stomped on the spike of irritation at the way her gaze lingered on Kevin's physique. Realizing the damage I'd done, I took a moment to decide my best response. This time I didn't have to fake the derision in my attitude. "I'm thirty-five. Kevin is twenty-eight. I've known him since he was a teenager. I don't look at him in a romantic light. I never have."

Which was kind of, mostly true.

Kevin's expression seemed to freeze, but the explanation was the best I could do considering the hole I'd already dug.

Brennan scraped her nail across her notebook with a sound reminiscent of nails on a chalkboard. "You're not dating anyone right now?"

Sure, rub it in. I fisted my hands on my hips. "I work three jobs and I have an eleven-year-old son. I have no time for dating."

"Just like you have no time to see your ex on the side?" she asked again.

Don't. Panic. Whatever happens, don't panic.

I shifted my gaze. "Absolutely not."

"Hmmm." The gust of wind that swept dust and leaves into the air didn't interfere with her unblinking stare. "If you haven't spoken in over fifteen years, why did Mr. McKiernan name you as a beneficiary on a million-dollar life insurance policy?"

I forced myself not to look at Kevin. Should I act surprised? Should I admit I knew? I decided to sidestep the issue with a dose of honesty. "The man didn't appreciate me when we were married. I have no idea why he'd consider leaving me anything."

"You and the dead woman were co-beneficiaries." The detective's gaze never wavered. "If Mr. McKiernan dies now, the money will be yours."

Not if I'm convicted of killing him. Or possibly her, I wasn't sure about that bit of legal trivia.

The detective should make up her mind. Did she suspect I was having an affair with Randy or planning to kill him? Either way, her chilly attitude turned the cool air arctic.

Maybe I should have copped to dating Kevin. That might have put Randy out of the picture.

On another day I might have appreciated her interrogation technique more. As it was, I kept my gaze locked on her and resisted the urge to look at Kevin. The last thing I wanted was to give this sharp-eyed cop another reason to tie him into this mess.

A light gleamed in Brennan's eyes. "Perhaps your ex-husband called you and you've forgotten? After all, you two grew up in Kentucky together before you ran away to Nevada to get married."

So, Randy and I got lonely and decided to off wifey-number-two? If that were true, did she honestly think we'd be stupid enough to put my name on his policy?

Actually, Randy was that dumb, but I certainly wouldn't have agreed.

Fear finally slapped my survival instincts out of hibernation. I had to get this woman off my scent.

My tired shrug was only partly faked. "My ties to Randy McKiernan ended a long time ago. My only involvement in this case is due to my job with Crawford Investigations. There's not much more I can tell you."

Or that I will tell you.

Crawford, my PI boss, an ex-cop, and another long-time friend, has said more than once that talking to the police is a person's biggest mistake. Finally alert to my danger, I adopted a zipped lip as my best defense.

Her iron gaze seemed to demand a confession. Goosebumps crept up my arms under Kevin's leather jacket.

All this and I wasn't even guilty.

Just when I was certain she'd drag us downtown, she held out her card. "You and Mr. Tanner will need to come to the station tomorrow and give a full report. We can talk more then."

I tried not to look too relieved. This close to being cut loose, I had no intention of giving her an opening.

"I can be there any time." I looked at Kevin with a raised brow.

He shrugged. "Morning's best for me. The construction site will still be closed."

"We'll be there first thing tomorrow." When she turned away, I grabbed Kevin's arm and headed in the other direction. "Let's get out of here before she gets out her handcuffs."

"I'm with you." Relief filled his voice. A minute later he executed a perfect three-point turn and headed toward the highway.

"I've never been so glad to leave the desert in my life." I popped on the heater and relaxed into the seat. "Even the ride is smoother."

Kevin turned off the deer path then onto a gravel road.

Though civilization beckoned, I turned around in my seat. Part of me expected to see a cop car on our bumper. Fortunately, the red strobe lights were already fading. I swiveled to face the front.

The specter of the police lurked over my shoulder. I feared they would be a constant presence until wifey-number-two's murder was solved.

4

---

17 Down; 8 Letters;
Clue: What distinguishes a person.
Answer: Identity

A s Kevin drove the Buick toward Langsdale at a steady purr, a wave of light-headedness made the world tilt and spin. My luncheon bagel had evidently evaporated.

Kevin nudged my shoulder. "Don't faint now. Fun's over. What say we stop at that old diner on the edge of town?"

"Mulligan's." My voice had an odd breathiness to it. The retro fifties diner had been a local favorite for years. A Cheese Frenchee with fries sounded like heaven. For anyone unfamiliar with that local treat, make a cheese sandwich, bread it, then deep fry it.

An hour later I licked a scoop of chocolate shake off my spoon. I'd have to make every bite last. The frosty metal container at the edge of the table was empty. The Cheese Frenchee and most of the fries were long gone.

"Where did you wander off to after the cops came?" I watched Kevin snag one of my fries. "I never thought you a crime scene groupie."

"Thanks for your faith." He munched his ill-gotten gain. "I recognized a couple of cops from the Dredge. I figured I'd do my part for your sleuthing biz."

The Dredge is a hole-in-the-wall tucked into a downtown alley. Free coffee for anyone with a badge makes it a regular stop for Langsdale's finest.

My saner half told me to stay out of it. As usual, my saner half lost. "What did they say?"

Kevin glanced around, but other than a family in the opposite corner and a couple at the counter, the diner was empty. He spoke in a low voice. "Based on the manner of death and the fact that the body was moved, definitely murder."

I hung on his every word while a bit of ice cream melted on my tongue. A mental image of the body made me swallow hard to keep my shake down. "Murder? They're certain?"

The waitress sauntered up and handed Kevin the bill as if I weren't present.

Kevin pushed the bill to me. He waited until she was out of earshot before he continued. "The pressure is on for a quick arrest. Especially, since they have a suspect with a motive."

"Don't joke." I glanced at the bill and calculated what I owed. "Brennan looked ready to arrest me tonight."

Kevin pulled out his wallet. "How much?"

I tallied his meal and added a tip. Cooking, cleaning, and finding my way without GPS might be beyond me, but numbers are my friends. I've rarely met a phone number I can't remember and there are few calculations I can't work off the top of my head.

Divvying up the bill didn't stop my brain from puzzling over the case. "Maybe it wasn't Randy. Maybe wifey-number-two discovered a burglar."

Kevin left the money, and we started toward the door. "How could a burglar hide the body so quickly?"

"Good question." Outside, I barely felt the dry breeze wash over my cheeks. The Buick's windshield reflected the hot pink neon sign. Leaning across the top of the car, I pointed at Kevin. "The burglar could have acquired a blueprint of the house in advance."

Kevin tapped the car. "Get in, Sherlock."

"It's not like I care," I told him after I slammed the door. "I just want to get the facts straight."

"Of course," he said in a placating tone.

I ignored him. Randy and wifey-number-two were clues in a puzzle. The compulsion to find some answers and start filling in the blanks pulled at me.

Kevin raised a brow. "You think Randy is capable of arranging his wife's death?"

"I can't eliminate him."

"Too bad for Randy," he said without a trace of regret. "A rich man won't garner a lot of sympathy from a jury."

"He's a gambler as well as a charmer. He might have seen murder-for-hire as another scheme." I eyed Kevin's profile. "You know the type."

Kevin snorted. "Don't remind me."

Thanks to his past, my bud has a working knowledge of every scam on the planet. But, unlike my ex, I have no doubt of Kevin's morals.

"You staying on the job?" My buddy, always eager to forget his past, shifted the conversation to me.

"The surveillance money is paying for Marcus's baseball equipment, not to mention next month's grocery bill. But it all depends on what Crawford wants. If he's still on the case, I will be, too." I chewed my lip while weighing my options. "But I don't want to give Marcus a reason to see this case as his personal murder investigation."

Kevin's stern expression crumbled with an evil chuckle. "Not to mention his seventy-plus sidekick."

I groaned. "What is it about old people and children that make them soulmates? Sometimes I wonder which of those two is the adult."

Kevin raised a brow. "You're talking about a woman who wore bedroom slippers to the bank to ask for a loan."

Despite my weariness, his deadpan delivery made me smile. His worry was also gaining traction against my determination.

"You're right." I exhaled through my teeth. "If Brennan doesn't arrest me during the interrogation tomorrow, I'll quit on Monday."

"Wow." Kevin shot me an overdone look of wide-eyed astonishment. "The mom gene wins out. I'm impressed."

"I guess I have to grow up eventually." I held up a hand. "But not until Monday."

BRENNAN DIDN'T jail me Thursday morning, but it was a near thing. Halfway through the session, I was ready to arrest me. By Friday night, I knew quitting was the right decision. I'd parried countless requests for inside info from my resident boy detective. I only wondered if I was too late to stop my son from going all Sherlock Holmes on the case.

My only consolation was that if the cops were half as dedicated as my son, they'd have the killer inside a week. I only hoped they arrested someone besides me.

Fortunately, Friday night was game night, a welcome diversion from bodies and investigations. I'd told Crawford I didn't do weekends. I needed time with Marcus and, no matter how much the boy begged, I refused to bring him on stakeout. Instead of watching Randy, I was watching popcorn pop in the microwave.

"Don't burn it." Marcus's yell showed his usual faith in my culinary skills.

When the buzzer sounded, I grabbed the bag and pulled the corners in opposite directions. The sweet aroma of warm butter tickled my nostrils. A childhood memory of watching movies with my parents and siblings brought a smile to my face.

I emptied the bag into a bowl and carried it to the dining room table where Marcus and the others waited.

"Finally." The boy snatched a handful of hot kernels.

I sipped my coffee as Mrs. C turned the Scrabble tiles face down. Marcus and Kevin sat on the one side of the table. Rabi and Mrs. C faced each other from opposite ends.

Marcus cast a sideways glance at Rabi then smiled at me with a triumphant gleam in his eyes. Despite a regular show of reluctance the man always let Marcus convince him to attend game night.

I picked out my letter tiles, determined to forget about the McKiernan case.

"The police confirmed the identification of Cassie Reed today," Kevin said.

I studied my tiles, only half-listening. "Is that the little girl who disappeared earlier this week?"

Marcus smacked his forehead. "I can't believe you said that."

"What?"

"That girl was found unhurt yesterday," Kevin said. "Cassie Reed is the maiden name of Cassandra McKiernan. Otherwise known as wifey-number-two."

So much for avoiding the topic. I'd have words with that man later. Unfortunately, the comment brought back the very image I'd been trying to forget. A half-buried body flashed before my mind's eye. To distract myself, I tossed a handful of popcorn in my mouth. "Oh, that Cassie."

The Cassie who had run up the staircase to get a ring her husband had bought her. A week ago her black hair would have been curled and arranged for her big evening. It would have bounced as she ran up the steps, yelling for everyone to wait, she'd be a minute...

But she never returned.

The whisper of her name had brought her to life. Despite my efforts to keep my distance, I could no longer dismiss her as a statistic.

My gaze flicked to Rabi, who studied me with eyes so dark they looked black. Marcus and Kevin watched me, curiosity on one face, sympathy on the other. I swallowed, but the popcorn remained stuck.

"She didn't deserve to die like that." My voice squeaked. I reached for my mug, gratefully wrapping my fingers around its solid warmth. A long sip sent hot coffee to loosen my throat. "I wonder if they've contacted her family."

I clenched my jaw a second too late to stop the words. My maudlin mood had sucked me into the conversation.

"The latest update says Randy broke down when he identified her body," Marcus reported. "That's a sign of a guilty conscience."

Mrs. C set down her cup of tea and took one kernel of popcorn. "She was buried in the sand for three days, luv."

"Just a formality." Rabi's low voice, scratchy from lack of use, pulled everyone's attention. "Guy I know picks up mail at the Medical Examiner's office. Under state law, they need dental records to confirm her identity. They contacted her hometown dentist in Kansas."

Kevin studied his letter tiles with an intense expression. "A cop at the Dredge said her Langsdale dentist couldn't find her file. The cops didn't want to bother Randy, so they traced Cassie Reed's hometown dentist in Kansas and asked for her dental x-rays. Then her Langsdale dentist finally sent the films over this morning. Now they have two sets."

"They don't match." I'd overheard Crawford utter that phrase during a phone call this afternoon. A thunderbolt of amazement struck me dumb as I realized for the first time what the context of his words must have been.

Stunned silence greeted my announcement.

Kevin fixed his gaze on me. "Where did you hear that?"

I stared at the Scrabble board, which so far didn't show a single tile. "In Crawford's office today. He got a call from Detective Brennan."

"Why didn't you tell us?" Marcus leaned over the table, shoving the board in his excitement.

"I just realized what he was talking about." I leaped to my defense. "He didn't act like the call was anything special so I waited. He listened for a minute then said, 'The x-rays don't match?' in this shocked voice. When he looked up and saw me, he waved me out."

"Maybe one office sent the wrong x-ray." Mrs. C's matter-of-fact tone calmed me.

Perhaps it was that simple.

"The police would've checked." Growing up with scam artists had exposed Kevin to police procedure at an early age. "They'd make sure before admitting to a problem on a high-profile case."

"Why would the detective call Crawford?" Rabi asked.

Good question. I wish I had an answer. I shook my head.

"Old times sake?" Mrs. C offered.

"He acted dumbstruck." I remembered the way he'd slumped in his chair, as if he'd been hit with a body blow. "Why does he care about this case?"

No one ventured a response to my rhetorical question. They knew less about Crawford's reasons than I did.

"I wonder which set doesn't match." Mrs. C met our gazes with a calm expression and held up a tile. "Am I first?"

"Go ahead." Despite my best intentions, the murder had me in a stranglehold. "The x-rays in town would have to match the body."

"We didn't draw for turns." Marcus glared at the older woman. "I should get to go first. I'm the youngest."

"You try that every week." Mrs. C shot a narrowed gaze at him. "I'm the oldest. I should go first."

"Last week you said Rabi was oldest," Marcus pointed out.

That caught my attention. Rabi was still in the work-force. Mrs. C had retired long ago.

The older woman drew herself up. "I said he *might* be older."

I smothered a chuckle and grabbed the box of tiles. We obviously weren't going to get anywhere until we started the game. I held up box. "For once, we'll do it by the rules. Everybody grab a tile."

Rabi got to go first.

"The x-rays in town have to match the victim," I repeated.

Rabi nodded as he laid out a word using the center square.

Silence reigned as I captured the score.

My gaze drifted to Marcus who'd been amazingly silent the past minutes. His eyes held a curious glint.

"That can only mean one thing." Kevin uttered the words in a steady voice. "The real Cassie Reed, the one from Kansas, is dead."

No one spoke. He had to be right. Wifey-number-two had lived in Langsdale for most of ten years. Two people can't share the same identity for that long.

Marcus picked up some tiles from his stand and looked up to meet my gaze. "I wonder if Randy knew about the switch."

The comment sent me reeling. I stared at my son's black hair and golden skin as he made his play. My gut reaction was denial. Randy *must* have believed the woman he married was the real Cassie. He'd met her not long after we split up.

Kevin eyed me with a quizzical gaze. The others were staring as well.

I'd missed something. I hate when that happens.

"Marcus's score," Kevin said.

My son pointed at the pad. "You didn't put it down. I got a triple letter with a Q."

I started guiltily and checked the board. Time to be a mom. "Quietly. Good job."

Marcus preened. In an instant, his expression changed. "You think he knew?"

The boy's death grip on a goal reminded me of me. "I don't know. The identity switch could have happened before they met."

"She had time to set it up," Marcus said. "She was older than he was."

"Really?" A shocked note ran through Mrs. C's response.

Marcus nodded. "When they met she was dancing in a floor show at some casino."

I'd heard it was a stripper club, but I didn't want to look tacky by saying so. Besides, I might have to explain the difference, and I didn't want to go there either.

"He was twenty-four. She was twenty-seven," Marcus continued, happy to show off his knowledge.

"Kevin, it's your turn." Mrs. C's gentle reminder spurred him to check his tiles, but the woman wasn't done. "Maybe she was in witness protection and the mob finally tracked her down."

The idea of a gangland hit had her voice pulsing with excitement.

"This doesn't have any earmarks of an execution." I was trying to get a handle on a murder, and she was writing crime fiction. "Besides, witness protection would create a brand new identity."

Mrs. C's expression fell. "That can't be true in this case. The dead woman was using the name of a real person. After all, the Cassie from Kansas had dental records."

She was right. The real Cassie had to have left her hometown as an adult or a teenager for x-rays to be on file. I wondered when she had crossed paths with the wifey-number-two.

And if the real Cassie Reed was dead, how had she died?

5

3 Down; 7 Letters;
Clue: A gathering for someone who has died.
Answer: Funeral

Nine o'clock on Saturday morning had already brought a re-hash of wifey-number-two's murder investigation. I blamed myself for stoking the fires last night around the Scrabble board.

Marcus scooped a bite of eggs into his mouth. "The problem is nailing his motive."

No need to ask who. Randy McKiernan, otherwise known as The Suspect, was the only topic of note in our house. And only one crime had been committed in the entire city.

Marcus's steely-eyed gaze drew me out of my reverie. No doubt, he was waiting for me to crack and discuss Randy's motive for murder. I had no illusion that remaining silent would end the conversation. He could give Brennan lessons in interrogation.

"There's no evidence she was cheating on him. He didn't have life insurance on her," the boy-child explained as if I hadn't heard this before. He pointed his fork at me. "If you were investigating, what would you look at next?"

"Opportunity." I clapped my mouth shut one second too late. He'd sucked me in. For once I wished Mrs. C was around to distract my miniature Sam Spade.

"Randy was downstairs with his guests." Marcus pounced on my response. "There's no proof he knew about the secret passage."

"Maybe he's innocent." I decided to play along, for the heck of it. "The latest statement from the police said they don't consider Randy a suspect."

"They have to say that. He's rich." A cynic to the core, my boy. "If he were a bum, he'd be in jail by now."

Being a cynic myself, I had to stop from nodding. Randy's donations to the mayor's last election undoubtedly eased the police pressure. However, public statements aside, Randy was the main person of interest, and he would be until rock-hard evidence proved him innocent.

That was the rule book according to Crawford. Cops start with the victim's inner circle then work their way out —spouse, lover, friends, co-workers. It's a known fact that people closest to a murder victim are most likely to kill them.

Gives me a warm, cozy feeling just thinking about it.

So, even facing a total lack of means, motive, and opportunity, the Langsdale police were playing the odds.

I could only hope Randy would pull out in front and leave me in the backfield.

"Are you still watching him?" Marcus asked.

"Where do you think I've been going every night this week?"

"Just checking my facts." Giving a bad imitation of Bogart, Marcus eyed me with an inscrutable gaze. "Who are you working for?"

"You know that as well—Crawford." I couldn't keep a trace of impatience from my tone.

"Who hired him?"

Good question. One for which I had no answer. When I'd asked my boss, I'd gotten the run-around. I'd questioned the other investigators, but no one knew. I'd even sounded out the bookkeeper. Turned out no money was coming in for this case.

No good-faith deposit. No cash up-front. Nothing.

Which sounded like Crawford might be footing the bill, except he didn't know Randy or the victim. Besides, my boss wouldn't investigate a jaywalker without cash in hand. Although, why would anyone pay Crawford for round-the-clock surveillance when the cops had their resources concentrated on the high-profile case?

Those questions puzzled me almost as much as the murder.

"I don't know who hired Crawford," I admitted. "I'm not sure he's getting paid."

Marcus set his glass of orange juice down with a thump. "Then why do it?"

I shrugged. "Not a clue. But he's paying me."

Raps on the door brought an end to the question and answer period. With relief, I pushed my chair away from the table. "Kevin's here."

Marcus headed for the door. Lunch with Kevin was the highlight of the boy's Saturday. Today held the added attraction of his soccer game.

I swept crumbs off the table and looked forward to hours of silence. My Saturday ritual included catching up on sleep, taking time for myself, or mailing the packages that paid my rent.

Depositing plates and cups in the sink, I didn't pay much attention until the words "Belden residence" floated my way. Frowning, I turned and saw Marcus standing stock still in front of the door. Eyes wide and expression frozen, he nodded slightly.

I started over. Being on the second floor of a three-unit apartment building, we don't get many visitors we don't know, and I was in no mood for a traveling preacher. I was just past the kitchen counter when the visitor spoke again.

"May I come in?"

My heart stilled. So did my feet.

Marcus slid a glance in my direction, then stepped away.

A second later Randy McKiernan rounded the door. His beer-gut from the trailer had been replaced by a hardened physique reminiscent of his days as captain of the football team. His tan looked better in person than it had through binoculars.

"Hi, Tracy." Straight blond hair and a square jaw rounded out an all-American profile. Kevin's family would've loved Randy. His voice oozed sincerity and his salesman's smile still extended to his brown eyes.

"Randy." I knew I should say more but I'd forgotten how to talk. Just as well since my mind was a total blank.

The familiar thud of Kevin's footsteps raced up the stairs. Relief filled me.

"Can't wait, huh? You have to stand with the door open?" Kevin strode in like a warm ocean breeze and put his arm across Marcus's shoulders. He stopped at the sight of Randy.

I locked onto his familiar presence like an anchor.

"Kevin, this is..." I searched for a name.

Randy squared his shoulders and stuck out his hand. "Randolph McKiernan."

"Kevin Tanner." His expression turned somber as he held out his hand. "Sorry about your wife."

I envied Kevin's aplomb.

"Thanks." Their gazes met then instantly locked in that subtle testosterone fueled 'size-up-the-other-guy' game men seem compelled to play. Their handshake tightened. After a few seconds, their grips relaxed.

I rolled my eyes and searched for a way to convince Randy to leave with Marcus and Kevin. Before that could happen, my mouth took over. "Marcus, don't forget your gear."

I snagged his gym bag on my way to the door.

"And this is?" Randy asked.

"I don't know where my head is." I brushed Marcus's hair and smiled. "This is Marcus Kwan Belden."

I automatically gave his preferred name. According to the courts, he's a loaner, but in every way that matters, we're family.

A glimmer of surprise sparked in Randy's gaze, but he held out his hand. "Nice to meet you."

Marcus shook his hand politely. "You too, Mr. McKiernan."

I preened at the visible proof that the social niceties I'd drilled into Marcus had taken root.

"Time to go, dude." Kevin nudged Marcus toward the door. "Or you'll be late."

Marcus's eyes narrowed.

I could see his brain searching for a reason to stay.

"Here's your stuff." I pushed his gym bag into his arms. "Where are you two going for lunch?"

"We haven't decided." Marcus got the words out before Kevin could speak. Since lunch was the main reason for the outing, the decision could take all morning. "We might come straight home."

Kevin's eyes met mine with a knowing glint.

"Okay," I said casually. I closed the door behind them. Unfortunately, when I turned, Randy remained. I fought to mask my disappointment as I gestured toward the kitchen. "Would you like some coffee?"

"Sure." Randy smiled. "It's the one thing you've never burned."

I ignored the dig and concentrated on a noise outside the door. I had a mental image of Kevin prying Marcus away from the keyhole and dragging him bodily down the stairs. Hopefully, the boy hadn't left claw marks in the wood.

Randy walked over to the table and sat opposite my chair. "Been to Kentucky lately?"

I shrugged as I got a mug from the cupboard. "I went home last year for my sister's wedding. Her third."

"We danced together at her first one," Randy said with a smile. "Remember?"

Unwilling to walk down memory lane, I ignored the comment and set a cup in front of him. "My brother went into business with Dad at the feed store. They're talking about combining some of their acres."

"Be a big help to your parents," Randy said. "Do they still have horses?"

"They'll be in their graves before they stop striving for the perfect saddle horse," I said with a smile.

Randy chuckled. Our sacrilegious boredom with horseflesh was one of the things that had bound us together in our teens.

"What's the flavor of the month?" he asked lightly, glancing around the apartment. "Smells good."

"Pumpkin Spice." I poured two cups and set the pot on the warmer. "What kind of creamer do you want?"

"What do you recommend?"

"Vanilla-hazelnut."

His smile had a nostalgic air. "I'd never second-guess the expert."

The sweet scent filled the air as we sipped our drinks.

A slight smile touched his lips as he set his cup down. "You always did brew the best."

My lips curled, but my mind raced. Did he know that I was watching him? That I'd found his wife's body? And what was my ex-husband doing parked in my kitchen a week after his second wife's murder?

Our eyes met. After a moment, his gaze slid to one side then to me then away. "Delicious, as always."

"Thanks." The word came out clear and casual. One point for me, grace under pressure. I didn't even know I had an automatic pilot and here it was kicking in when I needed it.

The respite gave me time to wonder why Randy wouldn't meet my eyes. I clamped my lips together and refused to ask.

If Brennan found out about his visit, I'd have more questions to answer. As the thought formed, my heart sank. Crawford's crew would have followed Randy to my doorstep.

Maybe if I didn't talk, Randy would drink his coffee and leave. I took a sip and let the flavors linger on my tongue. I mentally cataloged my shipping deadlines for the day, then stacked my orders against the supplies in stock. I was in mid-list when my gaze fell on Randy again.

He settled both elbows on the table. His hands surrounded his cup. "Wondering what I'm doing here?"

"The thought crossed my mind," I admitted.

"I heard that you found the..." he stopped and cleared his throat, "the bo... body."

So, he did know. Would the police have told him that wifey-number-two dental x-rays didn't match the real Cassie Reed's x-rays?

"I'm sorry for your loss." When my traitorous hand moved toward his, I pulled it away.

Even in his thirties he had that little-boy-lost aura that made most women want to clasp him to their breast.

"Ever since..." He cleared his throat again. "Ever since she disappeared, I told myself to expect the worst."

Maybe he just needed to talk to someone who wasn't the police or the press. Although surely he had friends.

His eyes glistened. "The best I could hope for was she'd been kidnaped or had run away. They both seemed impossible, but at least she'd be alive."

That could only come from a man in love. The empty expression in his eyes undermined my cynicism.

He rubbed a hand across his eyes and wiped away tears on his lashes. Taking a deep breath, he collected himself. "The police think she might have disturbed a burglar."

As long as the robber knew where the passage was so he could dump her body.

I nodded as though Kevin and I hadn't dismissed the possibility the other night. "Did she keep jewelry in the house? Do you have a safe?"

"You sound like the police." His jaw tightened. "Is her murder just another puzzle for you?"

I felt my face stiffen. If Randy didn't want questions, he should have known better than to knock on my door.

In a heartbeat, his antagonism wilted. "Other than her ring, the most expensive things we had were pieces of Mexican pottery she'd collected in Latin America. They're not rare."

Anyone who'd done enough research to know about the secret passage would have known they didn't keep anything of value. "Makes a burglar seem unlikely."

"That's what I told the cops," he said.

Yet, he hadn't told them about the secret passage or they might have found her body sooner. I wanted to ask, but that would only extend the conversation.

"Is my finding her body a matter of public record?" I still had hopes of staying out of the limelight on this case.

"Not while the case is active." He frowned. "You think the press will get hold of it?"

"I've been worried they might track me down."

"Then why did you get involved?"

The very question I'd been asking myself. "I knew if I didn't check out the story, the question would haunt me if she were never found. I never expected to find the bo- her."

"You always did jump in before you thought." He tossed out the verbal jab with a casual air. "But once you got involved, you never quit until you unraveled the puzzle."

"You know me, never say die." I cringed when I heard my words. "I can't imagine how hard this must be for you."

Sorrow filled his eyes. His hands grasped his coffee cup. "I keep thinking she'll walk through the door and explain."

She'd certainly have some explaining to do. However, saying so seemed inappropriate even to me.

"I don't know how to go forward." His voice trailed away, and he stared into his mug.

I wasn't sure if he was referring to his wife's murder or why he'd come here today.

After another long silence, he met my gaze. "The reason I came... I was wondering..."

I cringed inside. This wasn't going to be good. I could feel it.

He plunged in. "Would you come to the funeral home and help arrange a service?"

If he'd pulled out a bat and smacked me, I couldn't have been more stunned. I fought a deer-in-the-headlights look and plastered my body against the chair. Maybe if I sat back far enough, I'd slip off his radar.

Swallowing convulsively, I managed my usual quick-witted response. "What?"

"I have no right to ask." He stretched his hand halfway across the table in a pleading gesture. "I was a lazy good-for-nothing when we were married."

True, yet he'd waited until he wanted something before admitting it.

"I know we haven't seen each other in over fifteen

years," he continued, "but seeing your name was like a Godsend."

I stared at his heartfelt expression and searched for a way to squirm out of helping my ex plan his dead wife's funeral.

"It's not like I don't know people," he said. "I have plenty of friends."

None of whom had evidently taken the course in 'How to bury a loved one 101'.

He put his head in his hands. "I don't know where to start. I don't know what to do."

This help-me air had sucked me in when I'd fallen for him at sixteen. I'd learned some things since then.

"I never thought I'd be burying her." He looked at me with tear-filled eyes. "I don't want to drag my friends into this mess. Come with me to the funeral home. I don't know anything about making arrangements."

And I do? For a woman I'd never met? I was already in this mess deep enough. I opened my mouth to tell him to contact his friends. "Of course, I'll come."

Wait a minute! I can't be bound to something my automatic pilot agrees to. I hadn't even been consulted. I gritted my teeth. Too late. The words were out.

The tension left his shoulders. "Thanks, Tracy."

Sure, let the autopilot save you once, and it takes over.

I didn't want to go to a funeral home. I had flower bulbs to pack and mail.

How long did planning a funeral take? If I didn't get the orders out by the final mail pick-up at five, the company would exact penalties. I cast around for a way to back out.

Randy dabbed at his eyes and blew his nose. "You don't know how much this means to me."

I sighed in defeat. Mrs. C would help package the orders. I'd even pay her. Better to give her the money than the company. Kevin and Marcus I could browbeat. Rabi would help.

I sighed and promised myself to fire my automatic pilot first chance I got. "When do we leave?"

And how soon would Brennan pull me in for questioning once the tail on Randy told her I had consorted with my ex?

6

---

1 Down; 5 Letters;
Clue: A drama set to music.
Answer: Opera

When I entered the Nash Funeral Home a short hour later, crystal chandeliers sent prisms of light dancing on my dress. Plush blue carpet enveloped my black pumps while wildflowers in etched vases added a tantalizing aroma to the elegant atmosphere.

Good thing I'd changed out of my T-shirt and jeans. Death obviously paid well in this part of town.

A slim man in a charcoal gray suit glided toward us as silently as a wraith returning for a visit. I wouldn't have been surprised to see him float through a wall. Instead, he came to a stop and held out his hand. "Mr. McKiernan?"

The funeral guy had evidently passed Solemn Tone 201 with flying colors.

Randy shook the man's hand.

Distracted by another millisecond of gawking, I missed the other man's name. No matter.

"I was sorry to hear of your tragic loss." Funeral Guy steepled his hands. Catching sight of me, he quirked a brow.

I shared his confusion. I wasn't quite sure where I fit in either. However, I'd come prepared. "Tracy Belden. Mr. McKiernan asked me to assist with the arrangements."

I used my professional voice and gave no explanation. Another point from Crawford's rule book: the guilty talk too much. Innocent people feel no need to explain.

The man's shoulders relaxed. He pegged me as an assistant. We were good.

Then Randy stepped close and put his hand on my arm. "Tracy is an old friend of mine."

Funeral Guy masked a knowing glint almost immediately.

I kept my expression neutral and fought the impulse to slug my ex. I'd gone from assistant to mistress in one sentence, and still Randy kept talking.

"Cassie's death has been very difficult for me. I asked Tracy to come for moral support." His voice caught in his throat.

"Of course. These are trying times." The professional mask reappeared. "Let's step into my office, and we can begin."

Half-an-hour later, I sat in a leather chair worth at least two month's rent and debated kicking off my black heels.

Thirty minutes of my life to decide the service

would be Monday at ten-thirty. The police would release the body Sunday evening. That only gave the funeral home overnight to prepare the body. Randy passed on a wake. It would be closed casket and he didn't want gawkers.

"Do you do the cremation on-site?" Randy asked.

"Cremation?" I perked up. Though an autopsy was being completed as we spoke, a quick cremation seemed suspicious.

Randy turned to me, his gaze solemn. "Cassie wouldn't want to spend eternity boxed in."

I wanted to point out Cassie was long gone. All we had was her body. Instead, quick-thinking soul that I am, I nodded and said, "Oh."

Funeral Guy continued his spiel. "Would you like to look at the caskets?"

"For a cremation?" I couldn't mask my shock. "Why not rent out a loaner?"

From Randy and Funeral Guy's appalled expressions, I was pretty sure they didn't have a good answer. I decided not to ask what they planned to do with the casket afterward. It wasn't like Randy could trade it in for store credit. Could he save it for next time?

After a quelling look in my direction, Funeral Guy pulled out a catalog of caskets.

Randy chose a pearly-white, gold-trimmed affair with peach silk lining.

I liked the cherrywood with copper trim and mint green satin, but I wasn't being buried. I couldn't afford it anyway. So I kept my mouth shut and prayed we'd pick up speed.

"Excellent choice." Funeral Guy smiled happily. "That one is fifteen thousand."

Dollars? I tried not to swallow my tongue. My car hadn't cost that much.

Randy agreed to the exorbitant fee.

After my heart resumed its normal rate, I glanced at my watch and realized we'd been here most of an hour. At this rate, my feet would be numb when we left, and I'd have to crawl to the car. When the guy pulled out two thick handouts and started in on readings and music, my toes cringed.

Randy leafed through pages of scripture readings and essays with the speed of a snail on sleeping pills.

I couldn't take it. I smiled at Funeral Guy. "Mr. McKiernan will look this over at home. He'll call you tomorrow with his selections."

The man nodded. "That would be fine."

Moving this whole thing along would be fine with me. I flipped the booklet closed and set it in Randy's lap. He opened his mouth but I didn't give him a chance. I pasted on my polite smile. "And the music?"

The funeral director's eyes gleamed. "We have contacts with professionally trained vocalists who would be happy to sing any piece you select. Did Mrs. McKiernan have favorites?"

I'd give it a few minutes then pull the call back tomorrow ploy. I was thinking classics: "Amazing Grace", "Danny Boy".

My throat tightened at the very thought of "Danny Boy". It had been my granddad's favorite. When they'd sung it at the end of his service, my sodden tissues had disintegrated under a waterfall of tears.

"She loved opera," Randy answered with a nostalgic smile. "We scheduled trips around performances. The Austrian opera houses were special favorites."

Touring old opera houses could be interesting, but sitting through arias sung by high-pitched warblers made my ears hurt worse than my toes.

"As grand as those houses were," Randy continued, "Cassie couldn't help comparing them to the Met."

The other man glowed. His eyes took on a dreamy air. "Ah, yes."

Were these two going to launch into reminiscences of every opera house on the planet?

"Cassie grew up in Brooklyn." Randy's face had a far-away expression. "Her family struggled to get by, but she had a passion for music. She snuck into the Met when she was young. She swore someday she'd have the best seat in the place."

What about the family in Kansas? I kept my eyes wide and, hopefully, innocent. "Will her family be at the service?"

"She has no family." Randy's answer came so quickly the words ran into each other. His sorrow filled gaze was touching, but endless poker games had perfected his acting ability. "She was an only child, and her parents are dead."

I tucked the information away. "Did she live in New York City long?"

"She was born and bred in Brooklyn." Randy's gaze was distant. "She sang in the chorus at a small New York opera house during her last two years in high school."

My suspicion meter shot to the red zone. Again, where did the dental x-ray from Kansas fit into this history?

Answer—it didn't. Further proof there were two Cassie Reeds. The real one and the dead woman. The knowledge that the victim came from Brooklyn might buy me points with Detective Brennan.

The funeral guy leaned forward ever so slightly. "Your wife was a trained vocalist?"

"She sang soprano." Pride rang in Randy's voice. "She resumed vocal training once we settled here. Thankfully, her New York accent didn't come through in her singing."

Wifey-number-two had spoken with a New York accent. I filed the factoid away in my book of knowledge.

"Did she ever attend a public audition at the Met?" The glint in Funeral Guy's gaze seemed more than casual.

I smiled at the man's unknowing help. I couldn't have steered the conversation better myself.

"When she was seventeen," Randy said. "She didn't make it."

Seventeen seemed young but what did I know about opera? "Can anyone try out?"

Funeral Guy spoke first. "You can sign up for an open audition. I tried out several years ago when my wife and I visited New York."

"That must have been exciting." I don't know if cops comment on tangents, but I'm not a cop. I'm barely a real private eye. Besides, it seemed a shame not to let Funeral Guy relive the moment.

"It was such a thrill to stand on the stage and face the theater." His voice held a note of reverence, and his eyes were focused on the past. "I imagined I was Caruso, playing to a packed house. I'll always treasure the memory."

"How did it turn out?" The story obviously had a happy ending. I could use a little pick me up.

"They invited me to join the chorus." He preened, but

he was allowed. Not many people get to touch their dream. "I have the embossed letter framed in my den."

"Congratulations," I said, happy for him.

An inner glow animated the man's thin, pale face. "Did your wife try a second time?"

"She planned to after her voice matured," Randy said. "Unfortunately, her family ran into..."

Problems?

He tried again. "Cassie had to le..."

Leave town? I perched on the edge of my chair, waiting. Unfortunately, he fell silent.

"She never got the chance." Randy took a breath. "Life interfered."

"It has a way of doing that." Which of us ends up where we intend? Some of us, like me, don't even have a plan. Because if I had one iota of forethought, I wouldn't be here with my ex.

Funeral Guy pushed the music book toward Randy. "Why don't you look this over? Once you decide, we can finalize the arrangements."

Oh, goody, an uptown version of the bum's rush. I liked Funeral Guy more and more.

Randy put his hand on it, looking lost. His chronic inability to battle through a crisis was one more reason his sustained success in the stock market amazed me.

"This is a difficult time." Funeral Guy leaned forward. "It's easy to get overwhelmed."

When Randy didn't answer, I stifled an impatient retort and touched his arm. "Perhaps when you get home and relax, you'll remember some of the songs she liked."

Randy still made no move to stand. "If it's not the police, it's the press. I can't begin to get a handle on the business."

Odd words for a supposedly self-made man who'd been buying and selling stocks for over fourteen years.

Suspicion ran through my veins. I dredged up an eye-dropper full of sympathy. "Take one thing at a time. You'll get through."

Randy finally pushed himself upright. He turned toward the door then stopped. "I just remembered. Cassie once mentioned an aria she wanted sung at her funeral."

The funeral guy, rising from his own chair, perked up. "Which aria?"

"We were attending *Pagliacci* in Vienna. She mentioned the scene where the wife tries to carry on despite her world crumbling around her. That was Cassie. Someone who persevered no matter what."

What part of her world had been crumbling?

"We'll be happy to accommodate your wishes," Funeral Guy said.

All the way home, operas and arias, murders and funeral homes chased each other around in my head. The few facts I'd garnered pointed to a troubled past for wifey-number-two. But however much I wanted Randy to overtake me on the suspect list, he seemed the epitome of a man grieving for the woman he'd loved. Still, he and the victim had had their share of secrets.

Though my saner half tried to call a halt to messing with this case, a crossword puzzle with overlapping clues began to form in my mind. I'd already dug myself in hip deep by going with Randy. Now, I'd have to explain my actions to both Crawford and Brennan. Having new facts in my pocket was the only way to mitigate the damage I'd done to my cause.

Moments later, the car stopped in front of my building's faded brick façade. Hope surged. Freedom was in sight. Then Randy turned off the ignition.

I fought the urge to flee.

He turned to face me. "Thanks for coming. It meant a lot to have someone on my side."

Who said there were sides? And why did he need someone on *his*? Unlike me, he had an alibi for the murder.

Randy stared at me with sorrowful eyes, apparently waiting for an answer to the 'being on his side' comment.

I was ready to be gone. "Don't worry. The police will find whoever's responsible."

Which, if you're guilty, isn't a comfort.

"I wish I had your self-control." Randy pressed his lips together. "I've always been too passionate. You never let emotion get in your way."

My iota of sympathy exploded in a tiny puff of smoke. I pulled my fingers out of his grasp. "I hope things turn out all right for you."

I opened the door and slammed it in one quick motion. A minute later, I stood with my back against the inside door of my apartment building.

Not so much to keep Randy out, I'd already watched his BMW drive away. Mostly, I was trying to figure out why I was acting like a flame-retardant moth. The puzzle kept drawing me in, but this case was turning into an inferno.

And getting too close could get me accused of murder.

7

---

8 Down; 6 Letters;
Clue: A communication in written form.
Answer: Letter

I returned from the funeral home in time to muster the troops. One o'clock on Saturday afternoon found us positioned around the ten-foot oblong table in the storage room packaging bags of tulip bulbs for delivery.

For the past several years, I've worked for a local company that takes orders from the made-for-TV commercials. They send me bulk boxes of the latest inventory. I break the items into individual orders and send packages out to the customers.

It's a family-owned, old-school company. With the rapid growth of on-line ordering and shopping channels as competition, I don't know how they've lasted this long, and I can't help but wonder how much longer they can hang on. So far, I haven't found anything else that works with my schedule.

Marcus, on my right, stood at one narrow of the table. Rabi faced me from across the table. Mrs. C sat next to him with Kevin completing the circle.

The company paid me a flat fee for each package shipped. The others were helping me out of the goodness of their hearts. Our assembly line had been tested before so the operation was going smoothly. At this rate, Rabi would be on time for his last drop-off.

"One red, one white, two pink frills." Marcus wrinkled his nose. He handed the box to Rabi to tape shut. "Yuck. Frills."

Reaching for another order slip and a box, I wiggled my toes in my cocker-spaniel slippers, Marcus's last Christmas present. "Thanks for helping. I'd never get these done on my own."

Kevin looked up from a packing slip with a straight face. "I'm only here for the free pizza."

"I'm in it for the money." Mrs. C shot Kevin a triumphant smile. She pasted a mailing label on a box Rabi had taped shut.

I grabbed four packages of Broadway Reds then smiled at Marcus and Rabi. "At least you two are doing this out of the kindness of your hearts."

Rabi froze in the act of taping a box and eyed Marcus. "Don't we get free pizza?"

"I was shanghaied," Marcus said. "My captor told me nothing."

"Great, I'm surrounded by wise-cracking pizza-grubbing mercenaries." I slid my box toward Rabi then ruffled Marcus's hair. "If pizza is what you want, that's what you'll get."

"Good, because I'm starving," Kevin said.

"Oh, no." Mrs. C's moan stopped the action. "I've ordered pay-per-view downstairs for me soccer team tonight."

I let out my breath. After arranging a funeral for a woman I'd never met, this crisis was child's play. "We'll move the party to your place. That'll give me a chance to clean up and Rabi time to return."

"Oh, that'll be lovely," she crooned in her British accent. "I'll make us a special English treat."

"Candy?" Marcus asked.

"Better," Mrs. Colchester assured him. "Fresh baked biscuits smothered in butter and topped with sliced to-mah-toes."

Marcus grimaced, but the woman was too wound up to notice. In the midst of reminding myself to get him ice cream, I remembered an English exchange student in high school who had described that exact dish as a British favorite.

Could Mrs. C *truly* be from England? Maybe she was a war bride who'd been faking an American accent all these years.

That made less sense than faking a British accent for the past month.

"Are you going to fill that order?" Kevin tossed a wadded-up label at me. "Or have you decided to supervise?"

I shoved more bulbs in the box. "I was thinking."

"Probably about the suspect," Marcus informed him.

"I was *not* thinking about Randy or his wife."

"Wait a minute." Marcus pointed at me. "Do the police know Randy's wife was from Brooklyn?"

All he needed was a spotlight to make the interrogation complete. Fortunately, Mrs. C saved me by jumping into the fray.

"A person's accent isn't something family or friends would mention." The older woman mused. "You'd take it as a matter of course, wouldn't you?"

Unless the accent started less than a month ago.

"I told Crawford everything I learned today as soon as I returned." My boss had let loose with both barrels. I grimaced at the memory. "He promised to update Brennan. She'll find the real killer. I have nothing to worry about. I'm innocent."

"Lots of innocent people end up in jail." Mrs. C tossed out this none too comforting comment without blinking an eye.

"She's right," my son chimed in without missing a beat. As he spoke he checked a packing slip against the contents of a box before giving the order to Rabi. "Besides, it's our civic duty to help. The police wouldn't have found the body without you and Kevin."

"I am not saying another word about this case." I made a slashing gesture. "I'm not involved."

"You've done your part," Marcus assured me before addressing the others. "Anybody else hear anything new?"

"A cop I know said the Kansas police contacted the Reed family." Kevin shot me a sideways glance and shrugged sheepishly. "The family confirmed Cassie married Randy, but they say she left him a long time ago. They also swear she's alive, though she hasn't been home for over a decade."

"I'll just bet she hasn't." The words were out before I could stop them.

Kevin shot me a knowing look.

The others took my comment in stride. Evidently, they hadn't taken my vow of silence seriously.

"Do they have proof their daughter's alive?" Marcus's eyes practically whirled in his head. "Have they spoken to her?"

The logic behind his questions impressed me even as I told myself to concentrate on the orders.

Kevin shook his head. "She contacts them by e-mail."

"Yet they won't believe she's dead?" Mrs. Colchester asked.

"Hard to prove them wrong when the cops don't have the right body." With a flick of his wrist, Kevin sent a box skidding across the table to land in the cart. "No one knows when the real Cassie Reed disappeared. The only fact everyone agrees on is that the victim isn't her."

My gaze locked on Marcus. The thought of anything happening to him chilled my blood. "To believe the police would be admitting she's dead. A parent would do anything to avoid facing that fact."

"The police are retracing Cassie's last-known whereabouts," Kevin picked up his commentary. "Finding someone who knew her is going to be tough. Fifteen years is a long time for a dancer to pound the boards in Vegas."

Even as my hands filled orders, my brain knotted the strands of the puzzle together. The addiction seduced me with ease. "With no idea when the switch took place, how will they know which Cassie they're talking about?"

"That's why we're amateurs, and they're pros," Kevin said.

"And I intend to keep it that way. None of us needs to investigate this case," I added the comment for Marcus, but he kept checking invoices. In the momentary silence that followed, my foolishness in accompanying Randy returned full force. "Why I went with Randy I'll never know."

"To get rid of him." Mrs. Colchester calmly added a box to the stack by Kevin. She met my gaze. "The greatest asset men like him have is they don't take no for an answer."

"You're right." Having a reason for my lapse of judgment made me feel better. "Randy would never have left."

"Why did he come here in the first place?" Kevin tossed a box over my head. It banked off the wall and landed neatly in Rabi's cart.

Marcus made a noise as he read a text on his phone.

"What's wrong?" I looked at the box in front of him.

The boy's expression froze. "I have to go to Steve's. Now."

"Can't it wait until tomorrow?" I frowned. "We have to clean up; then I'm ordering pizza."

He shook his head. "He's going to show me the body of his dead angelfish."

"If you'd grown up in a harbor town, Ducky, you'd have seen enough dead fish to last you a lifetime," Mrs. C said with casual nonchalance.

I stored her comment in my memory bank before turning to Marcus.

"The fish died four days ago," he explained. "His mom won't keep the body in the freezer much longer,"

The image made my housekeeping look good. I couldn't stand in the way of someone getting a dead fish out of her freezer. "I'll give you a ride."

Steve's house was a ten-minute ride by car, maybe fifteen by the frequent, well-maintained buses that stopped on every corner.

"I'm not a little kid." Marcus headed for the door. "I'll hop on the bus. Be back in less than an hour."

It was late afternoon, but the September sun would keep daylight in place for a little longer. A constant police presence that kept the city safe for the tourists also made it easier for me to give Marcus a quick nod. "Call me when you get there."

I held the final box shut for Rabi to tape as I heard the door shut behind my son.

Kevin helped Mrs. Colchester load the second cart. "Any ideas?"

I started at his question. "On what?"

"Why Randy came by today." Kevin raised a brow. "You think he's after your bod?"

"No, my fortune," I said in a deadpan voice. "My svelte body and savoir-faire are icing on the cake."

Rabi and Mrs. Colchester's laughter mingled with Kevin's.

"It wasn't that funny," I muttered.

"We were laughing with you, luv." In the face of Mrs. C's British lilt even I couldn't pretend to be upset.

"I have no idea why Randy showed up." I admitted. "My only hope is that he never returns."

BY ELEVEN O'CLOCK SATURDAY NIGHT, the pizza party disbanded. I trudged up the steps with my arm around Marcus's shoulders. "I'm glad we can sleep in tomorrow."

He rolled his eyes. "I used to stay up all night when I was on my own."

I smiled. I'd heard the tough guy talk before.

He shrugged. "Having a bed's kind of nice."

I kissed the top of his head as I got my key out. The clock chiming the hour mixed with the phone's ring. The shrill tone was still assaulting my ears when I got the door open.

"You go on to bed," I told Marcus as I struggled with my key. "That must be Brennan."

After Crawford's grilling, he'd warned me to expect Detective Brennan's call. I'd assumed it would be tomorrow, not this late on a Saturday. As Marcus pounded up the stairs, I picked up the landline. "Hello."

"About time you got home." Randy's voice sounded in my ear.

Too late I saw his name on the portable phone's read-out. I didn't need this, not twice in one day. I plopped in a chair. "What do you want?"

The pause lasted only a heartbeat. I could almost hear Randy's mental gears shift as he re-assessed the situation.

"I know you've had a long day," he said softly. "I'm sure I didn't help by taking up so much of your morning, but I have to speak with you."

I had the refusal ready before he finished talking. "Anything you have to say can wait until morning."

"You're right. It is late." A weary sigh punctuated his words. "However, this is important."

My irritation grew with each passing second. Did he think I wouldn't remember the times I'd seen him pull his games on other people?

The line fell silent. He was probably waiting for me to take my cue and be sympathetic.

"Are you going to tell me what you want or not?" I asked. "Better yet, don't tell me. I'm going to bed."

"I'm in trouble." Surprise mixed with outrage in his voice.

"You have my sympathy." My flat tone made the words a lie. What could he do? Hang up? My luck wasn't that good. "It's not my problem."

"Actually, it is," he said in an edgy tone. "You've been spying on my house for a week."

"It's routine surveillance." I was beyond caring. "They needed people. They tapped me."

"Your buddy Kevin helped find her body." His tone was accusatory.

Anger burned away the edge of my fatigue. "Don't cause trouble for Kevin."

"I didn't call to argue." Randy backpedaled quickly at the hard note in my voice. He knew that attacking my friends was a sure-fire way to stoke my temper. "I need answers from you."

"I don't know anything about the investigation." I remained wary. "If you're innocent, you have nothing to worry about."

And if you're guilty, I'm not going to be the one to catch you.

"I have to talk to you. Tonight. In person."

I raised my brows at his imperious tone. "Not gonna happen."

"I found the letter."

Had I missed something? "What letter?"

"Why did you write Cassie?" His raised voice sounded in my ear. "What news did you have for her?"

The thought of me writing a letter was laughable. Since the electronic age dawned, the only time I put pen to paper was to sign my debit slips. At one point my mother claimed she'd given me up for dead because she hadn't gotten a signed Christmas card in years.

Why would Randy make up something so obviously ludicrous? "I never contacted your wife. I certainly didn't write her a letter."

A rustle of paper carried over the line. "I'm holding it in my hand right now, with your signature, name, and address."

I raked a hand through my already unruly hair. "What does it say?"

"That we were married and you have news about me she has to know, a matter of life and death."

I would never be so cliché. "You must be kidding."

"Did you kill her?"

"Of course not." I looked guiltily at the loft bedroom and lowered my voice. Hopefully, Marcus was asleep. "Wait a minute. The police searched your house."

"They were looking for a body, not papers," he said. "This was in a folder in a drawer."

I buried my head in my hand. I couldn't see any way out of it. "I have to see this letter."

"I'll be waiting." The peremptory note in his voice annoyed me all over again.

"I am not driving out to your place at this time of night." I remembered to keep my voice low this time.

"Well, I'm not coming into the inner city," he said.

I gritted my teeth at his snobbery. I didn't need him parked at my curb anyway. "Meet me at Romeo's diner at the edge of town. Fifteen minutes. Bring the letter."

"No need to remind me of the obvious." His conciliatory tone had vanished. "Don't get lost."

He hung up before I could find a comeback.

I made a rude face at my phone. Marcus's steady

breathing sounded in the stillness. I tried to delude myself that he hadn't heard anything, but I didn't buy it.

My watch read eleven-ten. If I intended to be at the diner in fifteen minutes, I'd better hustle downstairs and ask Mrs. C to sit with Marcus.

Luckily, the woman's a night owl. She'd agree to sack out on the couch until I returned. I headed for the still open door, reviewing the facts. When the trail hit Crawford, I stopped in my tracks.

Randy was going to lead the surveillance team right to me again, not to mention the police. I turned for the phone. Then stopped. Fifteen minutes hadn't left leeway for either of us. To make it on time Randy would have to leave immediately and he hated to be late. Besides, he wouldn't listen to any arguments for caution. Playing it safe wasn't his style.

The thought of skipping the meeting came and went. With my luck, if I didn't show, he'd drive to my apartment out of spite.

I gritted my teeth and headed for the door. Between Detective Brennan's suspicion, Randy's arrogance, and my too fast mouth, I'd be lucky not to wake up in jail.

8

5 Down; 7 Letters;
Clue: A wrong action from a bad choice.
Answer: Mistake

Fifteen minutes of waiting for Randy in a diner on a dead-end road hadn't improved my mood. Nor had the realization my cell was dead and I couldn't call him. I scanned the empty tables as if Randy would appear out of thin air. When would I learn?

At least if he never showed, Brennan wouldn't know about this failed meeting. I sipped my cup of decaf then grimaced at the cool liquid.

"Want a fresh cup?" A coffee pot materialized along with the waitress. Years of hard work had stamped their mark on a face decorated with gray curls and bifocals.

The delicious aroma of roasted coffee filled my nostrils.

"Oh, no." The woman's low voice remained casual despite her words. "You had decaf, didn't you?"

I waved away her regret. "Caffeine could only help."

She finished filling the cup then raised a brow. "Been stood up?"

"Looks that way." I sounded as disgusted as I felt.

"Dump him," she advised without hesitation. "Married men who cheat are no good. If they leave their wives, all you get's a cheater. You can do better. You're a sweet young thing."

She needed new specs. Nobody had called me sweet even when I'd been young. "You think he's married?"

"When two people arrive in separate cars at this time of night, it only means one thing." She took my question as an invitation and sat with a tired groan. "Trust me, sweetie. Everyone knows."

"Speaking from experience?" I asked.

She threw back her head and let out a gravelly laugh that turned to a hacking cough. After she settled, she grinned. "Nobody but Chester'd have an old sourpuss like me, baby girl."

"Chester?" I asked.

"Chester!" She yelled at a wide built man sitting at the counter whose face had met an anvil or two. She jerked a thumb at me. "Lady wants to know if I'm having an affair."

The man's somber expression didn't waver. "That's why I work with her, to keep the men away."

"We met at a diner thirty years ago, been together ever since." She pointed a stubby finger at me. "I married him for his hashbrowns. You want an order? On the house."

I shook my head, but she paid no attention.

"Chester!" Her wall-rattling yell could have been heard in the back forty. "Hashbrowns for the lady, grilled onions."

"No, onions." I'd never liked them cooked.

She sighed as if I were a personal disappointment. "No onions."

Fifteen minutes later, I all but licked my plate clean. "You're right. He's the best."

"In more ways than one," she said with a wicked smile.

I chuckled and came to a decision. "You're also right about waiting for losers."

She slapped the table hard enough to set the salt and pepper shakers dancing. "Good for you."

"That rat has wasted my time for the last time." I stood and fished in my purse for money. I didn't know Randy's game but I'd deal with his alleged letter in the morning. "How much for the hashbrowns?"

The woman shook her head. "Eight bits for the coffee. The advice is free. We'll call it good."

I found a ten and three ones the pizza guy had given me as change and threw in the ten on an impulse.

She frowned at the bill. "Hon, that's too much."

The reproach sounded real, but I smiled and walked away. "The advice was worth it."

I waved to Chester and walked outside. Pine trees rustled in a refreshing wind. Though I felt okay to drive I was so bone-tired the coffee wouldn't keep me up once I got home. I'd give Mrs. C the bum's rush then collapse in bed.

HALFWAY UP the steps to my apartment, I realized the light flooding the hall came from my place. A spurt of adrenaline fueled my rush up to my second-floor apartment.

Mrs. C stood inside the door with her cell phone in her hand and fear in her eyes. "Marcus is gone."

Fear sluiced through me. It was getting close to midnight. I grabbed her shoulders. "What?"

"I checked him after me movie ended," she said. "There's naught but pillows in his bed, bunched up to look like a body."

I turned toward the stairs. The phone's shrill ring spun me around.

Mrs. C stared at her cell phone. Surprise and hope warred in her eyes.

I pried it out of her grip. "Hello?"

"Why are you answering Mrs. Colchester's cell phone?" Kevin's voice sounded in my ear. "Better yet, why is yours off?"

"It's out of juice," I yelled into the receiver. "What's going on?"

"Don't bite my head off, I just found out. I didn't think you'd know."

"Mrs. C told me."

"How did she hear?" he asked. "Rickson only called me a minute ago."

"Rickson?" I put my hand to my head. Crawford had him watching Randy tonight. "What does he know about Marcus?"

"What happened to Marcus?" Kevin's voice sharpened.

I took a deep breath. "He snuck out. Isn't that why you called?"

"No." He bit off the denial. "Your ex has taken a powder."

I struggled to keep up with the shifting topics. "Randy?"

"How many exes do you have?" Kevin asked. "How long has Marcus been gone?"

"Maybe an hour." Where had Randy slunk off to? The rat was supposed to meet me. "How long has Randy been gone?"

"The cops got suspicious when he didn't leave to meet you," Kevin said.

"How did they know about that?"

"News flash," Kevin said. "Randy's phone is bugged."

How could I have forgotten? By now, mine was probably bugged as well. I urged my frazzled brain to concentrate as Kevin continued.

"When he didn't drive off to meet you the cops rang the bell. No one answered. They used some legal loophole and went in. No Randy."

Talk about deja vu. "How many hidden exits are there in that house?"

"No telling." Kevin's voice turned serious. "I called to warn you."

"I didn't do anything," I protested. Chester and his lady would swear to it.

"A little paranoid?" Kevin asked. "The cops know you were meeting Randy to talk about a threatening letter you sent wifey-number-two."

Worry and fatigue shot my irritation off the scale. "I didn't send a letter."

"The cops think you did," Kevin said. "Now it and your ex are missing. Guess who the cops think is covering her tracks on wifey-number-two's murder? Guess who they want to take downtown and possibly arrest?"

I sucked in a lung full of air. I could feel the dark walls of a jail cell closing in around me.

"When the police couldn't find Randy, they pulled in Rickson, who confirmed he hadn't seen Randy leave." Kevin laid out the facts in a steady voice. "As soon as Rickson got clear he called me. He didn't figure you'd be home."

"I can't spend all night at the station." My shock evaporated under the growing fear of being trapped. "I have to find Marcus."

"Then get out. Now." Kevin's voice was low and urgent. "'Cuz they're coming."

"I'm gone." I shoved the phone at Mrs. C then spun on my heel. When she grabbed my arm, I struggled against her grip.

She shoved her face closer to mine. "Listen."

I stopped. A siren wailed in the distance.

"If you go out front, they'll catch you before you get to the corner." She spoke in a fast soft tone. "They'll have an APB on your car. Either way, they'll nab you."

"I'll go out the rear." There was an exit out the storage room that led to an alley.

She shook her head. "The new padlock, remember?"

I groaned. Drat all security measures. "Where's the key?"

She grimaced. "In my office desk."

I didn't have time for her to trundle downstairs. The

siren had faded, but I could feel the cops closing in. I refused to waste time on their mindless suspicions. My brain suddenly clicked. "The fire escape upstairs faces the rear of the building."

I headed for Marcus's bedroom. The fire escape outside the bathroom window had to be Marcus's avenue of escape. Once at the top of the stairs, I picked my way across his bedroom.

Mrs. C's voice floated up to me. "She's headed for the fire escape."

A ribbon of shock ran through me before I realized she still had Kevin on the phone.

"I'll settle on the sofa again." Her footsteps crossed the room. "By the time they get past me, she'll be gone."

Skirting past the bed, I noticed Marcus had finished putting together the electric model car I'd bought him. I also realized the other woman's British accent not only hadn't wavered, it had deepened.

I stopped for a crucial second. Could the woman be British? The front door clicked shut and the television rose in volume. I tried to focus, but my mind seemed intent on jumping from one random topic to another.

Slipping inside the bathroom, I squatted in front of the window. A wedge propped the screen open. I should have figured. When I was young, I'd climbed out my window and shinnied down an oak tree.

Once on the fire escape, I shifted my purse strap over my head and surveyed my choices. The stairs looked tempting, but Mrs. Colchester was right. The cops would catch me on the first block.

The building on the other side of the alley had a metal ladder leading to the roof. I measured the inter-vening space. The handrails stuck out from the wall about a foot, but they were still a good four feet away. My stomach clenched.

I'd take my chances on the ground. A car screeched to a stop out front. A lack of laughter or voices cinched the deal. Someone was being quiet.

Too late to risk the alley. Cursing my lack of choices, I stepped over the banister. Amazingly, the gap looked even wider from here.

My hands locked onto the railing with a death grip. I swallowed. The one thing everyone says in situations like this is don't look down.

Of course, I looked.

A vise-like pressure squeezed all the blood out of my heart. If you think two stories up doesn't sound like much, climb out on a ledge sometime. It's a long way down. Fortunately, heights don't bother me. However, crashing into the concrete petrified me.

Another car braked out front.

I held onto the rail then stretched to the ladder. Way short. If I jumped high I'd have a second chance if I missed the first time.

What a confidence builder.

I zeroed in on the ladder. Then on my heart thudding its way out of my chest.

The night sky and the scattering of stars faded. Before I could change my mind I bent my knees, gave a short three-count, and leaped.

Wind whistled past my face. For two breathless heartbeats, it whistled below my feet. The brick wall flew at me with blinding speed.

My hands collided with cold metal. The rough brick scraped my skin raw. A heartbeat later my ribs slammed into the steel rungs.

I grabbed blindly. Stinging from the impact, my hands slipped off the smooth metal.

I fought for a handhold. Something. Anything.

My feet scrambled vainly for a purchase.

Panic choked me.

I was falling.

13 Across; 13 Letters;
Clue: Sherlock Holmes's opening salvo.
Answer: Thegamesafoot

With nothing between me and the ground but air, panic took control. I flailed around wildly. One arm hit the side rail and went numb. By sheer luck, the other hooked on a rung. My body jerked to a stop. My relief ended in agony when my ribs slammed into the un-giving metal.

Clutching the ladder with a white-knuckled grip, I scrambled to get my feet firmly on a rung. Gasping for air, I rested my head against the cool metal and swallowed my heart.

Maybe I'd stay here all night.

The squeal of a walkie-talkie shot adrenaline into my battered body. Heart thudding, I fought the agony of scraped skin and bruised muscles. Fear of capture fueled my slow climb up the ladder, rung by painful rung. Once at the top, I rolled over the ledge and fell to the roof like a bag of wet cement. Fresh waves of pain wracked my body.

"Alley's clear." The businesslike voice sounded all too close, even over the jazz music playing nearby.

My body broke out in a cold sweat.

One second sooner and he'd have seen me.

The squeak of a walkie-talkie interrupted the drumbeat of my heart. " -ay in position."

A scattering of stars stared at me with their cold gazes. After a moment to catch my breath, I sheltered my wounded side, gathered my feet, and rose.

A piece of gravel caught under my heel and screeched like a cat in a blender.

I froze. No sound of alarm arose from the alley. Sighing in relief, I pushed myself upright then walked to the door.

Hopefully, the padlock would be broken. Otherwise, my escape would turn into an embarrassing rescue plea. Though our resort town touted its clean, safe image, the hooligans win a few rounds.

Four feet from the door, the dim light showed the padlock hanging ajar. In the next heartbeat, a gaunt figure rose out of the shadows and blocked my path.

I bit back a scream.

A thin face smiled above a soiled brown shirt that blended with the roof tiles. The guy, I think it was a guy, had less weight on him than your average kite. "Could you spare a quarter?"

Why couldn't people warn you before they jumped out? Too stunned to think, I stumbled past him. Good thing, I had the coffee and hashbrowns to sustain me.

Guilt stopped me. I turned around.

The guy watched me with a guarded expression. I suppose in his business you can't be too careful. His expression changed to a gap-toothed grin as I shoved my last three singles into his hand.

When he opened his mouth, I shushed him and resumed my trek to the door. Before I sprain my sore shoulder patting myself on the back, I have to confess I'm not above trying to bribe the karma wheel.

I opened the door, thanking the universe for well-oiled hinges. Air vents let light into the stairwell. My eyes adjusted quickly. On the second landing, the shrill ring of my phone jump-started my heart. I found my cell—I'd plugged in the portable charger before I'd left—as another ring echoed off the walls. "Hello."

"Where are you, the bottom of a well?" Kevin's voice sounded abnormally loud.

"Hello to you, too. I'm fine, thanks." I kept my voice low and picked my way down the steps. The roof wasn't the only place vagrants hung out. "I'm in the stairwell of the building across the alley. I jumped from the fire escape."

"Without a net?" He whistled softly. "You hurt?"

My aches got better as I walked or maybe the adrenaline muted them. "Jarred shoulder. Bruised ribs. I'll live."

"I got wheels," he said. "Can you make it to Mike's?"

"Five minutes." The small grocer was two blocks away. However, pain was already making a return appearance. My feet were dragging. "Maybe ten minutes."

"I'll be on the south side by the corner."

"Okay." My breath wheezed as I stepped onto the ground level. I searched the darkness.

"Keep talking until you're outside," Kevin said. "I'll practice 'Feelings' for karaoke night."

"Please don't," I pleaded. "It's been a long day."

"That's my thanks for roaring in on my white horse?"

"I'll thank you when I've actually been saved." I focused on the door, only feet away. A creak sounded behind me. I spun on my heel, catching my breath.

"You okay?" Panic overcame Kevin's teasing. "I can be there in a hot second."

I saw nothing except dark pillars and barred windows. "Stay put. The cops are too close. I'm on the street now."

I stepped into the night air. Minutes later, I slipped into the passenger seat. When I swiveled to face him, a lancing pain sent waves of heat through my chest. I gasped and settled in. As the car roared away, I breathed a grateful sigh. "My knight in shining armor."

Kevin touched my arm. "You need to go to the ER."

I breathed slow and steady. His touch distracted me from the residual pain. "When they ask what happened I'll tell them I jumped off a fire escape to avoid the police. I don't think so. I'll live, just no sharp movements."

"If you die on me, I'll shove your body out of the car and drive off."

For the first time in hours, I laughed.

"If not the ER, where are we going?" Kevin asked.

"To roust Steve out of bed and find out why Marcus went over there tonight. How could I buy that 'dead fish in the freezer' story?"

He turned at the corner. "You realize it's fifteen minutes after midnight?"

I clicked the seat belt with more force than necessary. "You realize my son's missing?"

"Just checking." Kevin tapped a staccato rhythm on the steering wheel.

To keep my mind from imagining Marcus chasing a killer, I dredged up a safer topic of conversation. "When does Jimbo start his second job?"

Jimbo is one of Kevin's high-school buddies. He breezed into town two weeks ago, announced he was gay, and asked to crash at Kevin's place. Kevin took him in without hesitation, but for days every time Kevin mentioned that Jimbo was gay, my buddy also informed me Jimbo had been a linebacker.

To which I responded that there are no disqualifications for being gay. It's like being pregnant. You either are or you aren't.

I only cared that Jimbo had gotten a part-time job stocking shelves at a grocery store within a week. A few days ago, he'd received a call back on a second job. Though neither paid much, I gave the guy major points for working.

"Tonight's his first night." Kevin stopped at the next corner. He looked both ways even though it was the dead of night and no headlights shown for two blocks.

I frowned in puzzlement. "How did Jimbo get to work?"

"I dropped him off," Kevin said, shooting me a puzzled look in return.

"How? My Buick's at my place surrounded by the police."

He pointed at the seat.

I looked around and realized for the first time we were in his blue Chevy. "You got your car out of the garage."

He rolled his eyes. "If you're the brains of this outfit,

we're doomed. Good thing Marcus got some detecting genes."

"Shut up and drive," I said without any venom.

I swayed with the movement of the car. My shoulder ached but I didn't want to admit it. I concentrated on counting the streets leading to Steve's house. At the last corner, my amen turned into a cry of outrage as we drove past.

I pointed at the sign. "Steve's house is there."

"So are the cop cars." Kevin pointed out as he drove past the intersection.

I looked along the street. Townhouses sat side-by-side all along the block. Right in front of Steve's door, two black-and-whites sat grill to grill. Their blue and red flashing lights painted the street a kaleidoscope of colors.

My gaze remained locked on the scene until we drove on and the corner house blocked my view. "What do you think?"

"I think we have two missing children." Kevin's calm tone held an undertone of fear no one else would have caught.

"Steve is our only lead to Marcus." My throat was so tight I barely got the words out. "I have to find out what happened."

"Rule number one of successfully eluding the police is *not* to hunt them up first chance you get." Despite his words, his fingers tightened on the steering wheel.

"These cops aren't looking for me. They can't know anything about Randy so soon."

"Ever hear of things called radios?" He spoke as if talking to a three-year-old. "Besides, telling this group your son is missing will get you to the station for sure. You want your death-defying leap to be for nothing?"

I wanted to jump out of the car and run back. "What if the boys are there?"

"If the boys were there, the cops wouldn't be," Kevin explained as he turned right at the next block.

"What if the boys are dead?" My clenched hands were ice-cold. Blood thudded in my ears.

"Breathe, Tracy. And calm down." Kevin stared at me with a gentle look in his eyes. His fingers covered my hand for an instant, sending a rush of warmth up my arm. "If they'd found any bodies they'd have more than cops there."

"I've never lost a kid before." I sat back, striving for control. "We have to find out what they know, when Steve was last seen, if he said anything tonight."

"I agree." Kevin turned right at the next corner, completing the circle and coming up on the other end of Steve's street.

I sifted through possibilities as Kevin parked the car. "You have to talk to them."

"I agree," he repeated, his hand already on the door handle. His body was tense, ready for action. "The first requirement for a good lie is to stick as close to the truth as possible."

He was willing to lie? That was so sweet. After a childhood built on deceit, he tried to steer clear of lies.

"I'll tell them Mrs. Colchester was watching Marcus." His eyes narrowed. "When she discovered him missing, she panicked and called me."

"What about me?"

"You're on a bus to visit your uncle who had a heart attack," he said. "Old Nick still in Vegas?"

"Yes." Appreciation at his inventiveness momentarily

distracted me. Being raised by con artists had advantages. "You're a natural at this."

He cracked open the door. "All in a good cause."

I put a hand on his arm. "Come back as soon as you can. Tell them you have to call Mrs. C. Tell them anything."

"Don't get impatient," he said with a knowing look in his eyes. "Concentrate on where the boy detective might have gone."

"Hurry," I whispered as he started to straighten.

"Stay. Here." He pointed to the seat. "No matter what."

Already fidgeting, I watched him walk away.

What could Marcus be up to? His escapade had to tie in with wifey-number-two's death. But what role could Steve play? What did I know about the boy? Only that he was a surprise baby. His mother had been forty-four when he was born. That put her in her mid-fifties. That was no help.

His mother works at home, like you. Marcus's voice piped into my brain. *The mayor says it saves money.*

The mayor! I opened the door and raced after Kevin, scaring a pair of pigeons into flight.

Kevin turned around as the birds flew by his head. He rolled his eyes. "I haven't even gone yet."

"Steve's mother works for the mayor."

All I got was a frown. "Good for her."

"Listen, you nimrod." I pulled him closer to the building. "Randy contributed to the mayor's campaign two years ago. Steve's mother is the mayor's accountant. She talked to Marcus's class last month. She works from home."

Finally, a light sparked in his eyes. "Randy, the mayor, and a computer full of files."

One thought led to another. "Marcus would've gone after the files like a bloodhound on a hot scent."

Kevin shook his head. "Marcus wouldn't know the password for her computer."

"Oh, please." As if Kevin didn't ask Marcus for computer help all the time. "You think Marcus and Steve couldn't ferret out any passwords she came up with?"

Kevin nodded. "You're right."

I stepped toward the car. "Ask Steve's mother what he's been talking about, that'll sound natural."

"Get in the car." Kevin pointed behind me while walking in the opposite direction. "Stay put this time."

I checked over my shoulder in time to see Kevin turn the corner. Sighing, I slid into the passenger seat and closed the door.

Nothing to do but wait. Not my strong suit. Telling myself Mrs. C might have news I called her cell. After five rings I was ready to give up.

"Hello?" The sound of running water muffled her whispered greeting.

"Mrs. C? What's up?"

"The bobbies are here," she whispered. "Luckily my cell phone's on vibrate. I'm in the washroom."

Another British phrase. "Do they know Marcus is missing?"

"Haven't asked about him. Have you found him?"

"No, Kevin and I are at Steve's house. The cops have the street lit up like a Christmas tree. We think he and Marcus took off." I eyed the deserted street. "What have you told the cops?"

"A daft old thing like me?" she said with a chuckle. "It took them ten minutes to get me to the door."

I laughed with her. "Good for you."

"They found your car still warm. I told them a friend borrowed it but I didn't know who or why. I did say you'd gone out of town," she admitted. "But I'd lost the address. I don't think they'll leave without something definite."

"That's perfect." I updated her on my Las Vegas visit to Old Nick. I hesitated to tell her she may have a second set of cops but she had to know. "You may get more action. Kevin's gone in to find out what he can. He's going to tell these cops Marcus is missing. So they may show up."

"Mmmmm, I'll have to plant the seed, won't I?" A hint of excitement edged her words.

"Sorry to do this to you." Bad enough I had cops after me. I felt doubly guilty setting them on her.

"Don't worry about me, dearie. I'll say I was late getting to the door because I was looking for the little nipper. Then I was so distraught I couldn't think straight." She spoke in a matter-of-fact tone.

Her calmness took me off guard. Either she was a natural or this wasn't her first time telling tales.

"They're amateurs," she continued in a blithe tone. "And they'll need more than guesses to drag an old lady to the station. If they do, it won't be the first time."

Once I found Marcus, I *had* to find out more about this woman. "Thanks again. You're a real trooper."

"I haven't had this much fun in years." The flush of the toilet sounded over her amused tone. "You just find the little one. I'll set up for the second wave."

I clicked off and gave thanks the woman was on my side. The amateurs comment stuck with me. Few cops in a resort city stay naive for long. Rich tourists mean money and crime follows money like summer follows spring.

I checked the corner again. Not a leaf stirred. I was ready to go in after Kevin.

An interminable fifteen minutes later, a swirl of blue and red lights shot past. Two black-and-whites turned at the corner.

My breath caught in my throat. Why did they need more police?

10

19 Across; 6 Letters;
Clue: Round and round and round we go.
Answer: Circle

A black hole had formed at Steve's house. People went in—no one came out.

According to the clock, ten minutes had passed. That had to be wrong. Kevin had been gone at least fifty minutes. Maybe I was in a time-warp. Maybe I should peek around the corner to make sure aliens hadn't transported everyone off planet.

Kevin couldn't blame me for that.

Checking for aliens is a reasonable precaution.

I'd just go peek. I cracked open the door. The inside light lit up the sidewalk as a dark figure turned the corner. Recognizing Kevin's walk, I snapped the door shut with a guilty jerk.

After a couple of steps, he glanced over his shoulder,

broke into a run, and didn't stop until he slid into the driver's seat.

"What's up?" I checked my seatbelt, ready for a quick getaway. "Are the cops after you?"

The engine roared to life. The car swung into a U-turn. "I want to be gone before they think of more questions."

No one came running after him. "What took so long? What did they say? Were they suspicious?"

"They know less than we do." He flipped on the head-lights and picked up speed. "Steve went to bed as usual. When his dad checked on him later, he was gone."

My heart clunked against my bruised ribs as it fell. Hope I hadn't realized I'd been clinging to evaporated. "That's it?"

Kevin glanced my way. "You expected we'd find them hiding in the closet?"

"It only sounds silly when you say it out loud." I slumped against the seat. "So much for dreams."

Kevin drove past a mix of dark streets interspersed with the garish lights of after-hour businesses. "I asked Steve's mother what the boys talked about and if she thought they'd been acting strange lately."

"Stranger than usual?" The quip was out before I could stop myself. Probably just as well I hadn't talked to the cops.

"Glad to see you back to your old self." Kevin gave my shoulder a reassuring squeeze. "His mom helped him with a school project on financing political campaigns."

"Bingo!" Unfortunately, the confirmation only proved Marcus was hunting a murderer. "Did they mention Randy?"

"With Randy's name in the news, he came up as one of the mayor's supporters in the last election."

I waited for a bombshell. "Then what?"

Kevin shrugged. "Randy contributed the maximum. He appeared at fund-raising dinners. His career as a commodities trader has brought him a lot of connections in the city. He introduced the mayor to other business leaders, the whole bit."

No grand revelations? No finger pointing? No leads? "What if the mayor's link to Randy is a coincidence?"

Kevin raised a brow. "You believe that?"

"No way." My gut answered before my brain did.

"Neither do I. But we need something to go on at zero-dark-thirty in the morning."

Only one idea had surfaced while I had been chewing my nails to the quick. "Casinos."

Kevin raised a brow. "Hunh?"

"That's where the boys went."

"How do you figure?"

The dark streets flashing by held dangers aplenty for a young boy. If I guessed wrong, Marcus and Steve would be on their own. "Marcus could've gone sleuthing during the day with far less trouble. He chose the middle of the night for a reason. One of the places those two would attract less attention at night than during the day is a casino."

"Someone would spot them," Kevin said. "Security would run them in."

"Anyone in a casino is only looking for matching sevens. And Marcus could dodge a dozen security guards."

Kevin spoke. "You're right, but—"

"And—" My raised voice drowned him out. "The boys

are following Randy's trail. I don't know how they found it or why they think it's important, but my gut tells me that's what Marcus is doing."

Kevin turned onto a main boulevard. "Let's assume I believe your gut. What led from Randy to the casinos?"

I made a rude noise. "All roads for Randy lead to gambling."

"The man's on the run. Even in a casino in the dead of night, he's going to be noticed."

Despite his comment, he headed for the strip. I'd like to think it was because of his confidence in me, but it was probably because, like me, he had no idea where else to go.

"Playing the odds is his life. His thrill. His addiction."

"He's rich," Kevin protested.

"People don't gamble to make money any more than your family runs con games to retire. They make and squander fortunes regularly." I'd watched Randy spend pin money, rent money, and grocery money at the casinos. "Scams are in their blood like gambling is in Randy's."

A look of understanding filled Kevin's expression. As usual, he refused to comment on his family, so I continued.

"Hitting triple sevens or winning at poker with a bluff is a thrill ride." I sighed. "At least according to Randy, I've never won enough to know."

"Tell me." Kevin's shoulders shook with laughter.

With his gaze focused on the street, my glare was wasted. "This insight is all I got out of my marriage, so you better appreciate it."

"I do." His smirk made it hard to take him seriously.

"People don't change."

The laughter in Kevin's eyes died. "Some do, Tracy."

I wondered if he was thinking about my role as a mother or how he'd gone straight after breaking with his family. I was certain Randy wasn't his focus.

"It's been a lot of years since you and Randy split." Kevin shifted lanes and sped up. "Maybe playing the stock market took the place of poker."

The picture of Randy studying portfolios and fact sheets didn't jibe with the man I knew. Sitting across my kitchen table from my ex, I'd gotten the same impression of the live by his luck guy I'd known in Kentucky. "Learning new things and changing who you are inside are two different things. You were never a criminal at heart. You're an honest man who couldn't stand to hurt people."

Kevin met my gaze then silently turned to stare at the street.

"Randy's a hustler."

"People change," Kevin reiterated, just in case I hadn't heard it the first three times he'd said it. "Steve's mother said Randy and his wife attended every dinner and luncheon the mayor gave. They did everything but stuff the ballot box."

"Randy had to be up to something."

Traffic thickened. Billboards lit the streets, and the glow ahead had nothing to do with stars or heavenly bodies. We'd hit Langsdale's version of the strip.

"Where now, oh wise one?" Kevin asked.

Casinos flashed by. What if I was wrong? I smacked the question hard. "We'll start with the bigger ones. Even if they couldn't catch them, someone may have seen two eleven-year-olds."

"It'd help if we had a clue what they were up to,"

Kevin said. "What could they have found at Steve's house?"

"I wish I knew." The ring of my cell phone diverted me. I reached into the depths of my purse. "I warned Mrs. C you'd be sending another group of 'bobbies' her way. Be interesting to see how she dealt with them."

"Once we find those two, we need to check her out."

"Sign me up for that investigation. I didn't tell you what she said about the cops." I fished out the phone. "Hello?"

"What the hell are you doing running from the police?" Crawford's deep raspy voice demanded.

I pulled the phone away before he deafened me. I'd heard stories about him quelling brawls by his voice alone. Kevin's grimace made it obvious Crawford's voice still carried.

"Well?" Crawford asked.

His demanding tone got on my last nerve. "I'm on a bus to Vegas to see my uncle who's had a heart attack."

"Don't feed me the same line of garbage your English stoolie fed the cops."

"I do have an uncle in Vegas," I said.

"I know Nick." Crawford's bass drowned me out easily. "You introduced us when we were in Vegas two years ago hunting that lost kid."

I grimaced. It was too much to hope Crawford hadn't contacted him.

"It took me ten minutes to hunt him down, at home, in perfect health, and hosting a wild party he was nice enough to invite me to."

Kevin shot me a look of sympathy I probably didn't deserve.

"You are not on the interstate," Crawford continued

without a pause. "You're on a highway in town, in a blue Chevy with a tan interior, driven by your favorite cohort."

I exchanged a shocked look with Kevin. "How do you know?"

"I'm a detective." Crawford's voice rose slowly but steadily. "What are you doing?"

Kevin drove toward the bigger casinos. The parking lots brimmed with cars. Despite the late hour, people still sauntered along the sidewalk. Talk about looking for a needle in a haystack.

I exhaled. "Marcus is missing."

Silence greeted my news. It would have been more satisfying in other circumstances. Crawford's only son had barely survived a shoot-out on a traffic stop last year. Two months ago, we'd danced at his wedding.

"Tell me." Crawford's voice was all business.

I brought him up to date. "Randy never showed at the diner. When I got home, Mrs. C had discovered Marcus was missing. Then Kevin called and said the cops wanted to question me about a letter Randy claimed I wrote wifey-number-two."

"I know."

"The cops bugged Randy's phone."

"I know."

I don't know why I thought any of this would be news to him. He obviously had an in. "It's all lies."

"You're telling me? I've read your reports. You can't put two sentences together."

"Thanks for the vote of confidence," I said. "I plan to find Marcus first and talk to the police second. I don't know anything anyway."

"I'll vouch for that," Crawford said, always ready with a comeback.

I glared at the phone, regretting I'd given him an opening. "Kevin and I headed over to roust a friend Marcus visited earlier. The cops beat us. The other boy's missing, too."

"What's the kid's name?" Crawford's voice sliced in between my breaths.

I stopped to think. "Steve Warren. His mother is the mayor's accountant. Kevin found out Marcus had been asking questions about Randy's campaign contributions."

A harrumph was my only reward for this bit of news.

Kevin tapped me on the shoulder.

When I looked over, he gestured to the streets. The casinos were slipping behind us. I put my hand over the mouthpiece. "Where do high-rollers go?"

"I'm a construction worker," Kevin said. "How do I know?"

"The Palace Queen," Crawford said.

I told Kevin.

"That's back a couple of blocks." He pulled into the turn lane and swung around.

"That's not where you want to go," Crawford continued.

"Why not?" I asked, wondering what he was up to.

"Why are you looking in the casinos?"

I hesitated, but Crawford wouldn't rat me out to the cops. "I figure that's where the boys have gone."

"Why?"

"Marcus is determined to prove his detecting ability by solving this murder. To do that he somehow got a lead on Randy's money trail, and if I know Randy the trail leads through a casino."

"You may earn your junior decoder ring after all."

Kevin finished a U-turn.

I held up a hand to stop him.

Flashing me a mock glare, he pulled off the street and shot the car into park.

"What casino do we want?" I listened to the silence on the line for a few seconds. "Marcus is out there. I may not be good at this game, but I'm not quitting until I find him."

"Don't get your knickers in a knot," Crawford's growl sounded over the rustle of papers. "I'm looking for a name."

I rolled my eyes at the chance of Crawford finding anything on that mess he calls a desk. "We don't have all night."

"Head to the Silver Swan."

"The Silver Swan," I whispered to Kevin.

"Finally," he pulled into traffic.

At least, we were headed in the right direction. The Silver Swan and the Palace Queen faced off from opposite sides of the same corner. The Swan didn't have the bulk of the Palace Queen but it ran a close second and it had undergone a major facelift five years ago. "Tell me why we're headed there."

Crawford didn't answer.

"Here it is." He grunted and I imagined him settling his weight in his leather chair. "You're looking for an ex-chorus girl turned dealer named Lydia Storm."

"You're kidding." I wrote as I spoke.

"What'd you expect? Mary Poppins?" Crawford asked.

"Okay. Okay. What table does she work?" With Randy, it had to be poker.

"Craps." Crawford's answer dashed my imagined connection. "She's on tonight."

"All right." I threw the pencil in my bag with a careless toss. "Tell me how she's involved."

"Would you believe she's Randy's mistress?"

"No," I answered without hesitation. "I'm no fan, but Randy's not the cheating type."

Crawford made a clicking sound. "You get another marker on the board, Belden."

Maybe I could still read my ex. "Who is she?"

"Lydia knew Cassie Reed way back when."

I caught my breath at the connection.

"What?" Kevin looked over.

I relayed the tidbit then turned my attention to the phone. "How'd they find this Lydia person so quickly?"

"The local rag ran a story on the deceased Mrs. McKiernan asking people to come forward with information. The woman said she knew the victim as Cassie Reed in Vegas."

Kevin turned into the parking lot of the Silver Swan and parked under a glaring light.

I fought to keep the cast of characters straight. "Even if the victim called herself Cassie Reed—"

"The woman Lydia worked with came from Black Oak, Kansas." Crawford's raspy voice sounded like he'd just laid a trump card on a trick.

Kevin turned off the car and leaned close. Barely breathing, he listened intently to the conversation. The lingering scent of his cologne teased my nostrils.

Crawford continued, "The police showed her a sketch of the deceased when she wasn't three days dead."

I grimaced at the reminder of the body and concentrated on Crawford's build up.

"Lydia didn't recognize the victim." Crawford paused

for an instant. "The woman she knew in Vegas twenty years ago was the original Cassie Reed."

"But what about..." My thoughts and voice stumbled to a stop. The implications hit me like a bat between the eyeballs as Crawford continued.

"Lydia saw the Cassie Reed from Kansas take a header into the lap of a very drunk Randy McKiernan. That same Cassie showed up a month later with a wedding ring."

Kevin's gaze narrowed.

My brain finally filled in the picture. "The real Cassie Reed disappeared *after* the marriage, not before."

11

27 Down; 4 Letters;
Clue: Bright color. Casino signs are made of this.
Answer: Neon

My lips pursed in a silent whistle. "Randy knows what happened to the real Cassie Reed."

"The murder victim also knew Cassie's fate." Kevin eyed me with an intense scrutiny. "Good thing for Randy the dead tell no tales."

Crawford grunted. "Your ex vanished after the police started putting the pieces together."

A siren in the distance reminded me why I was on the streets in the middle of the night. "My only interest in this craps dealer is finding Marcus."

"Watch your step." A warning note sounded in Crawford's voice. "The police plan to re-interview Ms. Storm tonight. They'll take you in if they find you."

"Wonderful." Just when I thought I'd left the cops behind. "Let me know if you hear more good news."

"Call me if you need backup."

I knew I could count on the old fart. "Thanks."

"Next time your phone rings, check the ID before you start yapping," he said. "Cops have phones, too."

"Thanks for the vote of confidence." Grateful Crawford wasn't after me, I clicked off and climbed out of the car.

Kevin met me by the front fender. He eyed me with a serious gaze. "This means the dead woman isn't wifey-number-two. She's at least number three."

With that, he strode past me. I scowled at him while trying to wrap my mind around the fluid nature of Randy's wives. Finally, I found my legs and caught up to Kevin.

"We have a bigger problem." Not that we needed more issues. "Crawford never told me what Lydia looks like."

I felt foolish that I hadn't bothered to ask. After the night I'd had, I couldn't face calling him.

"We'll figure it out on the move." Kevin took my arm and marched me toward the building. "We have to get in and out before the cops arrive."

A moment later we strode through the wide glass doors of the main entrance. Lights blinked in a dizzying display. Bells and whistles warred with each other. A maze of dollar slots impeded our progress. Overhead, a haze of cigarette smoke swirled like a cloud looking to land.

One machine erupted in a fit of noise and light. The wrinkled woman playing it barely blinked. A few players paused long enough to eye her with envy. I headed for the crap tables.

Kevin blocked me with a subtle move. "The bar's over there. We need info."

I resisted the urge to rush forward blindly. Considering the lead the boys had on us, they could be anywhere. It was one o'clock, Sunday morning; maybe they were home. It was wishful thinking, but I pulled out my phone. "Order me a lemonade."

Three feet of emptiness around the bar failed to dim the noise on the decibel scale.

Kevin ordered the drinks as I dialed.

"Hello?" Mrs. C's voice sounded faint.

I cupped a hand over my other ear. "Any sign of Marcus?"

"Not a word. Where are you, lovey?" The English accent was still with us. "This is no time for barhopping."

"We think the boys came to a casino." I tried to moderate my voice so no one else could hear me, as if anyone cared. "What about the cops?"

"They've long since gone." Amusement sounded in her tone. "It was wild fun. The bobbies searched the building in case Marcus was hurt. They promised to call if they heard anything. They were so sweet. I made them tea and biscuits."

I'm chasing runaways, and my landlady's having a coffee klatch with a bunch of cops. "If Crawford calls, he knows the scoop."

"I'll tell him anything I can," she assured me.

"Thanks again." I clicked off and slid the phone into my purse. Taking a sip of cold lemonade, I joined the conversation between Kevin and the bartender.

"This craps dealer walked away from her table in the

middle of a game?" Kevin sipped his soda with a nonchalance I could only envy. "When was this?"

The bartender, a well-tanned blonde, crossed his well-toned arms over his chest. He aimed an inviting smile my way. "About an hour ago."

My heart picked up speed. That fit the timing of Marcus's disappearance. After he and Steve hooked up and hopped a bus, the boys could have arrived at the casino before the woman took off.

"Why did she leave?" Kevin asked, catching a peanut in his mouth.

"No one knows." The guy shook his head. "The security guard told me the roller had hit a streak. People crowded around the table so close no could move. A waitress served a couple right next to the dealer not five minutes earlier. But she didn't notice anything suspicious."

Scenes from countless movies of spies slipping a note in someone's pocket ran through my mind. It was so cliché I could see Marcus convincing a waitress to give the craps dealer a note to meet him.

The bartender filled a couple of orders then picked up the thread of the story as if he'd never left. "The security cameras showed she might be reading a note, then, with no warning, she put down her stick and signaled the floor boss. She vanished before anyone got there."

I sat on the edge of my seat.

Kevin glanced at a blackjack table and listened with all the interest of someone waiting for time to pass.

The guy leaned forward, evidently fearful he was losing his audience. "They even checked her apartment."

I hid my excitement by grasping my lemonade. I slid

the cold glass in the circle of condensation on the gleaming bar. "Her apartment?"

"The employees have the option of long-term leases in the hotel. I have a place upstairs." He cast me a simmering look.

"That's convenient." I met his smile with one of my own. "Did they find any clues in her place?"

"Nothing," he leaned my way. "By the time they checked, Jade had been gone over thirty minutes."

My balloon popped, scattering hope to the winds. Long practice kept my thoughts hidden behind a neutral mask. The woman had the wrong name. Still, how may craps dealers could disappear in one night? "Where'd she get a name like Jade?"

The bartender scanned the customers at the far end of the counter. When their attention remained fixed on video poker, he turned to me. "A stage name from Vegas. She said it was her good luck charm. Her real name is Lydia."

My balloon re-inflated.

"Maybe the INS found her," Kevin suggested as he casually sipped his drink.

The bartender and I exchanged puzzled looks.

"Illegal immigrants aren't only from Mexico." Kevin kept my gaze as he continued. "She may have snuck in from Asia years ago and somebody finally turned her in."

The bartender laughed. "The closest Lydia's been to China is San Francisco. She's a brown-eyed blonde with dark roots."

I gave Kevin three points for getting a description. Crawford would be impressed. I nudged Kevin's leg with my knee. We wouldn't get any more from this guy. "You want to hit the slots?"

"I suppose." Looking at the bartender, Kevin set two twenties on the counter. "Thanks for the conversation."

Four steps away from the bar the clamor of slots engulfed us again.

Kevin put his lips next to my ear. "We have to find the apartment."

"I have an idea."

Moments later, I hurried through a causeway lined with small shops and a string of lounges and restaurants. The hotel's registration desk came into view.

Kevin walked by my side with an athlete's grace. "Elevators are up ahead."

I scanned the lobby. "I don't want the main elevators."

"What are you looking for?" Kevin asked.

"I was a maid in Vegas, remember?" I pointed to an unmarked hall tucked into the corner. "Major hotels have a set of elevators for housekeeping. If you commit a crime, worry about the cleaning crew. They see everything and people pay them no mind."

A third of the way down the hall the buzz of conversation floated around a corner. I smiled at Kevin who graced me with a congratulatory nod.

A woman's voice with a southern accent filled the air. "I told that man I didn't care if he spent ten thousand on a throw, the next time his fingers *accidentally* ended up where they didn't belong he'd be playing one-handed."

Raucous laughter followed. The instant Kevin and I turned the corner, silence descended.

The half-a-dozen faces eyeing us ranged from tan to dark brown. Mexican. Asian. Black. In this profession, I'd been the minority. A grandmotherly woman smiled at us. "The main elevators are in the front hall."

"I'm sorry to disturb you." I gave her an apologetic

grimace. "A guard told me these elevators were the quickest way to the employee apartment. My son and his friend are with a dealer named Lydia Storm."

A young black woman who'd been stuffing towels into a cart turned toward me. "They were with her all right."

A rush of elation filled me.

"Your son's with a little Asian boy, isn't he?"

I stared in confusion; then I realized she'd assumed Steve was my son. I clutched Kevin's arm. I didn't have to fake the shaky relief in my voice. "They're here."

"Well..." A stocky Mexican man drawled the word out. "Not quite."

I frowned in puzzlement. "What do you mean?"

"How come those boys are running around at this time of night?" The young woman asked in an outraged voice. "It was after one when I saw them."

"My ex-husband." The venom I'd stored up against Randy poured out. If he hadn't dragged me away from my apartment, I'd have been home when Marcus took off.

Matching outrage filled the women's faces.

"Don't that just figure?" one woman said. "Men are useless."

"You got that right." I answered with feeling. "He was supposed to drop the boys at my place by ten. As usual, he didn't show. By the time I got a hold of him, he had the nerve to tell me he'd left the boys with this Lydia Storm. I could have killed him. I just may the next time I see him."

"You tell him, girl!"

I didn't see who said it, but the words kicked off a few minutes of trashing men in general and ex-husbands in particular.

The males remained silent. Except for Kevin who

muttered that men couldn't win in this argument. After things settled down a feeling of comradery filled the air.

"I came as soon as I could. A security guard sent me here." I ended my diatribe with an exasperated sigh.

Kevin put a hand on my shoulder. "We just want to get the boys home."

Who could resist such a plea?

Our audience exchanged looks; then the older woman spoke up. "Those boys aren't here, neither is Lydia."

My heart sank. "But ..."

"She walked away from her table an hour ago without permission." The woman made it sound as if murder would have been more easily forgiven. "I didn't hear mention of kids until just now."

She shot her co-worker an accusatory look.

"I didn't think of it until she mentioned her boy," the younger woman explained.

"Maybe she took them upstairs." Though I knew the casino personnel had found her apartment empty, I had to get a look at the place for myself.

"She's not home," a gray-haired black man spoke up. "I was doing rounds when the manager and security opened her door with the passkey. You could hear them yelling for her all the way down the hall. They left alone."

My shoulders slumped. I didn't have to feign my disappointment. This night was turning into a marathon.

"Did they find a note?" Kevin asked.

I latched onto the suggestion. "Maybe she left with the boys then came back after the manager left."

The man shrugged. "I didn't hear any talk of a note."

"Can I check?" I clasped my hands to my chest. "I

can't bear the thought of leaving, only to find she might be there. She could help me find my son."

No one said anything, then the matriarch of the group looked at me. "We're not allowed to let anyone into a private room without a search warrant."

I kept my lost puppy expression. I knew there was more to come.

"But if you take the elevator to the balcony for sight-seeing that's your choice." She glanced at the woman who'd seen the boys. "And if Wanda starts her two o'clock run in Lydia's room, it'd just be a coincidence."

My knees went weak with relief. I rewarded her with a smile of gratitude. This was a woman after my own heart.

"I've always wanted to see the city from the upper floor," I informed Kevin of this late discovered desire.

Wanda pushed her cart toward the elevator. "I'll get started."

With Kevin and I close behind her, Wanda flipped a switch and punched the tenth floor. I held onto the hope of a solid clue. The worry of being a murder suspect paled next to the thought of Marcus getting hurt.

12

30 Across; 4 Letters;
Clue: To give aid or assistance.
Answer: Help

B y the time the elevator passed the second floor, my nails were playing chopsticks on the decorative handrail. At the sixth floor, Kevin's smile looked like a grimace and his whisper to relax sounded like a threat.

I stilled my nervous fingers and shot him an apologetic look.

"You got yourself a good man this time, honey." Wanda winked at Kevin.

She was right. Who else would be chasing around the streets at two o'clock in the morning? Feeling mischievous, I stepped closer and put my arm around his waist. "He's a keeper."

Kevin raised a brow and sent a slow smile my way.

Just when I wondered what I'd gotten myself into, the elevator doors opened with a whoosh. Teasing forgotten, I followed Wanda into a corridor of muted blue and deep burgundy. The hall seemed cool without Kevin's warmth beside me.

"The sight-seeing balcony is on the right," Wanda tossed the comment over her shoulder.

"Thanks." An odd reluctance slowed my steps. Had I gotten us in too deep this time? What if Marcus was hurt or in danger?

As if sensing my hesitation, Kevin swept me forward. "Once the scam's in motion, stay in character. Never show doubt or fear."

I marshaled my resources and gave myself a talking to. What kind of a sneak was I if I balked this early in the game?

Wanda stopped at the fourth door on the right. A flip of her electronic key card opened the door. She turned to the apartment across the hall and repeated the maneuver. "You two enjoy the sights."

"Thanks again." I slipped into Lydia's apartment.

A combination dining room/living room was on the left. The alcove ahead on the right must be the bedroom.

Kevin shut the door behind us. "What are we looking for?"

"Anything," I shot at him. "I'll check the bedroom."

I only hoped the clue would have a big red bow tied to it.

Lydia Storm's taste was subdued. Soft blue flowers and white accessories accented pale yellow walls in the bedroom. An unplugged power cord for a laptop snaked across one corner of the desk.

A hiss from the living room stopped my heart. I

glanced around the corner. Instead of a desert rattler, Kevin stared at me from the middle of the room. "Careful what you touch. We don't need to leave fingerprints."

I refused to admit I hadn't thought of that. "This isn't my first rodeo."

Putting a tissue over my fingers, I slid a desk drawer open. A scattering of papers seemed at odds with the neatly organized desk. Too bad I couldn't confirm whether any were missing.

A sticky note taped to the bottom of the drawer caught my eye. At first glance the string of numbers and letters meant nothing. When my brain inserted a letter for each number, it spelled Garden Spot.

Silence roared in my ears. The last two blighted years of my marriage had been spent in the Garden Spot Trailer Inn watching my dreams wilt in the desert heat. Randy had stayed on there after I left him.

Why would that location have any meaning for Lydia?

My mind shuffled through possibilities. Had Lydia been more involved with the original Cassie Reed than she'd let on? How had Randy, Cassie, and Lydia all ended up in Langsdale?

"Time to go." Excitement thrummed in Kevin's whisper as it floated around the corner.

I slid the drawer shut and hurried to the closet. Conspicuous gaps marred three neat rows of shoes. A glance at a handful of empty hangers was all I needed.

The woman had bolted.

"Let's move!" Kevin's urgent tone snapped me out of my trance.

Out in the hall, Wanda was pushing her cart toward the staff elevators.

When he turned to follow Wanda, I snagged his shirt

and pulled him toward the front elevators. "We'll be less conspicuous if we slip out the main entrance."

After a step, I glanced the way we'd come. Wanda had disappeared. I nudged his arm. "What did you find?"

He pulled out a sheet of pale green paper. "Look familiar?"

"That's from Marcus's notebook." I touched the paper as if it were a talisman. "What's it say?"

"I didn't read it," he admitted. "I figured we'd better get out of there. Find anything?"

"She took some clothes. She's not coming back, and she did know Cassie in Vegas, possibly Randy as well." When I told him about the Garden Spot, Kevin gave a silent whistle.

The hall widened to a large open area. A bank of windows overlooked a panoramic view of the city. Balconies invited gawkers outside. The elevator ahead of us dinged.

"This view is amazing." Kevin executed a quick turn and gently but firmly dragged me toward the window. His slim build belied the strength in his corded muscles. "Look at those lights."

When I stiffened my legs, he stepped behind me and pulled me against his lean chest.

I leaned into his solid strength. Warmth frizzled my tired brain. A heartbeat later, I snapped out of it. "We've no ti—"

"Right this way, detective." The well-oiled voice of a management type sounded directly behind us.

Shock lanced through me like lightning. I almost swallowed my tongue.

"Isn't this gorgeous?" Astonishment reverberated

through Kevin's tone. "I've never been up this high before."

Taking a deep breath, I prayed my mouth would work. "It's beautiful."

A parade of footsteps marched behind us. The same voice spoke again. "Down the hall on the left. We checked after she disappeared, but her apartment was empty."

"No one has been in since?" an official voice asked.

"No, sir," the man said. "Has something happened to Lydia?"

"We don't know yet," the detective answered.

I wilted against Kevin. Thankfully, Wanda should be off the floor by now.

"Ms. Storm told no one where she was going or why she had to leave?" The detective's voice faded.

I snapped out of my shock in time to check their reflection in the windows. Their legs were just disappearing down the corridor. Kevin's head moved in the same direction. Half-a-breath later, we turned as one and ran to the elevator.

Kevin beat me by half a step and stabbed the button.

It took four rapid thumps of my heart for the elevator to come. Bolting inside, I smacked the lobby button. The doors closed with agonizing slowness.

Kevin let out a breath. "That was too close for comfort."

"I'm not cut out for this." I stared at the door, imagining the detective storming through it. "You don't suppose they left cops in the lobby, do you?"

Kevin shook his head. "They don't know we're here. They're interested in Lydia Storm."

Made sense, but when the doors opened, Kevin and I both peered around the elevator before getting out. No one stood by the doors acting noticeably nonchalant. I glanced at Kevin, feeling foolish.

He gave me an equally sheepish grin. "Let's go."

I walked toward the well-lit hotel doors.

"Belden, you don't know where you're going," Kevin said.

"I can't face that maze." I walked outside without a backward glance. The evening air felt like a splash of cold water. Blinking away the heaviness of my eyelids, I turned right. The car should be just around the corner.

Kevin grabbed my arm. "This way."

"You sure?"

He rolled his eyes. "Trust me."

Acres of parking lot surrounded us on all sides. The length of the casino stretched into the distance.

"This is going to be a long walk." Kevin eyed me with a searching gaze.

I sought for a witty reply. "Yeah."

"A woman of few words."

The distant corner of the building lay a good two blocks away. I started to re-think the odds of running into the detectives in the casino when a car stopped beside us.

"You two didn't stay long." Our friendly neighborhood bartender sat in the driver's seat of a blue Mustang convertible and flashed his pearly whites. "Did you win?"

"Not so you'd notice," Kevin said with a smile.

I was too busy thanking God to say anything.

"What are doing on this side of the building?"

"We wanted some fresh air, but it looks like quite a walk to the car." Kevin didn't so much as hint that he'd known where the car was before we left the building.

What chivalry.

"It's a nice night." I tried to act like I didn't care if the guy drove off and left us. I didn't convince anyone, least of all myself.

The guy laughed and jerked his thumb toward the car. "It's just as nice driving. Get in."

"Thank, God." I couldn't keep the relief out of my voice.

I slipped into the backseat. I was done charming the guy.

"You have enough room?" he asked.

"I'm fine." I forced out my last iota of cheeriness as my bones melted into the seat.

With Kevin riding shotgun, the car purred forward. The dark purple night flew by overhead. We turned a corner then wove through a dock area. One more turn and Kevin's Chevy came into view, sitting by its lonesome underneath a light pole.

I'd have collapsed onto the asphalt long ago.

When the Mustang eased to a stop, Kevin all but lifted me from the back seat. "Thanks again. We'll look you up next time."

My aches and pain made themselves felt as I struggled to remain upright. Kevin opened the door then waited until I sat, still protecting my right side.

As soon as Kevin got behind the wheel, he pulled out the green paper and smoothed it on his knee.

When I twisted for a better view, my ribs screamed. I clenched my teeth against the pain.

Kevin cast me a concerned look, but he flipped on the inside light without saying a word.

I wouldn't have listened anyway. I only had eyes for the note. Marcus had used the green marker from his backpack.

'Randy and his friends can't let anyone find out where

the money came from. He'll be after you next. Meet me by the rear elevators. A Friend'

"He's seen too many old movies." I read the note twice.

"'Where the money came from?'" Kevin read the phrase aloud. "Who are these 'friends'?"

I stabbed at the note, careful to keep the gesture small. "This proves there's something funny about Randy's money."

"It doesn't prove anything." Kevin countered. "Lydia's reaction does."

I stared at the words objectively. Green magic marker? How could anyone take that seriously? "The questions is, what scared her so much that she took off? And where are the boys? Did she take them with her?"

The thought drove a stake through my heart. The question still hung in the air when a whirl of blue and red lights cast a kaleidoscope of color across Kevin's face.

I watched Kevin's expression freeze at the same instant I felt my face stiffen. My eyes registered a flash of color before he snapped off the light, pushed me down, and slithered lower in his seat.

I make a lousy criminal. When would I learn to make a clean getaway when I had the chance?

13

33 Across; 8 Letters;
Clue: Uninformed; No idea what is going on.
Answer: Clueless

M y heart climbed into my throat, threatening to block my oxygen supply. Not only would I be taken in for questioning, I had dragged Kevin in with me. Even worse, Marcus was still unaccounted for.

Anxiety built in my roiling stomach. I nibbled on my thumbnail and tried to angle for a coherent scene in the rearview mirror. Even flipping on my back, I couldn't see anything useful.

"Are they coming this way?" I whispered.

Kevin had managed to fold his frame small enough that his head was well below the window of the Chevy. He cleaned his fingernails with the key while keeping a seemingly unconcerned gaze on the rearview mirror. "They've slowed. Spotlight is coming this way."

A wide beam of white light lit the night. It cut a swath through the Chevy and illuminating what little I could see of the parking lot.

"Could you have the decency to look worried?" I pressed my lips together as Kevin continued cleaning his nails. "You do realize you might be arrested for being caught with me?"

His blue eyes shifted to mine with a steady look before returning to follow the progress of the spotlight. "I've been arrested lots of times. Getting the charges to stick is the hard part. The cops have nothing conclusive on either of us. They'd have to release us. Eventually. At least they'd have to release me."

He shot a teasing smile my way.

"Great." I nibbled my nail, too worried about Marcus to think coherently. "I don't have time to go downtown for questioning."

I tried to work up a plan. But I had nothing. No plan. No Marcus. No answers. It was well past midnight. My Saturday had been way too long and Sunday wasn't starting out any better. I slumped against the seat. "Maybe we should give up."

"This from Tracy 'Never-say-die' Belden?" He stiffened like a dog on point. "Keep the white flag in your pocket. They're driving past the car."

His words roused my fighting spirit. From an opening in one of the windows, a cool breeze brought me to life.

I raised myself up on my elbows. His hand stopped me just short of the dashboard. This time, I was able to tilt my head enough to get a view of the police car. While not completely past our position, the black-and-white was to the right and slightly beyond us.

The driver panned the spotlight across the parking lot. Other than some buses in the hinterland and a handful of cars, acres of emptiness surrounded Kevin's Chevy.

"Is the guy on the passenger side wearing a cowboy hat?" Between the spotlight and the streetlights overhead I made out a slim silhouette. As I peered over the dash, the figure removed the wide-brimmed hat and swiveled around for a full view of the lot.

Kevin and I crouched lower.

When the passenger leaned over the backseat, I got a better look at him. He was male with a lean profile. His head brushed the inside of the cop car. A tall frame.

"Langsdale police don't wear Stetsons." I narrowed my gaze. "Who's the Cowboy Guy in the front seat?"

"Cowboy Guy?" Despite the circumstances, Kevin's voice held a touch of amusement. He knew my penchant for giving people nicknames. "If he's in the front seat, he's law enforcement. I don't see a uniform. Maybe he's from out of town."

"I'll run it by Crawford. See if it might be connected with this case or if it is just my random bad luck." I waited until the police car drove around the corner of the building before pulling myself upright in the seat. "Give me a heart attack."

"Let's get out of here before the cops do a second circuit." Kevin aimed the car for the nearest exit.

As the Chevy settled into the rhythm of the road, the day caught up with me. I closed my eyes and swayed to the rocking motion of the moving car.

A few turns later we picked up speed and a rhythmic

pattern of light and dark flashed across my eyelids. Streetlights. We were on a main drag.

On the verge of dropping off, I rubbed a hand across my face and forced my brain awake. "Where are we headed?"

"Home," Kevin said.

I shot awake. "We can't quit."

"Neither of us are in any shape to track a wily kid with a head start." He cast me a sideways glance. "Besides, your ribs have to be taped."

I hate it when logic interferes with my goals. But I barely had the energy to sit up straight. We had a note, not a map. "Okay, we'll catch some shut eye then regroup. Maybe by then, my boy-child will have called, and I can drag him home and ground him for the rest of his life."

"You're forgetting about Lydia," Kevin said.

I shook my head, too tired to think. "Somebody else will have to ground her."

"Marcus made her our problem when he pulled her away from that crap table." Unlike me, Kevin made no attempt to deny reality. He dealt with the issues head on.

"It's too much to think about." The day... the night was catching up with me. I didn't think I drifted off, but suddenly the gentle swaying came to a halt.

I blinked the sleep out of my eyes. The yellow stenciled letters of BAUM IRON danced on an old brick wall. The business has offices on the bottom floor of Kevin's apartment building.

"Wake up, Sleeping Beauty." Kevin turned off the ignition. "Your chariot has landed."

"You're mixing metaphors and fairy tales." I fought to gather my wits then opened the door. They were both a struggle, but I managed. My next trick would be to stay awake long enough to collapse into bed.

Chords of heavy music from the bar down the street laced the air. The beat was loud and steady. If I tried, I'd be able to catch the words. A screech of tires and a blaring horn sounded from the street. Early morning in the city.

Soon the nineteenth-century elevator that served the building ground to a halt on the second floor. Kevin pulled the brass doors open then reached for the accordion style iron grill. We usually didn't use the elevator. But it was either the elevator or have Kevin lug me up two flights of stairs.

Kevin nudged me toward his apartment.

I concentrated on putting one foot in front of the other.

"You can have the bed. I'll take the couch." He sorted through his key ring.

"Be real." I leaned on his doorjamb. "Your king bed is big enough for both of us to get lost in."

"Thank God," Kevin said with a tired sigh. "I can't stand sleeping on that couch. I swear your virtue is safe."

I've slept on his couch before. It's not bad. Right now, I'd have slept on the floor. "Nice of you to pretend either of us has any virtue left."

As soon as the door opened, I staggered across the threshold. A long marble-topped table stood against the edge of a red overstuffed sofa.

Marcus popped up over the back of the couch. "'Bout time you two got here."

14

Relief washed over me at the sight of my prodigal son alive and well. But when a quick scan showed no sign of injuries, irritation kicked in and rose to anger. It was after midnight, which made it Sunday morning. He had no business being out so late and scaring me half to death. I wanted to give him a lecture he'd never forget.

However, my eyelids each weighed a hundred pounds and the thought of lying down was already pushing aside the question of what Marcus had been doing and why. I advanced at my best speed, which turned out to be a slow crawl.

"If you ever run away again..." I tried to think of a

threat that didn't contain physical violence. "I'll have you barred from ever being a private investigator."

"I'd never run away." Marcus looked at me as if I'd just gotten off the boat. "Living with you is a good gig."

He jumped off the couch and flung his arms around me.

When I hissed in pain, he frowned and stepped away. I pulled him toward me, resting my cheek on his silky black hair. "It's just bruises."

After a second he stepped back. "I thought I'd be home before anyone knew I was gone."

"Why didn't you go to your place?" Kevin asked.

"The cops have it staked out," Marcus said.

"They do?" So what if I jumped out a window to avoid them? They should have known I'd be in touch when things calmed down.

Marcus met my gaze with those dark chocolate eyes. "I didn't mean to cause trouble."

Who could stay angry looking at that face? Not me. For one thing, I was too tired. "The important thing is you're here and you're safe. Don't do it again."

"No way," Marcus spoke quickly, then sighed. "I have a problem."

"Big surprise." The lines of tension had vanished from Kevin's face when he squeezed Marcus's shoulder. "A Belden with a problem."

My appointment with a pillow grew fainter. "Where's Steve?"

"He bailed." Marcus didn't try to hide his disdain. "I swore him to silence before he went home. He's probably in bed."

I wondered if Steve's mom wanted to switch children.

Just for the night. "What kind of problem are we talking about?"

"Nothing illegal."

Kevin didn't bother to muffle his laughter.

"Maybe I should cut to the chase." Hesitation sounded behind Marcus's bravado.

I folded my arms across my chest. "Tell me."

"Things didn't go as smoothly as they do in stories," Marcus admitted.

"Never does, dude," Kevin said with world-weary knowledge. "Where's Lydia?"

"She's the problem."

My legs shook and my eyes wouldn't stay open. I was hanging on by my fingernails. "I'm looking at my problem."

Marcus's smile showed how seriously he took me. But he wisely answered Kevin's question. "I stashed Lydia at a hotel, but I need more cash to pay the bill."

I didn't ask why she was in hiding or why I should keep her there. I didn't even try to think what hotel in this resort city would take cash. I only had strength for the essentials. I looked at Kevin and fought not to keel over. "If you drive, I can get money from an ATM."

"I'm not carrying you to the car." He walked toward me. "I'll get the money. First, we tape your ribs."

Marcus stepped away. "What's wrong with your ribs?"

"Long story." I ran my hand over his silky, black hair. "It's not serious. I just need to rest."

Kevin gestured me forward. "Starting now."

I turned toward the bedroom. "Come on, urchin. You can fill in the details."

The sound of a key in the door stopped us. Jimbo, Kevin's roomie and the former linebacker, stepped across the threshold. Still fighting with his key, he stopped and looked from Kevin to Marcus to me then back. He probably hadn't expected a greeting committee at zero-dark-thirty in the morning.

A cautious smile touched the corners of his lips. "Hey, gang. What's up?"

I'd never appreciated before how Jimbo filled a doorway. Wind would have had trouble getting past him. He stands six-foot-five and is built, as my father would say, like a brick outhouse. A silvery blond, hazel-eyed brick outhouse who outran us all when we played touch football.

Marcus raised a hand. "Hi, Jimbo, staying on nights?"

Jimbo nodded. "It's easier than switching around. My body clock is only on one shift."

He looked at Kevin. "One of the guys drove Svendon over to pick up the Buick."

Kevin slapped his forehead then turned to me with an apologetic look. "I was going to mention it but in all the excitement, I forgot."

I stared at him blankly. "Oh, *my* Buick."

"I mentioned to you the other day that Svendon wanted to borrow it today," Kevin said. "His mother's in one hospital. His wife's in another. His father's staying with him and their car got totaled."

I held up a hand. "Enough with the catalog of misery. The guy's life sounds worse than mine."

"I gave him the extra key I had and said if he didn't hear from me to take it," Kevin explained.

"They're welcome to the car. It's not like I can use it with cops staking out my place." An image formed and I started to laugh.

The guys exchanged puzzled looks.

"The cops are going to be chasing Svendon all over town." I gasped out the words between bursts of laughter.

Kevin and Marcus's eyes widened then they joined in.

Jimbo looked at us. "Police?"

The worry in his tone sobered us up. I realized there was no way to make sense of the situation. "It's been a long night."

He looked at me, his expression full of sympathy. "Looks like it."

I raised my chin. I couldn't look that bad. Then the room swayed. I gripped Marcus's shoulder.

He put his arm around my waist.

Kevin supported me from the other side.

I leaned against him. "I'm all right, just tired."

"You're not all right." Kevin's arm tightened around my waist. "You need your ribs checked."

"Anything I can do?" Jimbo asked.

Kevin and I exchanged glances.

"Actually, if you don't mind..." Kevin let the sentence fade away.

"Anything," Jimbo agreed unconditionally and, I thought, foolishly.

Kevin plunged right in. "We need to pay off a hotel so a woman Marcus stashed can hide out for a while."

"Sure thing." Jimbo accepted the bizarre explanation without a flicker of hesitation or surprise. "What hotel? How much money?"

I'd never thought to ask.

"I'll take you there," Marcus said. "A hundred should cover three to four days."

My mind struggled to make sense of his figures. A resort town like Langsdale didn't have hotels that cheap. I wanted to warn Jimbo, but I couldn't form the words.

"That's cool," Jimbo said. "I just got paid. We can get her some snacks, too."

"We'll work it out later," Kevin and I offered simultaneously.

"As far as we know, the woman isn't wanted," Kevin continued in a reassuring tone. "At least not for a crime, maybe as a material witness. Hiding her isn't illegal. If it is, it's probably a misdemeanor."

Kevin's explanation stirred me out of my stupor. Was he trying to reassure Jimbo or scare the man away?

Jimbo nodded so quickly I wasn't sure he'd heard the words. If he had, he evidently took misdemeanor crimes in stride.

The former linebacker motioned Marcus toward the door. "I'll get the money and we can deliver the goods."

"Don't let him talk you into pit stops of any kind," I warned, letting go of Marcus.

"I'll take good care of the kid." Jimbo looked at me with a slight grimace. "You better get some sleep."

Marcus, already by the big man's side, faced me with a concerned expression. "He's right. I've seen dead animals that look better than you."

"Thanks." I raised an eyebrow. At least, I tried. My facial muscles might have stopped obeying me by that point.

They turned and walked into the hall.

Kevin pulled me closer. "Want to go to bed with me?"

Barely able to keep legs beneath me or my eyes open, I met his gaze. "I thought you'd never ask."

I woke in a sea of downy comforter. Pulling it up to my chin, I snuggled into a soft pillow. Except my spread wasn't this nice. I forced my eyes open.

Sunlight glimmered around the window blinds on the far wall. Nothing looked familiar. How had I ended up in a strange bedroom? I propped myself up, wincing at a pain in my side.

My gaze rested on a maple dresser with carved legs. I'd helped Kevin pick out that dresser at an estate sale. I wilted into the bed and sighed in relief. Bands of something constricted my chest. I wondered when I'd hurt myself and why I was sleeping at Kevin's place.

My eyes drifted shut. Marcus was safe. The thought sparked a slide show of the previous night: the casino, Steve's house, the fire escape, the police, Randy.

I groaned and turned over to go to sleep. Then, my bladder reminded me why I'd been prodded awake. I tried to ignore it, but a full bladder waits for no one.

I stumbled out of bed. Holding my arms in front of me, I bounced through the bathroom door and off the sink like a pinball in play. Afterward, I sank beneath the comforter. The steady thrum of traffic sounded from the street. Shadows of light danced beyond my eyelids.

The next thing I knew the alluring scent of coffee filled the air. I drank in the smell. Mint with a hint of chocolate. If highways were scratch and sniff, I'd never get lost. I felt rested and almost human.

The mattress slanted and the scent of coffee grew stronger.

"I know you're awake. It's eleven-thirty in the morning. Marcus is on his second breakfast." Kevin's voice sounded within arm's reach. "Even if you hadn't slept for over ten hours, you can't remain unconscious with fresh coffee this close."

I opened my eyes, levered myself to a sitting position, then reached for the mug. Seconds later, hot liquid danced across my taste buds and scalded my throat. As soon as it hit my stomach, warmth sang through my veins to my toes. I put a pillow across my lap, then rested my mug on it.

"I could tell you it was mint chocolate with cinnamon," Kevin said, "but I'm sure you had it called before you opened your eyes."

"I missed the cinnamon," I admitted, taking a sip.

"I walked to the corner store two blocks away to get flavored coffee beans," he said in a martyred voice.

I touched his arm. "It was worth it."

"I figured you'd need to fortify yourself."

I didn't answer. For once the world could wait. Sunlight flooded through the open mini blinds. I made out the towers of the church that sits a block from Kevin's apartment building.

"Ten hours?" I couldn't believe I'd slept through the church ringing the hours. The bells start at seven in the morning and go until six at night. I'd made a crack once about why quit then, and Mrs. Colchester said six was the angelus, whatever that was. "I didn't hear the bells."

"They rang before I brought the coffee in."

Laughter rippled through his tone. I suppose at the thought that I could sleep through the bells but not the brew. No offense to God, but you have to have priorities. "God made coffee too, you know."

Kevin chuckled. "I don't think He likes it as much as you do."

I yawned. "Where's Marcus?"

"In the kitchen. He woke up about nine," Kevin said. "Time catches up even with eleven-year-olds."

"Thank God." I took a big drink of coffee, mulling the flavors over in my mouth before swallowing.

"Ready for the report?" Kevin asked.

"No." I knew I'd hear it anyway.

Kevin reached over to the table at the bedside. He picked up something and silently held it out to me; a chocolate covered biscotti.

"Oh, no," I moaned. "You not only spent money on 'a dried up old biscuit', but you're also risking crumbs in the bed?"

Kevin is an Oreo man and he despises crumbs.

Reminding myself that Marcus was safe, I reached for the treat. "Who's dead now?"

"It's just little things."

I dipped the biscotti in my coffee and remembered his non-comforting disclaimer to Jimbo last night. Or was it this morning? I shook my head and watched dust motes dance in the sunlight slanting through the blinds. A blue sky and soft white clouds filled the space between the slats.

"After you fell asleep, I told Mrs. Colchester and Crawford to take Marcus off the missing list. Steve is home. His story is he and Marcus wanted to check out the casino at night, no mention of a craps dealer."

I kept chewing and sipping, figuring he was working his way up from minor to major.

"Jimbo got the hotel bill settled for three days and bought her groceries and books so she can stay out of sight." He turned to me and his voice lost the professional reporting tone. "She's not in the Ritz. They like ID, but Marcus underestimated the money. We'll work that out."

At least the woman wasn't in a total dive. I felt responsible since Marcus had somehow precipitated her flight.

"Randy's still among the missing. No one has a clue where he's gone or how." Kevin continued with his list. "The papers say the police are concerned he might 'be a danger to himself in his grief-stricken state'."

I could hear the quotes in his voice. Translation: we want his butt back. Be his friend and turn him in. So far the report held nothing unexpected. The worst was yet to come. I took a bite of biscotti and sipped my coffee. For a brief second, I pictured myself in a Swiss resort, gazing at the mountains.

"There is a slight... complication."

The hesitation in his tone set my teeth on edge. "What now?"

Kevin looked at me. "Crawford explained to Detective Brennan about Marcus being missing. You're off the hook for being AWOL last night."

"Oh, goody." I waited for the punch line. What was he building up to? How bad could the news be?

"However, you're now a suspect in two murders."

15

25 Down; 7 Letters;
Clue: Information known only to a few.
Answer: Secrets

"Who else got murdered?" The shock coursing through my veins fueled the outrage in my voice. "You just said the police were looking for Randy."

"Doesn't mean they think he's alive." Kevin threw up his hands. "They want the body so they can officially charge you with both murders."

"They can't seriously buy the insurance policy as a motive." Though, admittedly, a million dollars was a lot of motive.

Kevin cast me a pitying look. "You wrote a letter to the dead woman. You lured her to a meeting. Wifey is found dead. Hubby visits you Saturday, sets up a meeting, and is also among the missing. You now stand to collect a cool million."

I stared at the dust dancing crazily in the sunlight.

"But... but..." I sputtered to a stop. "I was in the diner last night when he disappeared."

"For twenty minutes." Kevin's patent disbelief would have made him a great prosecution witness. "You were incommunicado the rest of the night."

"I was with you."

"Thanks for dragging me into this," he said in a note of mock outrage. "The police will tag me as the muscle. It's not like you could haul Randy's body anywhere by yourself."

I snapped my jaw shut, slowly absorbing the neat series of events that had boxed us in. "You're in trouble."

He cast me a mocking look. "Lucky for me I know a private investigator."

"I should have thrown Randy out yesterday morning and gone to Marcus's soccer game. That man always lands me in trouble then skates off." Panic fired my synapses. "We need to find Randy."

Kevin readjusted his pillow. "The police, the media, and Crawford are already looking."

"They don't know about Lydia." I tilted the mug up. Empty. "How am I supposed to think with no coffee?"

"Glad to have you back."

Throwing the pillow and the covers off my lap, I scooted off the bed. An oversized T-shirt hung past my knees. "We have, or had, a backdoor connection to the mayor's computer."

"Thanks to a miscreant child you wanted to punish."

"He's still on my list." I grabbed my clothes. "I have to get dressed."

Kevin stared at me from the bed. "You might want to watch those threats until the murder case is cleared up."

"Randy bolted because his scheme was unraveling and he couldn't face the music." My ex might have cleaned up his act over the years, but his instinct to flee in the face of trouble remained intact. "He grabbed a stash of cash and went into hiding."

"He left behind a lot of money," Kevin said, obviously unconvinced.

"He left behind a lot of years in prison." I sorted through my clothes and found my pants. "You better brew more coffee. We have to find out how Marcus knew about Lydia, then get the low-down on why she ran off. Then there's the question of the real Cassie Reed."

A gleam of anticipation grew in Kevin's eyes as he listened to my action plan. He slipped off the bed and walked toward the living room.

"Once we know the scheme and who had the most to lose, we'll have a clue what set this in motion." The door closed on my final word with a satisfying thud.

TWENTY MINUTES LATER, I sat by Kevin's kitchen window watching Marcus shovel milk-sodden cereal into his mouth with more enthusiasm than grace. "Take smaller bites and chew with your mouth closed."

He stared over his cereal bowl. "You wanted to know about Lydia."

"I don't need a view of breakfast going down," I said. "Lydia's not going anywhere."

"We'll check in later." Kevin pocketed his cell phone

and sat. "News and views from Crawford. Stay away from familiar places, especially home. He'll keep Mrs. Colchester in the know. He'll call the corner drugstore and have them take messages to her with a delivery if we need her for anything."

"Why couldn't it be her on the run? "That was her idea, wasn't it?"

Kevin nodded. "If you go down for murder, Crawford's going to hire her."

"I don't blame him." She obviously had more experience hiding from the police than I did.

"The cops won't hear any news from Crawford unless we turn up something that might clear you," Kevin continued.

"*When*," I said with added emphasis.

He looked at me with a puzzled expression.

"When we clear me," I said. "Let's try to stay upbeat."

"Oh, sure, absolutely." Kevin agreed without overwhelming enthusiasm. "Crawford also said he's willing to believe you're innocent."

"That's big of him." The moral support from that hooligan wouldn't keep a flea warm in Florida.

"If you get away with it, he wants a cut of the insurance money." Kevin poured himself a cup of coffee then topped off mine. "Me, too. It's the least you can do since I'm risking my good name to clear you."

"You don't have a good name to risk."

Marcus shoveled and chewed his cereal. His eyes got bigger with every mention of money. "If Randy turns up dead and you didn't do it, will we be rich?"

"Randy's not dead." The alluring smell of fresh coffee teased my nostrils. Whether Randy lived or died, being on easy street was not in the cards for me. "If he's found dead, I'll be fingered for it. So quit counting your pie-in-the-sky-money and start talking."

A somber look stole into his eyes. Marcus sloshed his spoon around, but the cereal was gone. "I didn't think it was going to turn out like it did."

I had to agree. "That's pretty much the story of my life."

My little wannabe detective pushed his bowl aside. "I planned to find out what Lydia knew and then leave. I convinced a waitress to slip her a note, but when Lydia came to talk to us, she was scared."

"It was her idea to leave the casino?" I asked.

"Of course, no way I wanted her tagging along." Marcus's tone reeked with attitude. "Once she got over us being kids, she acted like I knew the answers. I had to think of something."

Typical male, never willing to admit he didn't have a clue.

"What did you mean in your note by 'Randy and his friends'?" Kevin asked. "Who are these 'friends'?"

Marcus grinned and rose half out of his seat.

I thrust my hand in front of his face. "Start at the beginning. What led you to a craps dealer?"

My boy's face fell. Like a magician with a trick, he didn't want to explain where the rabbit came from; he wanted to dazzle.

"We need facts," I warned Marcus. "Especially if it involves hacking into the home computer of the mayor's accountant."

Marcus blinked in surprise. "You know about that?"

"I'm a PI. Remember?" Not to mention a good guesser. "You and Steve were looking for a video game, weren't you?"

"His mother bought a new one," Marcus said. "She puts the games on her computer to check for gore."

Since I was too poor to buy video games, Marcus played the ones his friends owned. I might worry more except Marcus had seen worse on the streets. Besides, I'd rather know what he was doing than have him hide things from me.

"Last week his mother had a late meeting at city hall. Their housekeeper was cooking supper, so we hacked into her home computer to find Hell Mouth 14."

If the woman was so concerned, why buy a game vilified by every do-gooder group in the nation? "Did you find it?"

"No, but we did find a link to remote into her work computer. Steve thought it might be hidden there. The grid card for the second level confirmation is in her desk drawer. From her work computer," his voice faded. He gave me a sheepish smile. "I hacked into the main server and got into the mayor's computer."

My blood pressure shot to the red zone. I gritted my teeth. Someday, I was going to find the FBI on my doorstep. However, with one dead woman, a missing ex, and the police looking for me, I couldn't afford the time to lecture. "Go on."

Marcus's tense expression relaxed. "I managed to uncover a file named Buffy's Pond."

Facing his look of expectation, I searched my memory, not wanting to disappoint. All I came up with was an old TV series Marcus and Steve had binge-watched last month. "you mean the character Buffy the Vampire Slayer on that old TV show?"

"Yeah." His eyes lit up like a teacher when a pupil

comes up with the right answer. "Buffy lived over the Hellmouth, a perfect place to hide 'Hell Mouth 14'."

Faultless logic. Mr. Spock would have been proud. But I spotted an obvious flaw. "Were you still in the mayor's files? How would he have this game?"

"I didn't stop to think. I just saw the title and went after it. Being on her computer got us through a lot of the firewalls, but when I managed to open the folder, no game." Despite everything, Marcus's voice held a note of disappointment. "The first line of the file read: Buffy equals Cassie. Below that was Pond equals Reed."

My eyes must have bugged out of their sockets. "Cassie Reed?"

Kevin tensed as if he'd been shot. "Talk about a link."

Marcus's smug smile said it all.

"You knew this yesterday and didn't say anything?" We'd spent Saturday afternoon discussing the case while we packed flower bulbs for mailing.

"Last week, I'd never heard of Cassie Reed," Marcus said. "It wasn't Hell Mouth, so we closed it. Last night, Steve texted me, and I remembered the file. But I had to be sure, or I'd look like a dork."

Slipping from King Rat to Dork would be a huge loss of face. I sipped my coffee and tried to look at the situation rationally. What would I have done if he'd mentioned it? "Is that why you ran off to Steve's?"

"I figured I'd double-check to make sure I was right."

Kevin spun his empty mug in a circle. "And you were."

"Steve's mother was gone and his father was in their den." Marcus smiled smugly. "This time I burned the file onto a CD."

My heart did a tap-dance. Proof. Evidence. "You have it?"

Marcus grimaced. "Not exactly."

My heart screeched to a stop mid-tap. "What do you mean 'not exactly'?"

"I accidentally stuck it in Steve's backpack." Marcus explained. "He moved the bags when I wasn't looking. I can get it at school tomorrow."

Our only clue and we had to wait until recess to rescue it. I bet Mrs. C had never had this problem. "Why didn't you tell us when you found us?"

"Hold it." Kevin held up a hand. "What was in the file?"

Marcus frowned. "There were word problems at the top, below that was a list of numbers and abbreviations."

I frowned. "What word problems?"

"Jade Garden equals Lydia Storm then great game equals Snake Eyes." He nodded as if that said it all.

After a quick review, my only conclusion was that both sides of each equation held the same number of letters. What did that mean? A code? "None of that explains what led you to the casinos or why you didn't tell us."

"I didn't have the facts," he said, exhaling.

"You wanted to play detective." I accused him. "You had the disk at that point."

"It was in Steve's backpack." His disappointment came through loud and clear. "Besides, I didn't know Lydia was real or in town."

I couldn't argue with him there.

Marcus shrugged. "I was hungry. I came home for pizza."

"Derailed by pepperoni."

I smothered a chuckle at Kevin's quip. "What led you to the Silver Swan?"

"That was all Steve," Marcus said in an admirable display of fairness. "He kept thinking about the names; Buffy equals Cassie. He said if there's an equals sign, the equations have to match. That's the way he thinks. Since we knew Cassie was real, Lydia Storm should be real."

The logic impressed me and he'd obviously been right, but I had to side with Marcus. "I'd never have figured that out."

Marcus agreed. "That's what I told him when he called me last night."

The phone had rung during Mrs. C's soccer game. I'd shooed Marcus into the kitchen to talk to his friend.

"Then Steve guessed Snake Eyes meant craps. He called casinos asking for a craps dealer named Lydia Storm. He told them he with the gaming commission." Marcus paused, a look of appreciation on his face. "The Silver Swan said they'd connect him to her manager. He hung up and called me."

"Why did you mention Randy and his friends in the note?" Kevin asked.

"The other file," Marcus said calmly.

I slapped my palm on the table and glanced heavenward. "There's another file?"

Marcus had the decency to look abashed. "Didn't I mention it?"

"No-oo." I prayed for patience. "What did this one say?"

"More names and numbers, but it didn't make sense."

"Why did you notice it?" Kevin asked.

"It was with the Buffy file," Marcus explained. "Steve and I opened it last night."

"And found what?" I prompted, none too quietly.

"It had Import Enterprise at the top, then a list of words: basement, first floor, second floor, up to twelve. Opposite that were amounts: four hundred thousand, a million, and so on. On the next page, amounts were on the left, names on the right."

"Different amounts or the same ones?" A worried look lurked in Kevin's too-serious gaze.

Marcus's face scrunched up. "Don't know."

"You said you recognized the names." I tried not to rush him. It was asking a lot when he'd only glanced at the file. "Do you remember any of them?"

Marcus eyed me. "The first one was comma-something."

"Commarragh?" I asked, not too surprised.

Marcus nodded.

Our beloved mayor who'd been re-elected two years ago with the help of Randy's generous donations.

"Any others?" Kevin followed local and state politics avidly. He would recognize any names from that arena.

"Scimitar." Marcus answered promptly.

I recognized the pattern. I'd taught Marcus to use mnemonics to help him with schoolwork. Being an apolitical type, I couldn't come up with a name that resembled the word for a long-curved sword.

"Scimirton?" Kevin asked in a too-casual voice.

When Marcus nodded again, I glanced at Kevin.

He turned toward me with a worried look in his eyes.

"Councilman?" I raised my brows in question.

"Gaming commissioner." Kevin informed me tersely.

My jaw clenched. In a state with legal gambling, the gaming commission is a combination of Midas and God's henchmen rolled into one. It was too far up the food chain for my comfort. I didn't want to hear more, but I had to ask. "Is that all?"

Marcus chewed his lip. "A Native American tribe."

"Any particular kind?" I felt like a game show host.

"Apache," the boy answered confidently.

"Apacini?" Kevin beat me to it again.

This time I didn't have to see his expression to know he was worried. The name sounded vaguely familiar, but I knew I'd never be able to place it. "Who's that?"

"The recently appointed head of the state zoning commission," Kevin said. "He used to be in the election office."

Wonderful.

"We're in way over our heads." Kevin imparted this obvious bit of news in a stage whisper.

I lifted my feet onto the rung of my chair. "Somebody let sharks loose in the minnow pond."

Kevin reached for a lifeline. "Time to pull in Crawford."

I shifted. "I wonder if we should talk to Lydia first."

"Why would she talk to us?" Kevin asked.

"She was scared enough to run away with an eleven-year-old." I glanced at Marcus. "No offense. You did good."

He preened, aware of the can of worms he'd opened. "She's nice. She'll talk to you."

Kevin leaned back. The movement stretched his T-shirt across his muscles. "If we don't check in, Crawford will think we're holding out like you did when Marcus took off."

He was right. Crawford would be righteously upset. "We better tell him in person. This is getting complicated."

Marcus sat forward, jostling his bowl and spilling milk on the table. "I can give him my report, too."

Kevin and I exchanged quick nods. It wasn't like we could drop him off with Mrs. C. Though Jimbo would watch him, I was hesitant to let Marcus out of my sight. Besides, he'd gotten us the leads. "First, clean up your spill and rinse your bowl."

Marcus gave a long-suffering sigh. "Come on, T.R."

"All good operatives clean up after themselves." Kevin set his cup in the sink by way of example. "It's in all the rulebooks."

That was all it took. Marcus jumped up and thrust his bowl into the sink with a crash then grabbed a dishrag and spun toward the table.

I hid a smile. "We better leave a note telling Jimbo what's up. Where do you think he'll see it?"

"I'll tell him when I get the car keys." Kevin walked into the living room.

I looked at Marcus. "What hotel is she in?"

Wiping the table with more flair than grace, he managed to splash more water on himself than the table. "The Shanty Inn on the interstate."

"That's less than a mile from the Silver Swan. Why go there?" I asked.

Marcus tossed the rag into the sink. "Who'd think someone trying to flee would be so close? 'Sides, a cab or bus driver would remember an Asian kid and a blonde traveling together."

I joined him as he walked out of the kitchen, impressed by his logic. "Weren't you together when you registered?"

"She gave me money and I went in alone. I told them my dad was sick and he'd talk to them in the morning."

Marcus informed me with a triumphant grin. "Jimbo came in handy there."

"Good plan." I should've known Marcus had worked up a cover story. "As long as she stays out of sight, no one can find her. Once we fill in Crawford and get the CD we'll have the proof we need. Then the cops can go after the real criminals."

"We have to solve the murder," Marcus protested.

"In real life, police don't like amateurs messing in their cases." I was more than ready to distance myself from this investigation. "We could get in trouble. I could lose custody of you. That's not worth any risk. So we're playing it cool."

His expression fell, but a second later he rebounded. "The cops will need my report. Think they'll put us in an interrogation room?"

"I hope not." Once was enough for me.

We walked into the living room as Kevin returned. He held out his hands, palms up. Both were empty.

"No keys?" I asked.

"No Jimbo, which means no car." Kevin held out his hands.

"Where would he go?" Marcus asked.

I didn't like the way this scenario was playing out. "What did you two do after you left here?"

"I filled him in on what happened." Marcus's brow furrowed. "When we got to the hotel, I unlocked the door, but Lydia had the chain on."

"You have a key?" I asked in surprise.

"I got two last night when we registered," Marcus said.

"Good thinking." He made a better detective than I did. "What did you tell Lydia?"

"I introduced Jimbo and told her to lay low until she

heard from us." Marcus thought for a minute. "Then I told her my mom's detective agency was working on the case."

I wondered what Crawford would think about my promotion. "How did she seem? Nervous? Calm?"

"Last night she was shook up. That's probably why Steve jumped ship." His voice held a note disappointment. "When Jimbo and I returned, she was quiet, like she'd been thinking."

Had the woman regretted her impulse to believe two boys and their wild story? I wanted to talk to her even more, but with no car, it was a moot point whether it was a good idea or not. "Did Jimbo say anything?"

Marcus shrugged. "After we left the hotel he asked about you guys. I told him the cops thought you and Kevin disposed of Randy's body. He didn't say much. When we got here, I fell asleep."

I glanced at Kevin. "You want to give him a call?"

A moment later Kevin was leaving a voice mail for his missing friend.

"Now what?" My voice rose toward the whiny end of the scale. "We're wanted by the cops and our transportation is non-existent."

"We could have Crawford pick us up," Marcus suggested.

"It's our best shot." Kevin reached for his phone. Its shrill ring split the air before he touched it.

"Maybe that's him," I said.

Kevin picked it up. "Hello?"

After a second, he held the receiver out to me. "It's the Colchester connection."

I took the phone. "Hello?"

"Morning, lovey." The lilting British accent held an

undercurrent of glee. "I had no idea your life would get so exciting so quickly."

Excitement is vastly overrated.

"We'll have to put our heads together later," Mrs. C suggested. "For now, I have a message from Jimbo."

"You heard from Jimbo?" Why call Mrs. C instead of Kevin? "Why did he leave Kevin's place?"

"I couldn't say." Her British tone was maddeningly calm. "He didn't have much time to talk. The police don't let you go on forever even if they do grant you the one call."

Surprise socked me in the gut. "The police?"

"Yes, ducks." Mrs. C spoke as if she were relaying a weather report. "The boy's in a bit of bind. He's been arrested."

16

29 Down; 4 Letters;
Clue: To entice someone into danger.
Answer: Lure

My brain whirled like an out-of-control carousel. "Jimbo's been arrested?"

Kevin crossed to my side. His eyes narrowed in thought.

Nothing made sense. I focused on something concrete. "What's the charge, Mrs. C?"

"I wrote it down." A rustling of paper came over the line. "Criminal trespassing."

"Criminal trespass?" I repeated the words, though Kevin had his head so close to my phone he must have heard. "Where did he trespass?"

"Evidently he made his way inside a locked gate and onto the patio of a city official," Mrs. C said.

The reminder of Marcus's list of names sent icy

fingers tiptoeing up my spine. Now I knew why cops didn't believe in coincidences. "Which official?"

"I don't know," Mrs. C admitted in a disappointed voice. "I happen to have an acquaintance who works at the police station, but they couldn't say, which I thought odd."

I happen to have an acquaintance? I bit back a laugh. The line was a classic. Good enough for *A Streetcar Named Desire* and *The Goodbye Girl*, one of our movie night picks. "The address must be on file. They could check where he was arrested."

"That wouldn't work at all." A note of reproach sounded at my attempt to jump ahead of her story. "He escaped the grounds and led everyone on a merry chase through the city."

"So... Where..." I sputtered to a stop.

"Let me explain," Mrs. C jumped right in.

"I'll put you on speaker." I hit the button on my phone, but Kevin still hovered close.

Adrenaline made me hyper-aware of the warmth of his breath on my cheek and the smell of coffee on him. Mrs. C's voice pulled me back to the latest crisis.

"At four o'clock this morning the bodyguard of a local politician noticed Jimbo by the French doors of the house."

That was roughly an hour and a half after he and Marcus left. What had Jimbo done to end up sneaking onto someone's estate? Was it normal for city politicians to have bodyguards?

"The police were called. The bodyguards gave chase, but they lost Jimbo on the north side."

Well past Kevin's apartment.

"They were combing the area by the new mall when the police spotted him leaving Prospect Hill Cemetery."

I glanced at Kevin. He had nothing to offer but a puzzled expression. "He hid in a cemetery?"

"Yes," Mrs. C confirmed. "Initially they charged him with fleeing arrest, but everyone admitted he stopped at once when the police hailed him."

She fell silent as if that ended the matter.

"Is criminal trespass more serious than regular trespass?" I blame the inane question on information overload.

"Not sure," Kevin clipped off the words.

"Don't know, luv." Mrs. C's British tone gave me the unilluminating answer in stereo. "If you're thinking of bail... "

I hadn't gotten that far. However, maybe I could persuade her to spring Jimbo. I'd done it for Kevin a few years ago in the dead of night. It just takes ready cash.

"It won't work," the calm voice on the other end of the line informed me. "He won't be arraigned today."

Kevin opened his mouth, but an off-key melody stopped him before he got a word out.

Marcus walked toward the couch. "Your purse is ringing."

"What now?" I turned to Kevin. "If that's the police, I'm ready to give up."

"Maybe we can trade you for Jimbo." Kevin turned to help Marcus find my phone. "He's never been arrested."

I rolled my eyes. "It's county jail not High Desert State Prison."

Marcus handed Kevin my cell phone. "Will Jimbo be sent to State Prison?"

Kevin shook his head as he answered my cell phone. "Hello?"

"Anything I can do?" Mrs. C's British accent brought me back to my own phone call.

I took her off speaker to avoid confusion while I considered the possibilities. "Where are you?"

"The drugstore." As if the fact should have been obvious.

"Well... " Before I could complete the thought, Kevin settled his well-muscled frame on the edge of the sofa and shot me an amused look. I covered the receiver again. "Who?"

Kevin tilted the phone toward me.

The loud, gravelly voice made Kevin's silent "Crawford" unnecessary. Unwilling to face another crisis, I turned away. If bail was out, all we could do was dig up answers. "Can you get him a message?"

"I can try." Her voice had a lilt to it. "Do you want me to go to the station if need be?"

Was it worth it? "Yes, tell him his family knows what happened and they're working on it."

"I'll let him know." Her quick response made me think of red coats going into battle.

"Thanks, Mrs. C," I said. "I owe you one."

"This is more fun than I've had in years," she assured me. "If things go badly do keep your head down. Ta-ta."

With her sign-off ringing in my ears, I hung up before I considered how she'd get to the station. Mass transit dirties her slippers. Kevin or I usually drive her wherever she needs to go, but right now we couldn't drive ourselves to the corner store.

With a slightly vindictive gleam in his eyes, Kevin held the phone out. "This one's for you, too."

I shot him an 'I'll-get-you-later' look and took the cell phone. "Hello."

"Ma Barker, I presume." When Crawford tries to soften a voice coarsened by years of smoking and drinking it's not good.

"Don't start," I warned. "Yesterday was forty-eight hours long and today isn't looking any better."

"Maybe I should turn you over to the police and let them clear their books."

"I haven't done anything and you know it," I said.

"Your boy has been active," he said. "Know anything about hiding a material witness?"

Too stunned to answer, I covered the receiver and met Kevin and Marcus's gazes. "They know we've got Lydia Storm."

"How?" Kevin's shock mirrored my own.

"You didn't think I'd put two and two together?" Crawford's bellow pulled my attention.

"I didn't have anything to do with her leaving the casino," I said, recovering some of my wits.

"Casinos have more cameras than Hollywood," Crawford said. "Once they fingered Marcus, his pal cracked."

I looked at my son. "Steve caved."

Marcus gritted his teeth. "Oh, man."

"Don't blame him," I said. "They caught you on film."

"The police want to know where she is," Crawford spoke in a stern voice. "And they want to know now."

With a rush of admiration for my little conniver, I covered the receiver one more time and whispered to Marcus. "They don't have her."

A wide grin split his face. "I told you."

Kevin slapped Marcus on the back.

Then I remembered the rest of the story. "Lydia Storm isn't the half of it."

Before Crawford could get a word in, I told him about the file containing the names and amounts on the accountant's PC.

"Unfortunately, Marcus accidentally stuck the CD in Steve's backpack." I winced at Crawford's groan. It would have been nice to have something solid to give the cops.

"I was about to call you when Mrs. Colchester phoned about Jimbo being arrested. It has to be involved. He was trespassing at the home of a city official. We don't know who and they won't set bail." I ended on this note of unsportsmanlike conduct.

No answer came. I was about to check our connection when he finally spoke. "Who the hell's Jimbo?"

"I thought that's what your comment about Ma Barker meant," I said. "You know, Ma Barker and her boys. Marcus and Jimbo both caught with their hands in the till."

"No-oo," he dragged out the word. "I meant Marcus and Steve and Kevin, not to mention the guy in your car. Recruiting new blood, are we?"

I'd forgotten about Kevin loaning my Buick to his friend. Must be why the cops hadn't traced me yet. I started to relay Mrs. C's news. I barely got two sentences out when Crawford cut me off.

"Stop." His voice cut across my story. "I've heard more coherent stories from drunks. I have my own acquaintances at the station. You don't know where he was headed or why?"

"Not a clue," I admitted. "He stashed Lydia, dropped off Marcus, then left. I wanted to see if Lydia could shed any light on things, but Kevin figured we should bring you up to date first."

If Marcus could give Steve credit, I could admit Kevin was the sensible one.

"Take a lesson," Crawford growled.

"I was about to call you when we found out Jimbo had taken off in Kevin's car."

"Speaking of cars, who's the nimrod driving yours and what is he doing?" Crawford asked. "Is this part of a master plan or are you out to confuse everybody?"

I had to laugh. "Kevin loaned my car to his buddy. I didn't know about it until two-thirty this morning. I hope the cops had a lovely drive."

"They've followed him all over town," Crawford said. "They're ready to shoot him."

I hoped they didn't shoot me when they caught me. Better yet, I could drop it all in their laps. Maybe I could get some rest in jail. "You want us to meet you at the station?"

"I have to warn the lead detective first." Crawford's response was quick and decisive. "Last thing she'll want is you spouting off for the record. We need proof."

"I hadn't thought of that." My stomach tightened. The specter of the dead woman floated in my mind's eye. I looked at Marcus. Whoever was involved had a lot to lose. "What do you want us to do?"

"I'll get that CD. Though it probably can't be used in court or as evidence, it might let them ask questions to get the information legally. Then I'll see what puddle your buddy Jimbo stepped in." He paused. I could almost see his brows furrow in thought. "How long would it take you to get to your witness?"

I covered the receiver. "How long to get to Lydia Storm?"

Kevin spread his hands out. "Using what? Bicycles?"

Marcus waved his hand like he wanted to be called on. "Thirty minutes. The hotel's on a main bus route. It's easy."

Kevin raised a brow. "Good thing we're not proud."

It wouldn't get me into the PI Hall of Fame, but it had wheels. I spoke into the phone. "Thirty minutes."

"Do it." A beep cut off part of Crawford's clipped response. "Call me in an hour."

I glanced at the readout on my phone. "My cell phone's running low. Call Kevin if you need to get in touch."

A murmur of voices sounded over the phone.

"Get out of that apartment," Crawford said. "The police are on their way to Kevin's place."

"We're gone." I clicked off and shoved the phone into my purse. My momentary illusion of the road's end vanished like smoke on the wind.

Crawford hadn't asked for Lydia Storm's location. Was that so he could honestly tell the cops he didn't know? Did that mean he was worried about an internal leak? The thought put my teeth on edge.

"I know when the next bus comes." Marcus ran to the kitchen where he'd left his backpack. "We have to hurry."

"The cops are on their way here," I whispered to Kevin.

"We'll go out this way." He moved as he spoke. "The stairs lead to the alley."

We met Marcus in at the kitchen door.

"We're sneaking out the back," I said, pointing over his shoulder.

"All right." His eyes lit up. He slipped his backpack on his shoulder and did an about face. "The bus stop on that corner is even closer."

"We have to keep quiet." I resisted the urge to reiterate the seriousness of the situation. I was scared enough for all of us.

Five minutes later, Kevin had led us through a basement, past a laundry room, and out the rear entrance of the next building. I'd had no idea the two were connected. Then again, I'd never snuck out of his place before.

We walked onto a patio bordered by a nine-foot wooden fence. Marcus pointed through the gate toward a bus stop half-a-block away.

I gave him a thumb's up.

Kevin touched my arm. I looked over my shoulder and found him studying the hall we'd just left. He gestured for silence.

Holding my breath, I strained to listen. It was nothing, I told myself. We were getting paranoid.

Then I heard it–a rhythmic thud, quick and hard, like running footsteps. Just as my heart geared up to some serious thumping of its own, the tense set of Kevin's shoulders eased.

He stepped toward me. "It's the washing machine."

The noise picked up speed. The heavy mechanical sound was clear now. My knees went weak with relief. "Give me a heart attack, why don't you?"

We hurried toward Marcus, waiting in the shadows.

As I watched, his eyes grew round. He waved us back with a frantic gesture. I plastered myself against the fence.

Kevin's breath fanned my cheek. His hand on my arm

was reassuring but it did funny things to my already racing heart.

"This the building?" The clipped voice of a man sounded from the other side of the wooden wall.

"Next one." The female voice held the same businesslike tone. A radio squealed so close I almost jumped out of my skin.

I opened my mouth to gasp. Kevin's hand covered my lips. I turned and met his gaze.

He mouthed one word. "Cops."

A one-word description of disaster.

17

4 Across; 8 Letters;
Clue: Formulating a course of action.
Answer: Planning

My pulse spiked with a thundering beat I was certain would alert the cops to our hiding place. With adrenaline racing through my veins, I listened to their fading footsteps.

Police presence eliminated the bus as a getaway vehicle. Just as well, Perry Mason's buddy Paul Drake wouldn't be caught dead on mass transit.

Good thing I knew the layout of this neighborhood as well as I knew my own. We were two blocks from Kevin's mechanic. I leaned toward Kevin. "We need wheels."

Kevin's expression changed to one of subdued excitement. "I love it when you go on the attack."

His husky voice wasn't fooling me. Like any man, he

craved action. I turned to Marcus and jerked a thumb toward the fence. "They gone?"

With a casual stealth that reminded me of his years on the street, he checked both ways then nodded.

Careful to avoid the broken glass and loose paper, I drew Marcus close.

Kevin's arm encircled my shoulder, but he kept his gaze locked on the fence.

I pitched my voice low. "We're going to Kevin's garage to get a loaner car."

Marcus agreed, all business.

"Step past the fence, then check Kevin's building. The cops don't know you," I said, the words more for my benefit than his. I was sure I was right, but what kind of a wretch sends a child out first?

Marcus glanced over his shoulder.

"If you see anyone, cross the street and go through that empty warehouse to the garage," I continued. "If we're not there in fifteen minutes, go home. Tell Mrs. C we'll be in touch."

His chin jutted out. "I won't leave you."

"No point all of us getting caught." It would have been easy to swear we'd get away, but I never make a promise to Marcus unless I know I can keep it. "We have to move before they realize nobody's home."

"I'm your guy." Without another word, Marcus sauntered into the daylight.

I was left clasping air.

Marcus glanced toward Kevin's building almost as an afterthought. He spoke without looking at us. "Nobody. C'mon."

The kid was a natural.

I stepped past the fence. Despite his assurance, I

looked. As I did, a skinny Vietnamese woman walked out the door of Kevin's building carrying a trash bag. I stiffened. "Uh-oh."

Kevin followed the direction of my gaze. Staring at his neighbor, he put a finger to his lips.

The woman glanced at the building, then at us and made a hurry-up gesture.

Breathing a sigh of relief, I sped around the corner. Not a soul in sight. I made a beeline for the door of the warehouse across the street. As I reached it, Marcus's head popped out.

"The path's clear to the door on the other side." He spun on his heel and dashed away.

Musty air inside the building caught in my throat. I saw Marcus run past piles of boxes on the right. Misshapen shadows rose up on the left.

A screech of metal sounded behind me. Kevin had pushed the door shut and was waving me on.

Lengthening my stride, I closed the distance to Marcus. He ducked under a wooden bar, turned the doorknob, and pulled.

Nothing happened. My heart fell.

Marcus adjusted his grip and tried again.

By the time I got under the wooden bar, he was halfway out the door, looking up and down the block.

A sprint across the street, through the melee of a water balloon fight, and we were a block from the garage. Five minutes later we raced toward the back of the garage doing a fast but understated jog.

Kevin pointed to a lopsided door hanging on loose hinges. "This leads to a back hall by the office. No windows."

I managed a nod. My breath came in short gasps. I

blamed the tape on my ribs. When I finally got within arm's reach of Marcus I grabbed his arm so he wouldn't barrel inside. I needn't have bothered. He opened the door with the stealth of a cat burglar, then shot me a conspiratorial grin.

For him, this was a lark, but the little wretch could have at least pretended to breathe heavy.

Every time I tried to catch my breath a stitch stabbed me in the side. I reached out to steady myself, then almost twisted my arm out of its socket to avoid knocking over cans of oil.

Kevin put his hands on my waist with a reassuring strength. "You okay?"

"As soon as the little yellow dots quit dancing the polka I'll be fine." I leaned against him and filled my lungs.

Sirens screamed in the street.

My whole body jerked. My head swung toward the sound.

Wrong move. The little dots started in on the rumba.

I felt Kevin tense. Marcus's head snapped around as well. I squinted through the grimy front window. The street remained empty. The wail of sirens faded.

"We have to get out of here. They may canvas the neighborhood." I didn't think they would, but Crawford's caution had added a new edge to my paranoia.

We walked into an office barely big enough to stand in.

With a gentle touch on my shoulder, Kevin squeezed past. "I'll see who's here."

I perched on the edge of the desk and practiced breathing.

Marcus studied the street.

A minute later, Kevin walked in with an Hispanic guy. I'd met the twin brothers who owned the place. One is Joe, the other's Juan. Joe never speaks to me. I don't know if it was all women or just my aura. Juan talked my leg off.

I slid off the desk and painted on my brightest smile. "I hope this isn't too much trouble."

He responded with a wordless smile.

This was Joe.

Kevin clapped the guy on the shoulder. "Juan has a car he can loan us."

My smile froze. "Juan?"

Kevin's brow furrowed. "Who'd you think it was?"

I shook my head. I give up. "Let's go."

The room emptied before I could move. Pulling in another breath, I trooped out behind the others.

A large well-lit garage opened to the street. The scent of oil and gas hung in the air. Juan slipped through a screen door in the corner. The spring twanged as it slammed behind him. He kept up a rapid pace to the rear of the lot.

A welcome breeze blew across the damp curls clinging to my face. Deep into paranoia, I kept the one-car garage he led us to between me and the street. Behind the building, a dusty yellow car sat by its lonesome. Rounded fenders might be back in style, but this was an oldie.

Who was I to complain? It had wheels.

"Hot damn!" Marcus's expletive cut through the silence.

"Marcus, watch your language. And keep your voice low." When I wheeled toward him, I saw another car revealed as Juan pulled off a tarp. My mouth went slack.

A Cadillac. Long, lean, and shimmery white. Fins rose

over a huge trunk and a red leather interior drew my gaze like an 'X' on a bomb drop. Did I mention it was a convertible? NASA could have spotted it on the dark side of the moon. Good thing we weren't driving this hulk.

Kevin had begun to drool.

I tried to break it to him gently. "Kevin, this isn't the car Juan's loaning us."

Juan, rolling up the huge covering, pointed at the ocean liner. "You take. We need room."

Kevin was undressing the car with his eyes. Marcus clambered into the rear and stretched his arms across the leather seat as if he'd found a new home.

I turned to the mechanic. "We need something smaller."

He smiled and nodded.

I relaxed and wondered if we'd be able to get Marcus out or if we'd have to leave him behind, which might not be a bad idea. Then Juan walked away.

"No," I took a few steps after him. "This is too fancy."

"No problem," he said with a wave. "You bring it back."

"Belden." Kevin's tone held a warning note. He'd heard me trying to deep-six his Caddy. "You wanted wheels."

"I don't want a pimp-mobile that might be stolen," I whispered.

"Juan bought it at an auction. His buyer fell through. It's taking up space. Gotta go." He tapped his watch with a triumphant expression. "We're on the clock."

I glanced at the time. We were ten minutes into the thirty I'd quoted Crawford. Instead of talking to Lydia Storm, we were wrangling about cars.

Cursing in my head, I looked from a disappearing

Juan to Kevin, already planted behind the wheel. The purr of the engine filled the air with a powerful hum.

Kevin groaned and Marcus swiveled toward the dashboard.

I rolled my eyes. My DNA strand lacked the lust molecule for four-wheel vehicles.

Kevin put the car in gear and gently rolled the white mammoth toward the street.

"We should get going," Marcus said in a righteous tone.

Kevin eyed me pointedly.

I gave up and slipped inside. "We're putting up the roof."

Groans sounded in stereo, but I held firm. "We need to make it a little harder for the space station to spot us."

"She has a point." Kevin flipped a switch. The roof whirred upward. A minute later, we rocketed down the street.

I refused to give the guys an opening, but that car had the smoothest ride this side of heaven. As the soft leather closed around me, I stifled a groan of pleasure. The only reason I didn't nod off was the realization that we needed to start solving problems faster than we found them.

I reluctantly straightened and faced Marcus who had his head perched over the front seat. "Tell me again what happened with Lydia last night. You said she acted scared."

"Take your time," Kevin said, glancing at him in the rearview mirror. "You were in the alcove when she rounded the corner. What did she say?"

Marcus's brow furrowed in thought. "She held out the paper and asked why we wrote the note. I told her Randy was running scared. She said, 'How do you know?'"

I frowned at the little-know-it-all. "How did you know?"

Marcus looked at me with a strange expression. "She kind of looks like you. Tall and thin. Talks like you, too."

"Don't change the subject," I warned him.

"I told the truth," he said with a shrug. "That Randy went to see his ex-wife Saturday then called her that evening. I heard you on the phone before I left."

That's what I get for yelling at Randy.

"She went ballistic," Marcus recounted with a gleam in his eye. "Wadded up the note and said 'why couldn't Randy stand on his own two feet for once? Why couldn't he be alone for a minute?' She said he'd panic and ruin everything."

"She knows Randy." I wondered again if she'd followed him and the dead woman from Vegas. "She nailed his weaknesses in a heartbeat."

Kevin's eyes narrowed. "Lydia did some panicking of her own."

"What then?" I turned to Marcus.

"She asked how we found her. Steve and I had agreed not to mention his mother. So I told her one of the laptops the mayor's office donated to our computer class had a file on it. When we hacked into it, we traced the information to her." Marcus informed me. "That's when she mumbled she had to leave. I told her we could stash her in a motel because if she drove off, they'd know."

"Who 'they'?" What else had the little know-it-all been keeping from me?

Marcus shrugged. "There's always a 'they'. She took off for her apartment, and we followed."

"Did she say anything else?" The Shanty Inn was just

ahead. Soon I could ask Lydia, but I wanted to be prepared.

"She yelled about Randy a little more, then threw the note in the waste basket." Marcus bit his lip, deep in thought. "She stuffed clothes in a bag. Steve and I were in the other room, but I watched her around the corner."

"Good move," I smiled at him. "What did you see?"

"She copied a file on her laptop to a thumb drive on her keying," he said with a smug look. "It looked like she deleted a bunch of files."

Kevin pulled into the turn lane by a neon palm tree pointing to the Shanty Inn. He eyed me with a knowing glance. "The woman is not shaping up to be victim material."

"I noticed." Disappointment settled over me. "Just what we need, another guilty soul on the run."

We pulled around the main building and into an open court. Two floors of rooms surrounded a central area.

"What room?" Kevin asked Marcus.

Marcus pointed toward the left rear corner. "One-oh-six."

"You have the key?" I asked.

"Yep." He sat back and fished in his pocket.

We clambered out and headed for the door. I got there first and rapped hard. No sound of movement inside. Kevin and Marcus caught up to me. Using my fist, I pounded on the door.

Marcus raised his hand, curled around the key.

I scanned the area.

"She's gone." A slightly accented voice sounded behind me.

I whirled.

An older Asian woman pushed a cleaning cart to the next room. "Your sister left this morning."

I'd always wanted another sister. "Was she alone?"

The woman nodded. "That other man, he miss her, too, by only a minute. He maybe caught her car."

"What did this man look like?" Kevin stepped forward.

Pulling out her key card without missing a beat, the maid motioned to Marcus. "Same one with that boy."

"Jimbo," Kevin breathed the name.

If I had to have a sister, I might as well put her to use. "Is it okay if we make sure she got all of her things?"

The woman shrugged. She slipped a key in the room next door and entered without a backward glance.

I nodded at Marcus. We slipped in and shut the door. It was your basic hotel room: a bed, a television, a table. Ready-to-eat foods and magazines were stacked on the table.

"Jimbo bought those," Marcus said. "Took almost all his money."

My ire rose at the woman casually spurning Jimbo's gift. Then my practical side kicked in. "See if any of the food is gone then re-sack it. We may as well take it with us."

"I'll check the closet," Kevin said.

"I'll take the bathroom." I flicked on the bathroom light. The shower curtain was open and the towels lay neatly in place. No hairbrush or makeup lay on the counter. I walked to the main room.

Marcus stood by the front door. The plastic sacks hung on his fingers. "It's all here."

The closet door clicked shut behind me. Kevin was on my heels. "Nada."

I reached past Marcus for the doorknob then stopped. "Where's the key?"

I rubbed it with my shirt then let it fall to the table. I did the same with the inside doorknob. Kevin went out first. I herded Marcus out then clicked the door shut. I smeared my hand over the knob. By the time I got to the pimp-mobile, Kevin had it running. Nobody said a word as he pulled into traffic.

I chewed on my thumbnail. Not that it took a lot of guesswork to make the pieces fit.

"Jimbo must have gotten suspicious and went to check on her." Kevin switched lanes smoothly.

When he paused, I jumped into his narrative. "When she pulled out, he ended up as a Peeping-Tom on the patio of a city official."

Marcus had his head perched over the seat again. "I bet whoever she talked to is named in the file."

And they knew about Jimbo. Fear coursed through me. I touched Kevin's arm. "Who on that list would have a place in town?"

"We only know the top three." Kevin expression turned thoughtful. "Apacini's state. He wouldn't live here. Whoever Lydia met, she's obviously in this mess with Randy and his wife. Too bad we don't know what 'this' is."

"Or how Randy figures in." I tried to find a thread to pull. Only one thing came to mind. "Randy's rich. He's invested in businesses around town. Art galleries. Restaurants. Retail shops."

"And he's legit." Kevin's tone underscored the last word.

A spider-web of connections popped to my mind. "Randy could exchange large amounts of cash."

Kevin nodded. "Dirty money."

Marcus gave a brilliant smile. "We solved it."

Hardly. The picture was far from complete.

"You have your cell?" I asked.

Kevin pulled out his phone.

I glanced at my watch. Twenty-two minutes since I'd hung up on Crawford. Not bad. As I congratulated myself, the phone rang. It figured Crawford would be watching the clock.

Kevin must have read my mind. "Bet I know who that is."

Remembering Crawford's warning, I checked the readout then grunted in surprise.

Kevin cast me a sideways glance. "Not Crawford?"

Instead of answering him, I clicked the button. "Hi, Mrs. Colchester."

Kevin cocked a brow in surprise.

"What's she want?" Marcus whispered in my ear.

"Hello, ducky." Her breezy greeting held a touch of warmth. Anyone overhearing her would've thought she was about to invite me to high tea. "I met that nice Mr. Crawford at the station. He asked me to let you know Jimbo has been put on suicide watch."

18

---

10 Across; 12 Letters;
Clue: Stubbornly resistant to change.
Answer: Incorrigible

"Jimbo is on suicide watch?" My voice rose in surprise.

As Kevin's head jerked in my direction, the steering wheel followed. The Caddy jumped the curb and barreled straight at a woman walking her poodle.

I waved frantically. "Watch out."

By the time Kevin pulled the car back onto the street, the woman and poodle had bolted across a parking lot.

They never looked back.

I subtly kneaded my ribs. With my remaining remnants of energy, I flipped my cell phone to speaker mode.

Kevin glanced at the phone. "Jimbo wouldn't try to kill himself."

"Of course not," Mrs. C responded to Kevin's comment without any prompting from me. "That nice Mr. Crawford said a big fish might get into small ponds. You understand."

"I do." Somebody was running scared and they had nothing to lose by silencing Jimbo.

Or the rest of us.

"Dandy," she continued happily. "Then you'll understand the rest of his message. He's going to retrieve the CD. You're to keep on the Lydia connection. He'll call in an hour."

With the English accent and the cryptic messages ringing in my ear I could almost believe I was in a James Bond movie. If only I could find a director to yell 'Cut'.

"I'm going home to watch the telly," she said. "By the way, I've picked up a disposable phone to make our calls more direct. I'll give you the number. If you need anything, do call."

"Oh, I will," I assured her. After copying the new phone number, I signed off. "Thanks again."

"It's nothing," she said. "Ta-ta now."

"What next?" Back to his unflappable self, Kevin continued along the main drag. "Drive around in circles until Crawford calls?"

"That would give me time to nap." I resisted the urge to melt into the soft leather seat. "But the CD won't tell us where Randy is hiding."

Marcus heaved mightily. "Real mysteries have clues."

"Too bad it's not one of my crossword puzzles. I could make up answers to fit." I could only wish this case was so easy. "I did find a clue in Lydia's apartment."

I explained about the sticky note and the Garden Spot trailer court.

"If they knew each other back then and they're both missing now, Randy and Lydia could be in this scheme together," Kevin mused.

I watched the scenery through half-open eyelids and tried out Kevin's theory. "I can't see Randy cheating on his wife. For all his faults, that's one thing I can't accuse him of. He's loyal."

Kevin gave me a long slow look. "I mean dirty money. Gambling is an excellent place to dump cash."

The comment fired my synapses. "Now you're talking."

"His criminal scheme went south. Wifey wants out. He kills her." Kevin laid out his theory with a casual attitude most women would find appalling, but I admired the way his mind worked. "Randy has you on his life insurance. He plants a blackmail letter in your name. You're halfway to life in prison."

His supposition roused me even more. "Sounds plausible, except Randy was never good at thinking."

"That's where Lydia comes in," Marcus added his two cents. "They framed you then ran off. They'll live in Brazil off a secret account while you waste away in prison, alone and unloved."

I pasted on an outraged expression. "You're not going to visit me?"

"I will." Kevin managed to infuse the simple words with a wealth of hidden meaning.

The warmth in his gaze sent a tingle up my spine. Not for the first time, those sapphire eyes tempted me. I squashed that train of thought before my brain got sidetracked.

"You won't go to prison." Marcus's belated show of support brought me to reality. "We'll thwart their evil plan."

"Thwart their plan?" I asked. "Is that a spelling word or is it from a Hardy Boys book?"

"Hardy Boys." Marcus loved the classics.

"In order to thwart them, we have to find them," Kevin said.

"That's doable." I leaned back. "Because Randy is still in town."

"What makes you so sure?" Kevin asked.

I scanned the horizon as if I'd find the answer in the blue-tipped mountain range. "Randy wouldn't run. He craves excitement."

However, with his picture plastered on every media outlet in town, he had to have a hidey-hole. But where?

"What's she doing?" Marcus whispered.

"Thinking," Kevin whispered back. "It takes her awhile."

I ignored the snide remark. An idea was inching its way into my brain.

A gleam sparked in Kevin's eyes. "You got something."

"What casino caters to hardline gamblers? Older. Out of the way. Lots of class."

"Blue Bayou." The guys answered in a unanimous chorus.

"Why does everyone know these answers except for me?"

Marcus rolled his eyes. "You have to get out more, T.R."

I raised a brow. "How do you know so much about casinos?"

"History class," Marcus said. "The Blue Bayou was the first big deal in town. It's got gold faucets and silk stuff."

Kevin agreed. "No big money anymore, but it caters to serious gamblers and high-dollar tourists. The penthouses are legendary for their service to high rollers."

I sat up. "That's where Randy is."

Kevin eyed me as if I was a candidate for the psych ward. "The hotel would turn him in."

I shook my head. "He's not wanted for a crime. Besides, how many people would have to see him?"

Marcus nodded. "For enough money, someone will hide him."

"Randy always kept money hidden," I said. "His stash would be enough to pay people to look the other way."

"It could work." Kevin looked relieved at having a solid lead. "The police think he split or he's dead. They're not looking local."

"I'd bet my Elvis albums on it," I said. "Besides, it's not like you have a better idea."

Kevin shrugged. "Blue Bayou here we come."

Ten minutes later the aging monarch of gambling came into view. Though a few wrinkles creased the exterior, the aura of grand old dame clung to both the hotel and the attached casino façade. Cracks might meander through the parking lot, but every bulb in the sign blazed, even in the late afternoon sunshine. A long threshold, covered by a low, well-lit dome, marched up to the casino. All it needed was paparazzi and stars, and it'd be ready for the Oscars.

Kevin drove around the building to check out entrances and exits.

Marcus turned to me with an eager light in his eyes. "Now what?"

I wished he hadn't asked. I didn't have a clue. "Where do you think is the best place to go in unnoticed?"

"Park by the front of the hotel," Kevin said. "Then walk in through a side entrance."

"When we leave, we go out the front." Marcus picked up the scheme as if they'd practiced it. "It'll be busier and they won't have seen us come in."

"Good plan." I was impressed. I also realized I was surrounded by sneaks.

We parked and got out, only to have an old couple in another car wave us over. I thought they'd ask directions, instead the old guy launched into a monologue praising the Caddy.

The woman threw in reminisces about their courtship in just such an ocean liner. Their admiration gave me pause. How could we make an unobtrusive getaway driving the white elephant?

"See? Everybody likes the car but you," Kevin said as we walked away.

"I like it," I corrected him. "I just don't want to have to make a getaway in it."

"We could abandon it." Marcus walked backward in front of us. "If anyone spots your home base, never return."

I perked up.

From Kevin's expression, you'd have thought we planned to kill his pet hamster. "That's only a last resort. We'd have to come back for it."

"Juan could pick it up," I assured him with a light step.

"We could steal another one," Marcus said to comfort him.

His words burst my bubble of contentment. "No stealing cars."

"I know how," Marcus assured me.

"So do I," Kevin added.

I stopped in my tracks. "Where did I meet you people?"

Kevin spoke first. "Standing over a dead body."

"The courthouse trying to steal your wallet," Marcus said. "You were quick for an old lady."

That hurt. I shook my head and walked on.

"We won't have to abandon the car," Kevin said in a droll tone. "Security will nail us before we get out of the building."

I glared at him then walked into a side corridor leading to the hotel lobby. A distant melody of bells and whistles from the slots from the casino carried on the air. Too late I remembered the security cameras that had tagged Marcus and his friend when they tracked down Lydia.

Kevin was right. We'd get caught.

A few steps brought us to the edge of a large two-story atrium. Movement caught my eye. I turned in time to see a man's figure, topped by a familiar looking Stetson, vanish around a corner. "That looked like Cowboy Guy."

"Who's Cowboy Guy?" Marcus asked.

"He's here?" Suspicion edged Kevin's tone.

"I didn't see a face." I'd only caught a flash, but the hat had been familiar.

"Who's Cowboy Guy?" Marcus repeated. His dark eyes studied the lobby with a subtle intensity. His gaze flicked up to a corner of the ceiling. "Cameras."

So, we were already on record. I sauntered toward a

seating area in the rear corner. "Cowboy Guy was riding along with the police at the Silver Swan last night."

Kevin's observant gaze scanned the lobby as well. By now, he would already know the location of the stairs, elevators, and every corridor in the area.

"You sure it was him?" Kevin asked as we stopped.

It wasn't like TV. No film replayed. Only a fleeting image of a man's figure and the association with Cowboy Guy. I shrugged. "Finding Randy is what matters."

"Agreed." Kevin's voice shifted to an all-business tone. "Housekeeping is the best place to start."

"T.R." Marcus nudged me in the side.

"Sir." An officious sounding male voice overrode Kevin's words. "Excuse me, sir."

Only when a hotel-liveried figure interjected himself into our trio did I realize Kevin was the object of his attention.

The other man's professional veneer couldn't mask the sheen of sweat on his lip or the nervous glance he cast over his shoulder. "Did you park the white Cadillac by the side entrance?"

Kevin stiffened. His concern shifting instantly from finding Randy to the great white beast. "What happened?"

"There's been a slight accident." No doubt the other man would have announced World War III in the same understated tone. "Would you come this way, please?"

As soon as Kevin's body turned to follow, I put a hand on his arm. "You can't leave."

"The car's a loaner." Kevin spread out his hands, then leaned closer. "You and Marcus reconnoiter. Text me with any leads you find."

"Marcus, maybe you could—" I glanced around, but

instead of a prepubescent boy, an old woman with an oxygen tank trudged past me, aimed at the slot machines.

My heart rate soared. A quick scan of the area showed no sign of my boy-child. "Marcus?"

At the alarm in my voice, Kevin stopped in his tracks. He searched the surrounded area.

"Sir?" A demanding note had entered the hotel employee's tone. "The other party involved is on a tight schedule. She has to leave."

"She can wait. Especially if she hit my car." Kevin's retort snapped like the crack of a whip.

"He's probably off investigating, like his mother." Kevin gave my shoulder a comforting squeeze. "You go that way. I'll check this way."

"So much for being inconspicuous," I muttered. I spun on my heel and found Marcus without taking a step. He stood inside the gift shop, peeking out from behind a revolving rack of four-hundred-dollar sunglasses. He jerked his head toward the hall behind him.

I nodded, and he ducked out of sight.

Kevin took my arm and started forward. "There he is."

I dug in my heels, forcing my buddy to stop. "You handle the car mishap. I'll find our scoundrel and text you with updates."

He grabbed my arm before I could escape. "Try to keep the trouble to a minimum."

"That's not working so far." We'd done nothing but accumulate problems. Once I got to the hall, the buzz of gambling grew to a noticeable hum. Slowing, I glanced around.

"Psst." The hiss came from a small alcove on my right.

With the security cameras in mind, I strolled along the corridor as nonchalantly as I could.

Marcus stood against the far wall, gesturing me forward. When we were toe-to-toe, he stopped his frantic movements. "This is a dead zone for their security system."

"How do you know?"

"A friend of mine from the old days works here," Marcus said. "He owes me a favor."

"Should I ask what favor?"

"Bernie worked at Tito's pawn shop till they caught him stealing," Marcus explained. "My diversion gave him a chance to escape. Tito calmed down and let him pay it off or Bernie would be sleeping under a dune."

"Would it be too much to hope he's gone straight?"

Marcus's raised brow said it all.

"I don't want to know," I said. "Next time, don't wander off without saying something."

"I had to catch Bernie before he disappeared," he explained.

The squawk of a walkie-talkie made me jump.

Marcus shot me a pitying look and raised his hand from his side. The walkie-talkie fit neatly into his palm.

"Racer One to Alley Rat," a man's voice spoke from the small machine.

"Alley Rat here. Go ahead." Marcus released the button.

"Third-floor promenade. West side. Racer One out."

"Roger. Alley Rat out."

"Isn't the rest of security going to hear you?" I asked.

"We switched frequencies." Pride edged his tone. He twisted dial to change the walkie-talkie channel again.

"Racer One?" I fell in step as Marcus turned to the hall.

"He's a fan." Marcus walked to the main room. A

whiff of cigar smoke wafted through the air. "The escalators are in the hall leading to the casino."

"I hope your friend found something. Progress would be nice."

Minutes later we walked through a pair of stained-glass doors onto a wide balcony. A white metal fence sporting old-fashioned lanterns on curlicue poles lent the place an air of nineteenth-century charm. I started left. Marcus pulled me right.

Though it wasn't quite three o'clock on Sunday, the sun had begun its descent. A soft breeze ruffled my hair, a welcome change from the closed in feeling in the building.

A wave of light-headedness shuddered through me. After sleeping until noon, my late morning breakfast had consisted of coffee and a biscotti. Dodging the police and searching for a killer was not the way I'd planned to spend my weekend. I rubbed a hand over my forehead as my feet stumbled over a crack in the cement.

"You okay?"

"A little tired," I said, striving to gather my wits. "Once we get some info, we can grab a sandwich. Do you see your guy?"

"By the railing talking to an old couple," Marcus answered without turning his head.

A Blue Bayou security guard chatted with a couple wearing Hawaiian shirts so gaudy I wondered if they'd gotten off the plane one stop too soon. The guard had curly brown hair and brown eyes an angel would have envied. He looked like he hadn't finished high school. "How old is Bernie?"

"Late twenties." Marcus smiled. "Everybody thinks he's sixteen. The guys loved using him as a shill."

As the guard's gaze roamed over the promenade, his eyes hardened from chocolate to stone. His attitude reminded me of Randy when he was ready to make a score.

I leaned close to Marcus. "Just remember, luck runs out, then all you have is Tito and a sand dune."

"Don't worry, T.R." Marcus's voice was filled with the easy confidence of eleven years. "I'm on the straight and narrow."

Easy to say. However, I could only preach so much considering I hoped to use Bernie to break into Randy's suite.

We walked by the guy without a glance. The promenade offered a beautiful view. Through the clear desert air, the pattern of the city gradually gave way to the rough outline of the mountains. The hues changed from gold to blue to purple as the late afternoon shadows started to settle on the horizon. Footsteps brought me back to reality.

"Got the goods?" Marcus asked without a turn of his head.

Bernie fell into step beside him. "You always did have the luck."

I glanced over. "He's here?"

"Someone is in the governor's suite. I didn't get a name." His gaze flicked over me and his charm notched up. "Wouldn't mind staying in touch with you though."

Marcus chuckled. "Give it up, boy. T.R.'s too much for you."

"Save it." I didn't waste energy making my smile reach my eyes. For Bernie coming on to females no doubt fell into the same category as breathing. "The high roller is all we need."

Bernie shrugged, not at all put out. "Only one maid is allowed in the room. I asked her if Brad Pitt's brother was in the suite. She denied it until I described a blond-haired, brown-eyed guy with a good build."

He paused for effect. "Stopped her cold."

A thrill ran up my spine.

"She looked like someone let the cat out of the bag. The next second she said it's an old guy who likes privacy," Bernie said. "But if the guest isn't the man-of-the-hour, it's his twin."

This time my smile reached my eyes.

For once, I couldn't wait to meet up with my ex. Randy's visit yesterday morning and his call last night had made me a suspect in a murder investigation. Now was my chance to return the favor by dragging him out of his hiding place and into the light.

That'd teach him to play games with my life.

19

---

42 Across; 8 Letters;
Clue: Unfaithful, deceive, or mislead.
Answer: Betrayal

My euphoria at having a lead on Randy evaporated in a hot second. We still had to *get* to my ex, currently locked in the top floor suite. As twilight settled on the mountains, the streetlights sparkled, and the desert colors deepened. The romantic aura held little allure as I picked at the problem.

"The hotel uses key cards, doesn't it?" Marcus asked.

Bernie nodded. "Entry can be tracked."

"Can't pick those either," Marcus noted with disgust.

Plans involving maids and cleaning carts came and went. Bernie had said only one maid cleaned the room, but if a frontal attack couldn't get us in, what did that leave?

I pictured the profile of the building, complete with the same white metal palisade that surrounded us. I held in a groan, not more leaping. Maybe the rooms just looked close together. "Do the penthouses have balconies?"

"Yeah." Bernie acknowledged a group of Japanese tourists as we rounded the corner.

"How far apart are they?" Ten feet sounded reasonable, especially in the interests of security. It would also be much too wide to jump.

Bernie shot me a narrowed slanting gaze. "Three feet."

I stifled a moan.

Marcus's eyes lit up. "We could do that."

I shook my head. "You're not coming. Besides, this won't work unless the room next to Randy's is empty."

"The management holds a suite in reserve in case a high roller stops by. It's right next to your boy." Bernie drew away, evidently worried insanity might be contagious.

I couldn't believe I was considering jumping off a balcony again. "What's on that side of the building? We don't need anyone calling the cops."

"It's highway all the way to the horizon." Bernie glanced around, but no one paid us any mind.

"Can you get us into the adjoining room?" My ribs were already aching. Maybe it was psychological or maybe they were smarter than I was.

"I'll get a key. Meet me by the lobby elevators in ten minutes." He tore his gaze away from me and looked at Marcus. "You weren't kidding. I'm glad she's not after me."

Marcus chuckled at his retreating form.

"You don't seem upset that you're not coming," I said.

He rolled his eyes. "You're doing your mom routine. Where would I go? We lost Kevin, and you may have to leave in a hurry. You wouldn't abandon me in a gambling establishment, would you?"

I narrowed my eyes. He was right. I had nowhere to send him.

"Three feet is nothing," Marcus continued. "I once jumped six feet over an alley when Three-Fingered Larry was after me."

His smug tone made it obvious he thought the three-fingered guy had been a fool. Losing two fingers would instill caution in anybody. I commended a man sensible enough not to leap into mid-air without a net, especially considering my crazy plan. "Come on, Daredevil."

We strolled across the blue brocade carpet in the main lobby. The fake gaslight sconces next to the elevators shone with fresh polish but Bernie was nowhere in sight. I realized I didn't even know what level we were aiming for. "How many floors does this place have?"

"Nine," Marcus said. "Don't worry. Bernie will be here."

"That's not what I'm worried about." Nine floors was plenty far to fall. I glanced at Marcus's shiny black hair and carefree stride. My stomach clenched. I couldn't risk him.

Unless this was a slam dunk, I wasn't going through with it. Risking myself was one thing. My grandfather always said I didn't know when to quit. But I'd take my chances with the cops before I'd endanger my son.

Bernie appeared out of nowhere. Crossing in front of us, he hit the elevator button while chatting up the tourists.

When the elevator dinged I had an image of someone putting a pinball in play. I shuddered.

Marcus looked at me. "What's wrong?"

I shrugged. "Just a weird feeling."

"It's okay." He nudged my arm. "I'll take care of you."

His grown-up tone made me smile and the moment evaporated.

We followed an older couple and a family of four onto the elevator. Bernie got on last. By the time the tourists got off, they and Bernie were laughing like old friends.

As soon as the doors closed, the security guard's expression turned businesslike. "The room is empty. The security cameras for eight and nine are now out. I've been sent on a quick patrol."

My estimation of Bernie's abilities rose. So did my distrust. This was a lot of trouble for an old debt to a boy he hadn't seen in years.

"What're you up to, Bern?" Suspicion filled Marcus's tone.

Pride washed over me. My boy, the cynic.

Bernie didn't even try to act innocent. "Might need a favor someday. Never hurts to stack the deck, especially when it doesn't cost me anything."

I relaxed a notch.

"It'll take five minutes to fix the cameras, long enough to get you in the room," he continued. "I'll open the door and slip inside. If anything goes wrong, keep walking. On the far side of the corridor go left. You'll be at the service elevator. Go to the kitchen or the dock. The dock's a quicker exit."

Bernie had things too well planned for this to be off-the-cuff. It felt like a practice run, but I didn't say a word.

I've learned, if you don't want to know the answer, don't ask the question.

The elevator opened. Bernie walked down the hall with a quick stride.

Marcus and I were right behind him. A camera, situated high in the corner, made me nervous. A hiss escaped through my teeth, but the thick green and beige carpet absorbed the noise.

Beyond Bernie's retreating form, the hall was empty. I pulled Marcus close. "If these balconies aren't all but touching, we're not doing this."

Disappointment filled his eyes. You'd think I'd refused him money for the ice-cream man instead of telling him he couldn't leap across a pair of balconies nine stories up.

Bernie lengthened his lead by a couple of strides. In a quick move, he disappeared into the near door on the left.

Marcus slipped in behind him.

Hot on his heels, I pushed the door shut behind me. Then I had to lean against it for support. "Oh, my word."

My apartment would have fit into this suite with room to spare. Chandeliers of faceted crystal dazzled my eyes. Parquet tables inlaid with several hardwoods glimmered beneath Baccarat chandeliers.

"Nice digs." Marcus spun on his heel in front of me then headed for the balcony.

Bernie waited outside one of three full-length French doors. Sheer drapes on the middle set fluttered in the evening breeze.

I walked forward on autopilot, brushed the curtains aside, and stepped into the evening air.

Streetlights rolled away in the distance to merge with

the dusky haze of the desert. Light pollution gave the sky a pale glow that contrasted with the deep purple mountain peaks ringing the horizon. No buildings blocked the view and there was nothing shabby about it.

Bernie barely glanced at it. "You're on your own."

His words brought reality back with a thud.

"Look, T.R." Marcus gestured at the railing. "Piece of cake."

He reached over and all but touched the wrought iron surrounding the balcony of the neighboring suite. The white metal bowed out at the bottom in an S-curve. A four-year-old could've gone from balcony to balcony.

What had the builders been thinking? Even for the overly trusting bygone days, this seemed absurdly close. I leaned over to look at the lower floors. Those balconies looked farther apart, but that didn't help me.

Marcus shot me a confident grin.

"All right," I said. "But I'm going first."

"That's my cue." Bernie's voice sounded behind us.

I'd all but forgotten him.

"Kid, I wish you luck. T.R." The security guard met my gaze. "He's right. You are something."

"Thanks for your help," I said.

"If anything happens, I don't know you." He stepped through the balcony door, closed it, and locked it from the inside. It sounded like the thud of a guillotine.

Marcus noted my reaction. "He had to cover his tracks."

I hadn't built up my reserves for the plunge, but there was literally nowhere else to go. Taking a deep breath, I gave the rolling view one last look. "I'll go first."

Marcus nodded solemnly.

Gripping the railing, I threw one leg over then the

other. With both feet on the outer edge, I tightened my hold on the metal bar and stepped across the expanse.

My foot landed on the wide bottom of the S-curve. My hand clenched the top metal bar. Setting my weight evenly, I pulled myself to the outer edge of the other balcony.

"Just like a pro." Marcus's triumphant tone didn't hide a breathy relief.

"Wait there." Telling myself not to look down, I tightened my grip on the railing and moved one foot to his balcony. "Step outside the railing. Hold on."

Marcus climbed over like a monkey. Seconds later he clung to the metal bar. With nothing between him and the night air, he shot me a smile. "It's cool."

My heart was in my throat and I wasn't sure I was breathing. "Keep one hand on the railing and step to the other side."

Before I could remember to breathe, he was balanced on the cement edge of the other balcony. I gripped his arm with my free hand. "Get over the railing."

"You're cutting off the circulation," he complained.

"Move." I waited until he was safe then joined him. I had all the energy of a wrung out dishrag. "Can I go home now?"

Marcus smiled. He glanced at the French doors. "How do we get in? Knock?"

I stared at the closed doors as if they'd sprung out of nowhere. Steeling my legs, I pushed away from the wall and motioned Marcus to stay.

He rolled his eyes but stayed by the railing.

Instead of sheer panels, drapes covered the French doors. The first set was pulled tight. A sliver of light showed through the second pair. I peeked in.

As luxuriously furnished as the other suite, this one looked just as empty. Then I noticed a plate with a thick slab of steak and a serving of potatoes on it.

My stomach rumbled. I had to promise it a deep-dish pizza with everything to silence it.

"Is he there?" Marcus whispered.

I shook my head.

A crash captured my attention. The tableau inside the suite unfolded like a scene from an old movie; Randy locked in a struggle with a guy dressed all in black. A stocking mask hid the attacker's face. His lean build didn't compare to Randy's but he was obviously wiry enough to hold his own.

"Who's the ninja?" Marcus's voice sounded below my chin. The boy had slipped in while I was distracted.

I shook my head in mute surprise.

In a sudden move, Randy twisted the other guy's arms above his head and slammed him into the wall.

My breath caught in my throat at the sight of the gun in the other man's hands.

Using Randy's grip against him, the ninja kicked Randy hard in the gut.

My ex sailed backward. Arms flailing, he pulverized an end table on his way to the floor.

My stomach noted the steak and potatoes remained safely intact on the food cart.

The killer brought the gun into a shooting stance.

"What do we do?" Marcus asked.

I wasn't about to face a gunman, but I could try for distraction. I pushed Marcus to one side and stood next to him by the stone wall. Then, taking a moment, I kicked at the lower pane of the French door.

As I pulled my leg to safety, a hole appeared in the

glass. A spider-web of cracks formed as a bullet zipped into the air with a mosquito-like buzz.

Inside the suite a yell cut through the night.

I looked at Marcus. "You okay?"

He agreed, his eyes big as saucers.

I peeked through the edge of the drapes and into the room.

Randy stood over his opponent. A broken table leg dangled from his hand.

The gunman lay unmoving amid the wreckage of end table.

I reached through the broken glass, unlocked the door, and rushed into the room.

Randy raised the table leg then his eyes widened. "Tracy? Where did you come from?"

"Is he dead?" Marcus asked in a hushed voice.

Randy stumbled, raking a hand through his hair. "I didn't hit him that hard."

I glanced at the man on the floor. What if the ninja came to? My stomach roiled in fear. "Hit him again."

"I don't want to kill him." Randy protested.

Now he develops a conscience. "Where's the gun?"

My ex glanced around, worry etched on his face. "I didn't see where it fell."

"Find it." I glanced around as well even as I turned to Marcus and pointed at the door. "Go to the end of the hall and call the service elevator. We'll be right behind you."

He collected himself and nodded. With one last look at the figure on the floor, he started toward the door.

"I can't go out in public." Randy's protest stopped Marcus in his tracks. "The police are looking for me."

"Security will be here in a hot minute." I moved

toward the man. "The first thing they'll do is call the cops."

He cursed silently.

I walked toward Randy while looking around for the gun. "This guy could have backup. He may wake up any second."

Randy's shoulders slumped as I drilled the message home.

"You've been found out." I took his arm and turned to Marcus. "Go."

Marcus stepped toward the front door.

"No," Randy's command came on the heels of mine.

I told myself not to smack him. Only the reminder that I'd come here for answers stopped me from leaving without him.

Randy pointed toward what looked to be the kitchen. "The rear exit is by the service area."

Marcus pivoted and ran off.

The doorknob to the corridor rattled.

I tightened my grip on Randy and pulled. "Forget the gun. Let's go."

He stumbled after me like a punch-drunk boxer.

Hoping Bernie had gotten the call and might delay, I pushed Randy forward.

The gunman moaned and braced his hands on the floor.

That was all I needed. My hand still gripping Randy's arm, I turned toward the hall Marcus had taken.

Randy didn't move. "But—"

I bunched his shirt in my fists and shoved my face into his. "Move."

The guttural tone hurt my throat, but the look on his

face was worth it. I spun him in the right direction then ran past him. I wouldn't leave Marcus an orphan again.

Thudding footsteps sounded behind me. I glanced over. Randy's frightened face was only inches away. Behind him, the dark form struggled to his feet. He reached for the weapon that had been hidden under his body.

Blood drained from my face.

Randy watched my expression. His eyes widened.

I turned around and sped up. Flashing through the kitchen, I eyed the distance to the hall.

A scream rent the air. Close on its heels, came a thudding sound, like a body hitting the locked door of the suite.

Fear froze my blood. That wasn't security. It must be the ninja's backup. I grabbed the doorjamb without slowing. Pulling myself into the turn, I looked their way.

The gunman raced toward us, gun raised.

"Down." I flung myself around the corner. Too fast. My foot slipped. Pain knifed me in the side. True to my high-school track-star days, I hit a three-point stance, but didn't go down.

Randy dove forward but kept his feet.

Next I knew, Randy had his hand on my arm, pulling me up. Within a step, I matched him stride for stride. The crash of breaking wood and angry shouts followed us. We bounced off the wall and around the corner.

I heard the mosquito-buzz again.

I didn't look back. I didn't want to know. At the end of the hall, Marcus stood in the doorway of an open elevator.

"Hit the button." My scream echoed off the walls.

Marcus stabbed at the control panel and frantically waved us forward.

Three strides away, the doors started to close. My breath came in short gasps.

Marcus gazed at the hall behind me. Horror replaced worry. "Down."

My blood froze as I felt a bull's-eye burn itself onto my skin.

20

18 Across; 9 Letters;
Clue: Acting together in secret toward a fraudulent end
Answer: Conniving

Seeing the blood drain from Marcus's face shot my survival instinct into overdrive. I leaped through the elevator doors and snagged my son on the fly. Momentum sent us crashing to the floor.

Randy lunged through the closing doors with no time to spare. He landed with a thud then rolled to the opposite corner.

As the elevator clanged shut, deafening gunfire exploded in the hall. Loud metallic thuds struck the door in quick succession.

With my arms around Marcus and my heart in my throat, I held my breath until the elevator started moving.

A heavy thud crashed against the elevator doors. The echoes reverberated along the shaft.

"That was wild." Excitement oozed in Marcus's tone. He wiggled in my embrace. "T.R., you're choking me again."

I pried my fingers loose then let my head fall against the wall. Leaping over balconies. Gun fights. This was crazy. Marcus could have been hurt.

Randy's gaze shifted from my son to me. "You saved my life."

I shot to a sitting position, happy to channel my fear into anger. "Remember that when the time comes for explanations."

A shuttered look flittered through Randy's eyes. Crisis over, he reverted to his usual priority—saving himself. His gaze slid sideways then returned.

Mine didn't waver. "I didn't come for the floor show. I want answers."

He grimaced, then gave what could have been a shrug or a nod. Didn't matter. He had no wiggle room left.

I kissed the top of Marcus's head to reassure myself he was actually in one piece. "Good job."

Marcus grinned at me with a smug expression. "It's in the blood."

I didn't have the energy to tell him murder and mysteries weren't a game. Promising myself we'd discuss that later, I glanced at the control panel. The light for dock was lit.

"The guys chasing us won't know we didn't go through the kitchen," Marcus explained. "It might gain us a few minutes, long enough to hotwire a car."

My better half protested, but my survival instinct crushed it. "Just this once."

Marcus smirked.

With three levels to go until we reached the dock, I

struggled to gain my feet, grimacing at the stitch in my ribs. "I'll text Kevin once we're safely away."

Marcus popped up like a jack-in-the-box. Putting his hand under my arm, he eyed my side as if expecting blood. "You okay?"

I ignored my weakness. "Just my ribs."

When the elevator doors slid open, I peered out while trying to control my rattled nerves. Not a soul in sight. "No time to waste."

We set out at a quick jog toward double wide doors. Beyond them, the parking lot beckoned like the promised land.

"I can't believe this area isn't locked up." Randy sounded suspicious.

I didn't care about anything but getting away.

Marcus looked around. "The garage is empty. You'd need keys to call the elevators. They'll have cameras here, too."

An itch burned between my shoulders. My ears strained to catch sounds of pursuit. Finally, the evening air surrounded us. Though the shadow of the building felt like a friend, we were twenty feet from the cars.

The faint ding of the elevator sounded like a death knell in the stillness.

"Run." My heart thudded with fear.

We sprinted for the vehicles.

I changed directions so I was between Marcus and where I thought the shots would come from. Glancing back, I stumbled and almost lost my footing in shock.

Two shooters raced after us. Neither was the ninja. One was a stout man in a suit. In my fleeting glimpse, the other looked like Cowboy Guy. Shock coursed through me, or it could have been the pain in my ribs. I turned toward the imagined safety of the parking lot, still too far away.

A screech of tires and the roar of a powerful engine sounded to my left. Panic filled me. Then, out of the corner of my eyes, I saw a streak of ivory race toward us.

With Kevin behind the wheel, the white elephant roared to the rescue. The top was down and the red interior beckoned like a bull's eye.

Relief lent me speed. Hope fired my tired legs with renewed strength.

Kevin screeched to a stop. "Get in."

Marcus vaulted into the backseat.

I dove into the front passenger side head first. Still airborne, I yelled at Kevin. "Take off."

He hesitated.

Impatience rose inside me; then I heard another thud in the back. Oh, yeah, Randy. I'd forgotten about him.

Bullets zinged overhead. Kevin ducked and floored the gas.

Yanking my feet inside the car, I curled into a fetal position.

Kevin leaned over me, his face inches above mine. With one eye looking over the dash and one hand on the wheel, he squeezed my arm. "Glad you could make it."

"Happy to be here."

The acrid smell of burning rubber mixed with the Spearmint on his breath. The car shot forward.

Foolishly, I raised my head and looked back. It was stupid, but I had to see if Cowboy Guy was one of the shooters.

A thickset man in a suitcoat stood in a shooting stance. His gun had a dead sight on the car.

A second guy, lean and lanky in jeans and a plaid shirt, ran toward him.

I knew that profile. I'd seen it last night in the police car at the Blue Bayou.

When he came even with the other man, Cowboy Guy brought his arm up beneath the shooter's arms.

I strained for a better view. The car slewed around the corner. I slid against Kevin.

He steadied me with a rock-hard hand. After a quick check, he shifted his gaze to the front.

"No one got shot." I breathed a huge sigh of relief. "Score one for the good guys."

Kevin and the beautiful white beast flew out of the lot and onto the main drag.

Wind whipped my hair. I sat back. For a moment, watching the landscape zip by like a slide show gone wild was all I could manage. Next thing I knew the desert loomed before us. "Where are you going?"

"Somewhere I know we're not being followed."

I rolled up the window to siphon off some of the wind. "It'd take a small plane to follow this thing."

"Admit it, the Caddy's growing on you." His words held a triumphant tone.

"I refuse to admit any such thing." I fought a smile. "How did you know where we'd be?"

Kevin rolled up his window as well. The wind swept around us. He slowed the car, and the noise level dropped. "I was in the administration office when the call came over the guard's walkie-talkie about trouble in a suite. I knew it could only be the Belden Detective Agency."

He winked into the rearview mirror.

Marcus, straining forward against his seatbelt, gave a thumb's up.

Kevin continued. "I bolted for the car and drove back and forth from the kitchen to the docks until I hit paydirt."

"Thank, God." I patted his shoulder. "We need a place to land. You have your phone?"

"Crawford called." He dug in his pocket. "He has the CD. I told him you were getting the *Wall Street Journal.*"

"What's that mean?" Marcus wrinkled his nose.

"It's a paper that lists the stock markets," I explained. God knew he'd never seen the paper in our place. "It's how Randy made his money. Kevin was being subtle."

"Good job." Marcus thumped Kevin on the shoulder and was rewarded with another wink.

Leaning forward to block the wind, I dialed Mrs. C's throwaway cell phone. I could only hope no one was tracking Kevin's cell phone, but I had no options left.

She picked up on the second ring.

"It's me," I said. "We need a place to crash."

"Let me work on it," she said in her calm little British voice. "I'll ring you in five."

"Thanks." A click sounded as soon as I spoke. I was about to relax when a thought struck me. "What happened with the car?"

"Wondered how long it'd take you." His white teeth flashed in the dying light. "An angry woman who keyed the wrong white car in front of a witness paid handsomely to make the problem, and me, go away."

For an instant, the smell of easy money masked all other issues. "How much did she give you?"

Kevin's expression held a leer that had nothing to do

with sex. "She gave up twenty-four-hundred dollars of her score on the slots."

My heart thudded. I met Kevin's excited grin then looked at Marcus.

"Tracy, do you have a destination other than the middle of nowhere?" Randy's demanding tone cut across my moment of victory.

Annoyance replaced euphoria. He hadn't even said thanks. "We just saved your butt, so pipe down."

Kevin leaned toward me as I turned around. "What makes you think Mrs. Colchester can come up with a hideaway?"

"What makes you think she can't?" I held up the cell phone. "Five minutes."

The words were barely out of my mouth when the phone rang. I flashed a triumphant smile and opened it with a flourish. With my luck, it'd be one of Kevin's buddies. But it wasn't.

"I've made the arrangements, luv." The mellow accent sounded as cool as ever. "Do you have a pencil?"

I dug in my purse for a pad and pen. "I'm ready."

Writing one-handed in a moving car with my knee as a table didn't make for the best penmanship, but the address was legible. I repeated it.

"That's the place. Will meet you—" A crackle of static interrupted her. "You'll be—good hands."

More static. I wasn't sure she could hear me, but I tried. "Thanks, I'll check in later."

I disconnected. "Turn this jalopy around."

Fifteen minutes later, we drove past a neighborhood bar and up a two-lane side street. The neighborhood was okay, not the best. Traffic was steady for a Sunday evening. A resort town never shuts down.

Kevin had waved aside the address after hearing it once. He drove like he knew where we were headed.

I had a growing sensation I should know as well. However, I'd spent my last reserves of energy to text Crawford about Cowboy Guy and his friend with an urgent request for any information on the new players. Now my brain cells refused to talk to each other. My eyelids drooped while the wind swept over me. I'd find out where we were headed soon enough.

"How much farther?" Randy sounded like a child on a road trip.

"Up ahead." Kevin pointed to an apartment building half-a-block away.

As the car turned into the drive the garage door rose.

Kevin maneuvered the boat in smoothly and stopped. The gears of the garage door caught with a metal clang. Seconds later it closed behind us.

By the time the lights went on, I knew who was waiting. I reached for the door handle.

"Rabi." Marcus stood on the seat. "Wait till you hear what we did."

I wondered fleetingly where he'd moved his Jeep, but the thought was gone before I could blink. I hoisted myself out of the car as the skeletal black man walked up.

Marcus didn't bother with the door. He jumped over the side to slap palms.

I shuffled forward with a tired smile. "Rabi, seeing you is the best thing that's happened to me all day."

The perfect waves of his shoulder-length hair glinted in the light as he shook his head. "You've had a mighty poor day."

"You'll hear all about it." I motioned Marcus to

silence, for all the good it did me. "Wait until we get upstairs. If I make it that far."

Kevin rounded the car with the expression of a proud papa. He gestured toward the luxury liner. "Beauty, isn't she?"

"She is fi-ine." Rabi's nod of appreciation was all Kevin could have hoped for. They stood side-by-side admiring our great white deliverer.

I headed for the stairs leading to his second-floor apartment. I'd need every inch of lead I could get.

Randy climbed out of the car on the far side. He eyed the garage with a raised brow. His lawn mower probably wouldn't fit in here. But once the conversation turned toward the car, he thawed. "Had it long?"

"Got it today from a friend." Kevin stroked the hood, not bothering to mention the car wasn't actually his.

"Not many around this nice." Randy's politician smile included Rabi as he eyed the car.

With the stairs looming before me like Mount Everest, I considered sleeping in the car. Lord knew, there was plenty of room. But it was early yet. Though the adventures had piled up, it was still shy of six o'clock on Sunday.

"Pizza's on the way."

Rabi's promise did it. If my feet couldn't make it, my stomach would get me up upstairs if it had to crawl. Though my snail's pace slowed progress, we beat the delivery boy. That's the important thing.

Thirty minutes later, the remains of three New York style pizzas, two orders of bread sticks, and empty liters of soda and water surrounded us. Randy and I faced each other over the coffee table in the cracker-box-sized living room. Marcus sat on a chair between us. Rabi and Kevin kept watch while leaning against the kitchen table, a yard away.

The throbbing in my ribs had subsided. I felt almost human. I graced Randy with my sweetest smile.

His shoulders relaxed. The smile he shot me could have charmed birds from the trees.

My smile slid away. "Start talking."

He drew back with an expression of wide-eyed innocence.

I remembered his act from senior year when I'd caught him going into the prop room with Mary Sue. I jabbed a finger at him. "You knew your phone was bugged. Yet you still called me about my writing your wife."

"I was shocked," he protested. "When I—"

"You weren't too shocked to save yourself." My voice hardened.

His expression froze, but he recovered. "Tracy, I swear—"

"Don't bother." I clipped off the words. "If you don't deliver answers, I'll tell the cops you came to me with a plan to kill your wife. If I talk first, I'll get the best deal."

He paled beneath his smooth tan.

I softened my voice to a casual tone. "You know I don't make idle threats."

I thought I heard Kevin whisper something about the cooking pot dream, but I didn't break eye contact with my ex.

Randy watched me warily. After a minute, he exhaled like a leaky balloon. "I don't know where to begin."

"Try the beginning." The words were barely out when I reconsidered. "Forget it. I'll tell you what I know so you don't have to make things up as you go along."

His eyes took on a hurt look. His brow furrowed.

"Everybody knows wifey-number-two wasn't the real deal." Why was he acting so innocent? The police had had plenty of time to confront him with the facts. "The dead woman was never married to you."

Randy rocketed forward so fast I thought he'd conk me on the head. "What are you talking about?"

I rolled my eyes. "The dental records don't match."

"They didn't need dental records," he said. "I identified the body."

"Confirmation by dental x-rays is required." Marcus dismissed Randy's naivete about police procedure with the wave of a bread stick. "Cops have to be sure they don't bury the wrong body."

Randy glanced at Marcus then at me. "Her dental x-rays would have confirmed her identity."

My ex obviously didn't know there were two, conflicting sets of x-rays. A fact the police had known since Friday evening.

Why hadn't Detective Brennan confronted him? She'd had plenty of time. Randy hadn't taken off until Saturday night. Could it be because of Randy's wealth and his connection to the mayor? Perhaps Brennan wanted to gather more evidence before accusing Randy of murdering the real Cassie Reed.

Marcus eyed my ex with a smug expression. The boy relished any chance to explain. "The dentist in town couldn't find her file. Since the cops knew Cassie Reed was born in Kansas, they traced her family and contacted her old dentist."

Randy paled. He jerked Marcus out of the chair. "They did what?"

I thrust my body between him and Marcus and grabbed Randy's wrist in a tight grip.

Kevin and Rabi were already beside me. The cold fury in their eyes chilled even me. If they got to Randy he wouldn't have to worry about the police, or anything else.

Only my history with Randy kept me from letting them loose on him. I dug my nails into his skin. "Let. Him. Go."

Randy looked at his hand holding Marcus then released the boy as if he was on fire.

"Sit." Still holding Randy's wrist, I forced him back until he plopped onto the chair. Then I put my hands on Marcus's shoulders. "You okay?"

"Yeah." He sounded more surprised than anything. No one had laid a hand on him since he'd been with me.

Randy held up his hands, palms out.

"I'm sorry, ki—Marcus. I didn't mean to hurt you. I swear." His face was pale, and his eyes held nothing of the usual façade. "I was shocked. I—I'm sorry."

I hugged Marcus close. "Why don't you get a soda? Then you can sit at the table with Kevin and Rabi."

"Okay." Marcus agreed casually and turned away.

Rabi touched Marcus' shoulder as he went by but his gaze didn't waver, neither did Kevin's. Their flat hard gazes could have burned a hole through iron.

I have to give Randy credit. He met their looks head on.

"I don't do stuff like that." His voice shook as he spoke. "I don't know what came over me."

Kevin trembled as if on the verge of losing control.

Randy looked at them for a minute longer then shifted his gaze to me. "I didn't mean to touch him. Tracy, you know I wouldn't hurt a kid. Never."

"I know, Randy." Much as I hated to give him an inch, I couldn't deny the truth. In high school, Randy had almost put a man in the hospital when he witnessed the guy beating his son. "You stay put from now on."

Randy took one look at Rabi and Kevin's steely gazes and succumbed. "I will."

I turned to Rabi and Kevin. "It's okay."

They finally dragged their gazes from Randy. Rabi walked to the table where Marcus sat sipping his soda. His wide-eyed gaze was glued to the drama.

When Kevin didn't move, I touched his arm until he met my gaze. Finally, his tense muscles beneath my hand relaxed, and he backed up.

Taking a deep breath, I sat opposite Randy. "Let's start again."

By this time, my heart had almost settled to its normal rate, and I realized what had sparked the violence. "You knew the Kansas x-rays wouldn't match the body. Which confirms the fact that you married the real Cassie Reed years ago in Vegas."

Which matched Lydia's story. She'd told the truth when she said she knew them both in Vegas. Where did that leave Randy? Was he a Blackbeard? Or a murderer?

21

23 Down; 9 Letters;
Clue: A fact beyond doubt.
Answer: Certainty

R andy looked at me with a stunned expression. "The cops know Cassie... my wife... "

My irritation reached a boiling point. I didn't have the patience for him to work out the details. "The police know that sometime after you married the real Cassie Reed, she exited stage-left and the dead woman took her identity. The cops know you're involved with the real Cassie's disappearance."

His expression looked like that of a trapped animal looking for an escape.

"The cops also know wifey-number-two hailed from New York twenty years ago." I added this morsel before he could speak. "No need to thank me."

His mouth tightened.

Evidently gratitude wasn't on his mind. Too bad. "You're in deep, Randy. I wouldn't care except you dragged me in, too."

I prodded him again. "I also know you're in some money scheme with illustrious members of our local political community."

He started forward. One glance at Kevin and Rabi froze him in place. "Wha... what do you mean?"

I rolled my eyes at his innocent tone. "The mayor had a directory with the names Cassie Reed, Jade Garden, and Lydia Storm on his computer. The other file in the directory has McKiernan Enterprises with a list of politicians and dollar amounts, large amounts."

By the time I finished, he was so green I worried he might throw up on Rabi's floor.

"The cops know this?" Randy squeaked out.

"The CD is being analyzed now." Not by the cops but he didn't need to know that detail.

His gaze turned thoughtful, then they lit up. "I can fix this."

I felt like shaking sense into the man. "One of your political buddies killed your wife."

"No, they didn't." His denial brimmed with derision. "Her murder exposed my affairs to scrutiny. None of them want that."

Put that way, I had to admit, he had a point. "Then who killed her?"

"I don't know." His exasperated tone came close to matching my mood.

"The cops think it was me."

"You'll be cleared." He waved away my concern. "You have no motive to kill Cassie."

"Except your million-dollar life insurance policy with my name on it."

"Oh." A light flickered behind his eyes. "I forgot about that."

"What was your plan?" I didn't have the slightest idea what lay behind that scheme. "Did you intend to kill her all along and implicate me?"

"No." He jerked upright. "I was out partying and got to feeling sorry for you and your pathetic life. So, I added you as co-beneficiary with my wife to a policy I'd taken our earlier."

I ignored the derisive comments. At least, it was explanation I could buy. "In other words, you were falling-down drunk and didn't know what you were doing."

"I did you a favor, and this is how you thank me?"

"Your favor gives me a motive for killing your wife," I reminded him. "I inherit a million dollars if you die. The cops think they've solved the crime."

"Lucky for you, I'm not dead."

"Not yet." I forced the words through gritted teeth.

His smirk evaporated.

When I was sure I had his attention, I continued. "I've run all over town in the past two days. I've bruised my ribs. I'm wanted by the police and I've been shot at by three different gunmen tonight."

Randy was up before I formed my next thought.

Kevin sauntered closer. Ready to leap in, but I held out my hand to forestall him.

Randy never took his gaze off me. "There weren't *three* gunmen. There was only one."

"Who cares about numbers? It only takes one bullet to make a corpse." My frustration boiled over into anger.

"Who do you think broke down the door as we ran out? Your attacker was on the floor."

My ex turned to Kevin still standing by us. "There was only one shooter in the suite. Only one."

Kevin eyed Randy for a moment before curiosity evidently won out. "I saw two in the parking lot."

Evidently, I'd been the only one from the room crazy enough to look at the two men in the parking lot. "The ninja wasn't in the parking lot. They were new shooters, like in craps."

How appropriate.

Kevin finally gestured Rabi back and the two men resumed their station by the table.

"Who sent the other two shooters?" Randy wiped a line of sweat off his lips. "I have to go to the bathroom."

"Forget it." I blocked his path. "Marcus snuck out on Mrs. C through a bathroom window and I crawled my way to freedom the same way. I don't care if you piss in the chair. Nobody leaves until I get answers."

"Man, she's tough," Marcus whispered.

Murmurs of assent didn't faze my concentration.

Randy's eyes zeroed in on me. "You led those two gunmen to me."

"What about the one in your suite?" My voice rose in shock. His crazy accusation made no sense. "You're not concerned about him trying to kill you?"

Randy's mouth opened and closed like a fish out of water.

As I watched him sputter, two sparks ignited in my brain. "You know who sent the ninja. You know who murdered Cassie. You've known all along."

It was all I could do not to pummel the man. My body

stepped toward my ex-husband as if under someone else's control.

Randy put his hands in front of his chest, evidently reading the fury in my expression. "I don't. I didn't. It's not them."

I stopped and took a moment. A day of aches, pains, and frustration ignited a cold fury in my gut. "Tell. Me. Now. Or the cops will have my confession in fifteen minutes and you'll be headed to jail."

Randy studied me for a moment before shaking his head. "You always took life too seriously. That was your problem."

Irritation at his cavalier attitude only added to my rage. "My problem is standing in front of me."

"The guy in my suite overreacted. I've resolved the issue related to the Jade file. I'll give you the background so you'll understand that the people involved didn't murder Cassie."

"Short sentences," I warned him. "Stick to the facts."

Randy exhaled in one short burst. "I had inside information on my first investment. A dealer who owed me a favor told me about a buyout of an import-export business."

"Don't tell me," I interrupted, thinking of Jade Garden. "Oriental goods?"

He nodded. "I had a feeling I was about to hit a jackpot."

For a minute I saw the devil-may-care boy who'd charmed me so long ago. I shook my head. God must love the dreamers.

He continued. "When I heard Tang Chi Electronics was involved. I hocked everything I owned and bought the stock."

My eyes widened. He went into debt on a rumor? How had Randy and I ever made it work? Oh, that's right, we hadn't.

Ten years ago Tang Chi had been a small firm chasing the electronic tech giants. Then, their fortunes underwent a meteoric rise. Now you couldn't swing a burned out toaster without seeing their logo on every electronic gadget under the sun. As a marketing ploy, they give away jade statues with big purchases.

I narrowed my gaze. "Years ago, when Tang Chi was an up-and-comer, they sank their liquid cash into a small time import-export company?"

Randy gave me a wide smile. "Shrewd, hunh?"

Visions of the shadier items import companies could bring through customs danced through my head. "That's a word for it."

"Anyway," he hurried on. "When I called a stock-broker to invest in Tang Chi, his assistant got suspicious and approached me. After I let her in on the secret, she bought stock, too."

Sharing information on insider trading is an easy ticket to the penitentiary. But it was Randy and a pretty girl and that made it all too believable. Then the pieces fell into place. "The assistant was wifey-number-two."

He smiled wistfully. "Cassie was a hell-raiser."

"What was her real name?" I asked.

"I've called her Cassie for so long." His eyes took on a distant look. "Duna... Orduna Grimmley."

Marcus and I exchanged horrified glances. I'd have opted for Cassie Reed myself.

"We moved in together, but with all our cash tied up in the stock, we got desperate pretty quickly."

"What about her job with the stockbroker?" I asked.

"She left shortly after I met her," Randy explained. "Some question of missing money."

Bend the rules till they break was evidently the McKiernan family motto. "Missing money. Insider stock deals. Some people call those crimes."

He shrugged away my comment. "Two months later, the stock went through the roof. We were rich. We decided it would simplify matters to introduce Duna as my wife. We bought a townhouse. Life was good."

"Why didn't you file for divorce and marry Duna?"

"I didn't know where Cassie was. She could have been dead." He scoffed. "Besides, Duna's boss kept hounding her. He lost his company and had to start over. He started a vendetta against her. Sent investigators. Harassed her family. Posted a reward. Luckily, the guy didn't connect her disappearance to me."

Randy cast a quick glance at me.

I returned his look with a flat stare. This rationalization was pure Randy. Nothing was ever his fault.

"We figured it best if Duna disappeared," Randy continued. "She was already using Cassie's name. We moved out of Vegas. She had plastic surgery and dyed her hair. Her own mother wouldn't have recognized her."

I waited, but he seemed to have wound down. Did he think he could shut me up with this feeble story? "None of this explains the ninja or Duna's murder. Get to the dirt."

"Duna knew the stock market from her old job. She had a nose for deals."

I'm not slow, just hit me over the head and I catch on right away. "You didn't make your fortune trading stocks. She did."

"I helped," Randy defensively.

"You were the front man." I stepped on his words. "She couldn't buy stocks in her name, and you couldn't run the deals. Cut to the chase. Who wanted Duna dead?"

He shot me a disgusted glance, but he started talking again. "After the dust settled, Tang Chi Enterprises contacted us."

"Why?" I was running out of patience with his epic explanation.

"Duna and I bought the biggest percentage of stock before the buyout. They threatened to turn us in for insider trading." Randy shifted his gaze. "Instead, we struck up a business deal with them. We took a percentage, and they kept quiet. It all worked out."

Rumors had floated for years that Tang Chi had ties to organized crime in China. The import/export company would be a perfect cover for smuggling. "Sure, life was good. If you don't mind selling your soul."

Randy leaped to his feet, fists clenched. "All I did was invest money. It was legitimate."

"I don't care whether your deal involved money laundering or major fraud. It wasn't legit." I shot back with a touch of derision. I also didn't care enough to sort out the details of the criminal enterprise. "Then what? You and Duna's ties to Chinese gangsters weren't enough? You had to expand your service to crooked politicians?"

"You have no right to talk like that." He jabbed his finger in my face. "The Tang Chi donate money to politic causes. The funding goes through the mayor, not us."

"My attitude is the least of your problems." I jumped to my feet, slapping Randy's hand away. "Duna's dead. Murdered. Get back to explaining how she ran afoul of the Tang Chi."

Randy licked his lips. "She skimmed money from their accounts."

A long, low whistle sounded from one of the guys.

That pretty much summed it up. My sympathy dropped to rock bottom. "Did the woman have a death wish?"

"She had stock deals to cover." Randy collapsed in the chair as if the strings holding him up had been cut. "She'd have been okay if the big investments hadn't gone south."

"The definition of embezzlement is clear even if you work for criminals." I waved off his burgeoning outrage. "Duna stole money and lost it. Next?"

"She planned to recoup her losses, replace the money, and doctor the files."

My mind did a quick circuit. "Enter the mayor and the hidden bank accounts. More free money."

Randy nodded. "The mayor was infatuated with Duna. She found out where he hid the thumb drive that held the encryption key for the payoff accounts. Duna got a matching thumb drive and made the switch."

I followed his convoluted story of criminals stealing from criminals with a growing sense of amazement. I couldn't believe these people. No wonder criminals get caught. "I would think thieves would know better than to trust each other."

My ex shot me a dirty look before continuing.

"Once Duna had access to the bank accounts, she did some high-risk-high-return trading." The more he talked, the smoother Randy's delivery became. "She said no one would know the money had been missing. She just had to get the original drive returned to the mayor."

"Then disaster struck," I spoke in the dark bass tone

of a movie trailer. When Marcus shot me a triumphant smile, I realized I'd been watching too many old movies with the boy.

Randy raked a hand through his hair. "The mayor had an unexpected visit from the Tang Chi. When he inserted the duplicate thumb drive and found it was blank, all hell broke loose. Bad luck."

One convenient rationalization to wipe away all the lies, deception, and theft. What a cop out. "Why did your partners tell you this?"

"They thought the cops or the FBI took the thumb drive," he explained. "They warned us the house might be bugged. The phones tapped."

Randy's luck was almost laughable.

He shook his head again. "We figured if we put the drive back in the mayor's office and he found it, things would cool off. Duna tried on Saturday morning before our party, but she couldn't make the switch. She hid the drive with the encryption on it. She planned to try again Sunday morning."

She never got the chance, I added silently. "Who killed her?"

"I don't know." Randy pounded his knees, his voice a combination of anger, frustration, and grief. "All I know is she went upstairs and nev—"

His voice broke.

Despite myself, I couldn't stop a welling of sympathy.

He slumped in the chair. "At first, I thought she'd been kidnapped. When no ransom demand came, I thought she'd surprised a burglar."

"Where is this encryption file everyone's looking for?" I asked.

"I have no idea." He ran a hand through his hair.

"After you found her body, I explained everything to the Tang Chi, including the fact that she'd hidden the drive. We searched the house a dozen times with no success."

I turned a defeated gaze to Kevin.

He raised a brow. "Did you expect this to be easy?"

A blaring of rap music made me jump.

Marcus pulled out his phone. His eyes lit up as he looked at the readout.

"Hey, Crawford." The boy listened for a moment. A serious expression covered his face. "T.R. hasn't had time to charge her phone."

"I haven't had time to breathe," I muttered, wondering if Kevin's phone had run out of juice as well.

A moment later, the boy covered the mouthpiece to address us. "Man says we got a problem."

"Tell me something I don't know." Kevin's expression was as calm as the eye of a storm. His childhood had taught him to roll with the punches.

As always, his steady nerves anchored me in a crisis. After my son passed me his cell phone, Crawford gave me a cryptic update on Cowboy Guy and the man in the suit-coat for my ears only. There were Kansas cops, alerted by the Langsdale investigation of Cassie Reed. He hadn't known they were in town. He couldn't, or wouldn't, say more.

I was careful to keep my expression neutral and my gaze fixed. This case got more baffling by the minute. My boss and I are old friends. He didn't usually play so close to the chest with background details.

Then Crawford and I caught each other up on encrypted files. Crawford's computer genius was working on the CD Marcus had downloaded from the mayor's computer, but without Duna's encryption key it would take time, which we didn't have to spare.

"Put me on speaker," Crawford demanded. "I want your ex to hear this."

I thumbed the button and held out the phone.

"If anyone finds out we have that payoff file; the fat's in the fire." My boss's gravelly voice rattled into the room.

Rabi leaned against the table looking as if he might fall asleep. The man could at least have the decency to appear concerned.

Crawford continued with his warnings. "I can't scream payoffs and throw this grenade at Brennan until I have the information and all the players in plain English."

A chill traveled up my spine. The waters were getting dangerous.

"Get the original thumb drive the victim stole and find the real Cassie Reed." Crawford's gravelly voice hardened even more. "If your ex won't come clean, bring him to me."

The underlying fury shook even me. From Randy's petrified expression, he hadn't missed the underlying threat.

What's the two-word phrase reserved for a condemned prisoner?

Oh, yeah. My ex definitely had the look of a dead man walking.

---

22

1 Down; 6 Letters;
Clue: A passageway or hole through the ground.
Answer: Tunnel

L ong after the call ended, Crawford's threat lingered. I stared at Randy.

"You do not want face Crawford," I told him in a hard voice. "Those payoff files got Duna murdered. We have to find that thumb drive."

Randy spread out his hands, palms up—clueless as usual. "I got nothin'."

I cast about for the next move. Where to go when my murder investigation had turned into a game of hide-and-seek? I faced my guys, lined up like movie-goers at a free showing. All they needed was a bucket of popcorn. "Any ideas from the peanut gallery?"

"The Tang Chi are still looking for the thumb drive with the encryption key on it. So Duna's killer didn't recover it at the time of her death." Kevin's brow furrowed in thought. "The problem is we don't know whether the drive is in Randy's house."

"You had to bring that up?" My low spirits dipped lower. I hadn't considered that possibility. "If it's not in the house, we don't stand a chance."

"It's there," Rabi spoke in his usual drawl. "Duna needed the encryption key close to decipher the entries."

Marcus nudged Rabi's arm and gave him a wink. "Good thinking."

Though Rabi's mouth barely moved, his eyes gleamed.

Kevin gave a thumb's up. "The team is on the job."

I fell silent, unwilling to face the next step. Kevin, always happier in action mode, had no such reservations.

"We have to go in and find it. Marcus can stay with Rabi." Kevin ignored my and Marcus's groans. Me for having to go and my son for being left behind. "You and I can take Randy to the estate and sneak in from the back. We can't risk being spotted if the cops or the Tang Chi are watching the house. How did you get out last night without anyone seeing you?"

Randy pulled himself up in the chair. "There's a tunnel from the basement to the far side of the hill."

"Then that's how we'll get in," I said.

My ex's gaze shifted to Kevin then to me. "There's a problem."

"There always is." Kevin delivered the comment in a deadpan voice.

"When the bootleggers remodeled the estate in the nineteen-twenties, they built an iron gate over the mouth of the mining tunnel so no one could sneak in. Four feet inside the gate, a latch is embedded in the ground. When an ore car came down the rail loaded with booze, a hook on the bottom pulled the latch to release the gate. After the car passed, the latch reset."

I didn't get what he was driving at. "So?"

"You can't get in from the outside," he explained. "I flipped the switch as I left. The gate locked behind me."

I buried my head in my hands. The only other way was via the main entrance. No telling how many binoculars were trained on it these days.

"Would a hook work?" Kevin asked.

"The latch is at an angle." After a moment, Randy slid a glance my way. "There is one possibility, but you're not going to like it."

His words made me wary. "What?"

"The bars are too narrow for an adult, but..." His voice trailed away as I narrowed my gaze.

"Yes-ss." Out of the corner of my eye, I saw Marcus jab his fist in the air.

Randy shrugged. "I said you wouldn't like it."

"What about me?" I asked.

"It's too small for any adult."

"What about taking out the hinges on the gate?" I'd seen that done on TV.

"The gate is drilled into solid bedrock," Randy said. "A demolition charge could bring down the tunnel and not loosen the hinges."

"If kids can sneak in, why leave it in place?" I asked.

"The gate sits behind a locked steel door," Randy said with exaggerated patience. "I have the key for that."

"Oh." I hated to admit it, but I was beaten.

I sighed in defeat. I may be stubborn, but I'm not stupid. "We may as well get started. Sitting here won't change anything."

Kevin looked at Randy. "Is there a road that leads to this tunnel?"

Randy looked around. "A dirt path, but a car can make it."

Kevin turned to Rabi. "The Caddy's too heavy for that terrain."

I met Rabi's gaze. "Any plans for the rest of the evening?"

He checked his watch. "Five minutes to eight o'clock. That's when *I Love Lucy* starts."

Marcus didn't buy his lame excuse for a second. His small fist rapped Rabi on the shoulder. "You have to be in on this. You're part of the team."

Rabi shook his head in mock sorrow. "I guess I can miss this episode."

"Good." Not that I'd doubted the outcome, but I wanted another pair of eyes on Marcus, not to mention Randy.

Rabi walked to the door. "I'll tell my cousin I'll be out."

The look in his eye said he might pick up a little hardware as well. Marcus wasn't the only one who'd seen Rabi's collection of weapons. The thought of someone on our side having firepower reassured me. Harsh language only does so much against bullets.

Marcus hopped off the table. "I'm going with Rabi."

"Not so fast." I put a hand on his shoulder and pulled him back. "You and I need to talk."

"Oh, man." Marcus rolled his eyes, a teenager's worth of attitude in an eleven-year-old body. "It's lecture time."

"You got that right, partner."

ONE SHORT MOTHER-SON talk and a long half-an-hour later, we closed in on the backside of Randy's palatial estate. So far the car had hit every rut in the trail. I sat in the backseat next to Rabi and Marcus. With every bounce that jarred my bones, I silently cursed Randy for not keeping the path repaired.

Kevin, watching Rabi fighting to keep his ten-year-old Jeep out of the stiff weeds crowding in on both sides, said as much.

"My property stops at the tunnel," Randy explained from the front passenger seat. "This belongs to the state."

"That would explain the upkeep," Kevin said in a dry tone.

The car's back wheels hit a rock and went airborne. Crashing to the ground, the car fish-tailed toward a tree. Rabi wrenched it back to what passed for a path, and we continued not-so-merrily on our way.

Sitting behind Rabi, I kept my arm around Marcus's shoulders and my eyes on Randy. He was only here in the hope we'd find the thumb drive for his Tang Chi buddies.

"I wish we hadn't lost the connection when we were talking to Crawford," Kevin said in a frustrated voice.

I tried to focus on the positive. "At least Crawford knows where we're headed and why. He's sending back-up."

"We know the code word for the backup," Marcus pointed out. "Roxie."

I watched the glow of the headlights leap around. "Nothing we can do except hope they know we're the good guys."

"It'd be a shame to get shot by our own side," Kevin said in a wry tone.

My hand tightened on Marcus's shoulder. "Nobody's going to get shot."

Kevin's gaze met mine over Marcus's head.

"Probably nobody'll even be there." Marcus sighed. "It'll be all quiet and boring."

"Good," Rabi muttered in a low steady drawl. "Anybody pops out of a closet, I'd be so scared I'd faint dead away."

Marcus chuckled. "You'd never faint."

Even I had to smile at the image of the tall man passing out from fear. Outside the car, stiff grasses flashed by in the darkness. "Are we lost?"

Kevin snorted. "We've had this discussion. Which of us got lost in Vegas? A city covered in neon lights?"

"The real Cassie did." Marcus's comment brought the banter to a halt. "Randy never said where she went."

My ex-husband's shoulders stiffened.

"Duna took Cassie's name, birthday, and social security number," Marcus continued. "The real Cassie would have needed a new identity."

"He's right." I frowned, realizing no one else had picked up the dropped thread. "How did the real Cassie get by all these years with Duna using her social security number?"

Randy remained silent.

"You killed her," Marcus said matter-of-factly.

My ex jerked around. "I did not."

"She came back and you killed her," Marcus repeated with a strain of ghoulish delight.

Randy's gaze narrowed. "Stop saying that, you little brat."

"You probably chopped her up into little bits and fed her to your piranha," Marcus continued relentlessly.

"We did no—" Randy stopped in mid-protest. "I've never even owned piranha."

"Too bad," Marcus replied in on off-hand manner.

I tapped Marcus on the shoulder. "Let's leave the gory details to the books."

"It was a cable movie. *Mega Piranha*," Marcus corrected me. "Lots of blood and body parts."

"I don't need details. Let's get back to finding the real Cassie Reed. That's on the top of Crawford's to-do list for me." I eyed my ex's profile. "What happened to her, Randy?"

He stared out the front window without answering.

"Her family swears she is alive," I said. "They're right, aren't they? She is alive, and you know where."

Randy looked away. "She contacted me after Duna and I made our money. I explained the situation and gave her a settlement to start a new life. She'd already moved on. She was happy to take another identity. That's all."

Yeah, and I have the winning lottery ticket in my shoe. If it were that simple, why did Crawford's client want her and why now? Cassie with a new identity? Sure. But living anonymously behind a white picket fence? My gut told me there was more to the story.

"We're here." Relief underscored Randy's voice. He pointed off to the right.

The headlights lit up a flat stretch of sand and brush. We bounced over one final rock before stopping under a fragile canopy of scraggly pines.

Under cover of darkness, Marcus nudged me. His teeth gleamed like the Cheshire Cat's. He put his mouth to my ear. "I got him, hunh?"

I stifled a laugh. The little sneak had deliberately egged Randy on with that stupid piranha story.

Before anyone could move, Rabi put a hand on Randy's shoulder and turned off the ignition. Even our breathing seemed loud. "Noise carries. Best not to talk unless needed."

Everyone nodded.

"You have the key ready, Randy?" I asked, my voice barely above a whisper.

"Here." The clink and clatter of metal rang in the stillness. The next instant he muffled the noise.

"Grab the flashlights and let's go." I opened the door and stepped into the cool desert air. A multitude of stars, cold and silent in the dark sky, sparkled overhead. Behind me, car doors clicked shut. I pulled my gaze to the ground and followed the others to the steel door.

Seconds later we stood in the mouth of the tunnel, four by six-foot square. Randy flipped a switch I hadn't noticed. A barred gate stood rock solid four feet in front of us. A row of fluorescent lights lit up the tunnel then continued past the gate and around a curve.

"I told you we wouldn't need flashlights," Randy said.

"I like to be prepared. A throwback to my days as a Girl Scout." Which had lasted all of two weeks before I was asked not to return. FYI—the tents they used for camping were flammable. I really thought they'd be fireproof. "Anyway, we need the flashlights. We're not going to turn on the house lights."

Before I could say boo, Marcus slipped through the bars of the gate as if he'd been greased. Talk about anticlimactic. "Marcus."

The little snot put a finger to his lips and turned away.

"Don't worry, Mom," Kevin whispered in my ear, amusement ringing in his voice.

"My heart can't take this," I whispered back.

My little criminal walked four feet up the tunnel, then he bent and pulled up a tarnished hook, offset at a weird angle. Marcus leaned into it but it didn't move.

"Uh-oh." Kevin's harbinger of disappointment sounded in my ear.

I held my breath against the ghost of failure. We'd brought no ropes or wires. They wouldn't have helped anyway, the angle was too skewed for a straight pull to work.

Marcus sat on the ground and put his foot against the latch. Bracing his hands behind him, he pushed with the sole of his shoe.

Nothing happened.

Putting his other foot on top of the first one, Marcus put his hands against the metal track behind him. Gritting his teeth, he shoved again. His arms and legs shook with effort.

I clamped my teeth around my tongue. Just when I thought I couldn't stand the pressure, the latch rose. Was I imagining it? No, Marcus's legs had straightened. In the next second, the latch swerved in a slight arc and rose perpendicular to the ground.

I grinned and bumped Kevin's arm.

He chuckled. "You're such a mom."

Randy waved us back from the gate.

Marcus gave one final push and a soft click sounded.

Rabi grabbed the bars and we all pulled the gate up and out over our heads. Rabi and I slipped in first, then Randy and Kevin. When we lowered the gate, it clicked shut with a loud snap.

Rabi smiled congratulations to Marcus. Kevin patted the boy on the shoulder.

I cupped his cheek and kissed his forehead. Keeping my voice as low as possible, I leaned forward. "Rabi will go first."

"It's called point," Marcus whispered. "I'll go with him."

"Randy goes next. He knows the layout." I slid a glance to Rabi as I spoke, trying to instill it with a warning to keep a tight rein on Randy.

Rabi's eyes narrowed. He nodded.

I didn't mention that, thanks to blueprints Crawford had acquired, I probably knew the layout of the house better than Randy, especially in the dark. I looked at my ex. "Could anyone in the basement see the lights in this tunnel?"

Randy shook his head. "The panel's tight. There's a light switch on this side of the door."

"Okay, Kevin and Marcus will bring up the back."

"The rear," Marcus inserted.

Not only a Sherlock, a miniature Patton. "We'll regroup at the other end and turn off the light to let our eyes adjust to the darkness. Then we open the panel. What's on the other side?"

"A weight room," Randy assured me.

I nodded. "We'll wait there and make sure the house is quiet. Remember, no flashlights at first."

Rabi jerked his head at Randy, and we set off.

A long walk down a short pier. The phrase ran through my mind when we reached the other end. The echo of our footsteps had died, and the walls looked closer than when we'd started.

Randy flicked off the lights.

I gritted my teeth in the inky blackness. Part of me yearned to remain hidden rather than stumble around in a dark house.

"Now," Rabi barely breathed the word.

A soft click sounded. The next thing I knew, a whoosh of air fanned my face and a gray rectangle the size and shape of a door appeared in the wall. Within seconds I could see the others, as well as the rough outline of a chair and a weight set.

I shoved my cowardly half in the closet as I walked into the basement. I slipped my arm around Marcus's shoulders and gave him a reassuring squeeze. The muscles in his neck relaxed.

Nice to know I wasn't the only one with butterflies.

Rabi stopped several feet inside the room. His head turned in a slow arc, surveying the long, narrow room, then beckoned us forward.

Kevin brushed my right arm with one hand and put his other on Marcus's back. A quick reminder of his presence. As we walked on, his touch vanished, but the warmth and reassurance remained.

We hadn't gone more than a couple of feet when Marcus slipped ahead of me.

Randy walked to the bottom of the stairs. They led to the kitchen on the main floor. As he turned toward us a light snapped on, illuminating his blond hair.

We were screwed.

23

4 Down; 5 Letters;
Clue: As far as something or someone can go
Answer: Limit

I braced myself for cops, criminals, or both.

"Motion sensors," Kevin whispered.

I tried to rein in my rising panic as I chided myself. I couldn't count the times I'd watched the motion sensors trigger the lights while doing surveillance. Anything from a low flying bird to a curious squirrel set them off. Unfortunately, if anyone was on stake out, they couldn't afford to dismiss any sign of movement.

Randy's gaze shot from side-to-side. His breath quickened. He turned to me with a scowl on his face. "You better have a plan."

"As a matter of fact, I do." An idea had flared to life along with the lights. "We need to go to the second floor.

The hall closet by the bedroom, where the cops think Duna was killed."

Randy started up the stairs.

Rabi's long stride kept him close to a pissed-off Randy.

Marcus hurried after them but I caught him by the collar and shoved him behind me. "You bring up the flank with Kevin."

"The rear, T.R." Disgust filled his whisper.

Leaving him under Kevin's watchful gaze, I dashed up the stairs. The other two were already climbing to the second floor. I took a long drag of air and ran up the next flight.

The back stairs swung out to allow for a turret. I ran up the twisting steps without thinking. The sight of Rabi clutching Randy's arm at the top brought me to a halt. Nobody said a word until Marcus and Kevin joined us.

"Best if we stay together." For all the emotion in Rabi's drawl, you'd have thought we were out for a walk in the park.

Marcus nodded solemnly. "In horror movies, splitting up is how people get picked off."

Randy's pointed gaze at Rabi's granite grip brought no relief. His jaw tightened. "Our bedroom is at the end of the hall."

I took the lead. "The hall closet has the secret passageway in it. That's what we want."

A moment later, I opened the doors to the closet. Crime scene tape covered the opening to the passage in the back of the closet. Built-in shelves lined both sides of the oversized broom closet. The shelves were mostly empty. The police had evidently confiscated whatever had been stored here.

I summoned up my confidence, aware that each passing second might bring either the police or the Tang Chi down on us. "Marcus and I will search. We'll close the doors so the lights won't be seen."

I walked in behind Marcus. Brushing past Kevin, I muttered for his ears only. "Hopefully, this will work."

He patted me. "Go get 'em, Tiger."

When Marcus shut the door, I flipped on the interior light, then squatted to his level. "Start on your side. Think hidden compartments or hidey-holes."

The light caught his grin and cast eerie shadows on his face. "I'll find it. I'm a good sneak."

I doubted the PTA would take his words or this situation as a testament to my good parenting. With a rueful shake of my head, I turned to my side of the alcove. I used both hands to feel under the lowest shelf. Time stretched endlessly as I worked my way up to the next shelf.

My legs were cramping, and sweat had pitted out my shirt. After what seemed like forever, I glanced at my watch. Three minutes. I was exhausted.

However, as usual, the part of me that was determined to solve the puzzle overrode my good sense. I straightened my legs and tackled the next shelf.

"Got it," Marcus whispered in triumph. "The lowest shelf had a hollow end with a fake cover."

I swung around. A rush of triumph filled me at the sight of him holding a key ring with a three-inch-long drive attached. I raised both fists in a silent cheer. When I stepped forward, he shoved the key ring in my hand.

I slipped it into the pocket of my jeans and pushed open the door. A waft of cool air chilled the sweat on my face.

"About time," Randy's fierce whisper greeted our exit.

Marcus shut the doors as I stepped forward.

"Let's go." I jerked my head toward the stairs.

A strong hand on my elbow spun me around.

Randy thrust his face into mine. "I'm tired of being ordered around. I want answers."

I wrenched my arm loose. "This isn't the time. We have to leave."

Marcus tugged at my shirt. "Kevin and I put a ca—"

A crash of metal from below interrupted him.

My heart jumped. Everyone froze.

Kevin finished Marcus's announcement in an ominous tone. "A cart at the bottom of the stairs."

Angry voices carried up the stairwell.

"Through the master suite." I grabbed Marcus's hand and sprinted toward the end of the hall. Kevin pulled Randy along. Rabi brought up the rear.

With the element of surprise gone, I flipped on the flashlight. Marcus's flashlight joined mine. Twin streamers of light bounced over the walls and floor.

The shouts and running feet grew closer, spurring me on. In seconds, the sitting room flew past, then the entertainment area. The stairs were tucked into the opposite corner. "This way."

"Watch the table," Marcus cautioned, his flashlight lit on a low coffee table holding a heavy crystal vase.

I skirted around it, hoping the others noted the warning. Grabbing the rails, I took the stairs two at a time. Three steps from the bottom a dark figure stepped into the doorway. The black profile of a gun showed in his hand. I caught a glimpse of the tie and suitcoat owner who had shot at us at the casino.

Assailants behind us. Guns in front of us.

Bracing both hands on the railings, I pulled my legs up and kicked his chest as hard as I could.

The man crashed to the floor with a heavy thud. He lay like a stunned rhino but he still had the gun.

A low curse sounded to the side of the bottom doorway.

The others crowded close on my heels.

"We have to move," Kevin demanded.

A crash of furniture in the entertainment room punctuated his words. Shots exploded. The acrid smell of gunpowder filled the stairwell.

"Roxie! Roxie!" Cowboy Guy peeked around the doorway. His gun was pointed down and away. And he hadn't tried to shoot me. "Crawford sent us."

I ran down the steps to the main level then leaped to one side to avoid stomping on Suitcoat. By the time Marcus jumped over him, the downed man had gained his feet with a speed and agility I hadn't expected in a man his size.

Rabi hurtled down the stairs and ducked around the corner.

A quick look confirmed our location on the first floor. "This way."

The eruption of gunfire cut off my words.

Suitcoat planted his feet and fired four booming shots up the stairwell. He gestured Cowboy Guy to follow us. "Go."

Cowboy Guy jumped to our side of the doorway.

Moments later, Marcus, Kevin, and I were in the basement running full tilt for the door to the tunnel.

Kevin's thudding footsteps followed close at my heels. Deep-throated yells and sporadic gunfire melded into a barrage of noise farther behind.

A laser of pain sliced through my ribs. I bit my lip and kept running, zigzagging around a jutting wall. I wouldn't last long. Fortunately, the entrance to the tunnel was at hand. Clutching at a set of shelves, I struggled to keep my feet.

Randy burst out of the darkness and hit the switch. Stepping into the tunnel, he flipped on the lights.

"Go, Marcus. Go." I shoved the boy forward.

Kevin was beside me. He glanced toward the hall where the gunfight continued then touched my arm. "You all right?"

I managed a weak shrug and stumbled into the tunnel.

Kevin stood astride the door and met Randy's gaze. "Spring the lock."

Randy flipped the switch on the inside.

Bracing his feet, Kevin held the panel open. He poked his head out and yelled at the three men running through the basement. "Hurry!"

Randy started up the tunnel.

I rested a hand against the wall. The pain in my side had grown to a red-hot poker. Reaching out, I touched Randy's arm. "Get Marcus to the other side."

His eyes widened, and he reached for me.

I must have looked even worse than I felt. I pushed him farther into the tunnel. "Go on."

"Come on, kid. I'll race you." Randy tapped Marcus on the shoulder and ran beside him.

Marcus started off then glanced over his shoulder. When he saw I wasn't behind him, he slowed.

"Open the latch, Marcus," I yelled. "We'll catch up."

His expression cleared. Turning around, he ran full tilt with Randy at his side.

I swallowed hard and pushed off the wall. Agony lanced through me. I watched the other two disappear, then leaned back. I'd never make that run.

Kevin's muscles strained with the effort of holding the panel open.

A thunder that brought back memories of stampeding horses echoed behind me. Rabi and Suitcoat swept into the tunnel.

Cowboy Guy sprang through last. "Close it."

Kevin let go. The door snapped shut. The hiss of a spring and the snap of a lock confirmed the panel had shut.

"No wonder everyone keeps disappearing from this place." A gruff voice, probably Suitcoat, observed.

"Move," Rabi urged.

"Your ribs?" Kevin's voice sounded in my ear at the same moment I felt his hand on my arm.

I nodded. Something in my side had snapped when I'd kicked Suitcoat; each jarring step had made it worse.

Without another word, Kevin put his arm around my waist and moved my arm across his shoulders. Tightening his grip, he took my weight on his arm. Rabi matched him on my other side.

Running footsteps sounded on the other side of the panel. "Where are they? They were just here."

"There was a door," a second voice said. "I saw the light."

Hard pounding rattled the wall.

Holding me between them, Kevin and Rabi took off running. My feet touched nothing but air. When we got to the other side, Marcus and Randy had the gate up and the door open.

The tunnel behind us remained silent.

"She okay?" Marcus asked, starting forward.

"She'll mend," Kevin assured him. "We have to get out of here."

Rabi and Kevin maneuvered me outside without a hitch. The night air had never smelled so fresh. "You two are good."

"We aim to please, ma'am." Kevin's gasps marred his affected drawl, but it earned a chuckle from Rabi.

"Don't make me laugh, white boy." Rabi's response set them off again.

I joined in until the stitch in my side protested.

A clang of metal behind us confirmed the gate had reset. With a flick of the wrist, inky darkness swept over the tunnel.

Maybe it was my imagination, but I thought I heard a noise in the tunnel. Thankfully, the others slammed the door and locked it before I could draw another painful breath.

Randy leaned against it. "Thank, God, I've got the only key."

Kevin glanced toward the car. "I'd still like to get out of here."

"Amen to that, brother," Rabi said in heartfelt tones.

I felt a little foolish with the two of them holding me. I tapped their shoulders and unwrapped my arms from around their necks. "I'll walk from here. Thanks for the lift."

"You sure?" Kevin held his hands toward me as if I'd fall.

I took a step, a smart-aleck remark at the ready. Unfortunately, a hiss of agony escaped, and two pairs of hands grabbed me. I gave in and put my arms around them again.

Kevin and Rabi clasped each other's forearm, brought them underneath my thighs, and lifted me into the air.

"You hurt?" Marcus came up in front of us.

"She's faking it so she can be the queen bee." Kevin tossed off the comment easily, but he eyed me with a worried gaze.

"I hurt my ribs." I pitched my voice soft and low, so it wouldn't carry. "But this is a nice way to travel."

Marcus shook his head. "No more jumping off balconies. You don't have the knack."

"From your mouth to God's ear. Why don't you scope out the path to the car and make sure they don't trip on anything?"

Though the night was clear and the stars were bright, the last thing I wanted was to pitch head-over-heels. Not only would it hurt; it would be incredibly embarrassing.

"What about them?" Marcus pointed behind us. Cowboy Guy was already following. Randy and Suitcoat stood by the locked steel door eyeing each other with naked animosity. "They coming?"

With the thumb drive in my pocket and my guys safe, I didn't care. "We can take them or they can fend for themselves."

"I'm not staying in the woods with those two." Cowboy Guy's voice floated on the night air. He snapped his gun into a holster and started after us.

Marcus chuckled then walked along the path toward Rabi's wheels.

"Not everybody will fit in that Jeep." Randy's arrogant tone cut through the still night and reverberated off the trees.

"Why don't you talk louder in case everyone hasn't

fixed our position yet?" My brain knew no one could hear us, but his whining grated on my last nerve.

Randy's head jerked in the direction of the house, blocked by the hill. With a rapid step, he crashed through the weeds.

Suitcoat, eyes thoughtful, looked like he had his own agenda. He followed on Rabi's heels, except he managed to stay on the path and make not a sound.

I reminded myself Crawford had sent him. The ex-detective's instincts hadn't failed him yet. Only time would tell if his streak would hold.

It took time to squeeze six adults and one child into the car. It was not pretty.

Rabi, after insisting Kevin drive, sat in the backseat.

I don't think he wanted his back to any of the other men. Marcus was perched on Rabi's knees on my left and Cowboy Guy's slim, jean-clad thigh was tight against me on my right.

With Kevin driving and the thickset man on the right, Randy had less room in the middle than your average sardine. Every time Kevin moved, his elbow jabbed Randy. Randy tried to shift, but the car wasn't wide, and Suitcoat was not small.

Kevin glanced over his shoulder more than once to eye Cowboy Guy. His gaze held the same look of mistrust I felt about Suitcoat.

"Do you know where you're going?" Randy asked.

"The highway. Then town. Then..."

"Crawford's." I finished his sentence smoothly, but Cowboy Guy's voice matched me.

Kevin's shoulders tensed.

I wondered if the day was catching up with him. He

was usually so easygoing. I exchanged a sideways glance with the man next to me.

One side of Cowboy's mouth quirked up in a slow country smile. "He's the only one we all trust. He can tell you we're on the same side."

I could live with that. I studied Kevin's tense jaw and perfect profile and wondered what he had against the cowboy.

"I hope I'm not squishing you," Cowboy Guy said.

"Actually, the less I move the better," I said. "And we're packed in here so tight, I can barely move at all."

"Everybody comfortable?" Kevin eyed me with a narrowed gaze. The car jerked forward. "Crawford here we come."

"Shouldn't you put the lights on?" Randy asked in a worried tone.

"In case no one figured out where that tunnel leads and they decide to check out this area?" Kevin asked.

"You could hit a tree," Randy continued.

"Close your eyes," Kevin said. "You won't see them."

"Imagine it's a roller-coaster," Marcus said gleefully. "Except neater because you could really smack into something."

I smiled in the darkness at the lilt in his voice at our possible impending doom.

Randy scowled at the boy.

Having painted this hopeful picture, Marcus thrust his head next to Kevin's shoulder to get a better view of the trees rushing at the windshield.

Knowing Kevin wouldn't endanger a hair on the boy's head helped me concentrate on protecting my aching ribs. The digital clock on the dashboard said nine forty-three. We'd left Rabi's place less than two hours ago.

Though I felt as if I hadn't slept in forever, I'd been awake less than twelve hours.

Conversation ceased as Kevin maneuvered through the twisting path. Though the groaning metal made it seem like the entire frame might collapse at any second, I got used to the noise. I also didn't mind the constant scratching of weeds and bushes on the underbelly. I imagined it was the surf rushing to shore.

The thing that got me was the noise the branches made when they broke off. The popping sounded like gunfire. After a particularly loud one, Marcus shifted.

"There went the gas tank," he said in a hushed whisper. "We're probably leaving a trail of gas. When a spark catches on the next rock... boom!"

The fact that a rock slammed into the undercarriage at that moment only added to his glee, especially when Randy and Suitcoat both flinched. In their lone display of solidarity so far they turned and glared at him.

He turned to me with a wicked grin.

I could have said something, but his little snips helped distract me from how low the car was dragging.

Five minutes stranded with this crowd and I'd go find whoever had been chasing us. Kevin was a keeper, but we'd have to ditch Randy and Suitcoat behind a rock.

"Can't you move any faster?" Randy asked.

"I could," Kevin said. "But I think I should stay inside the vehicle."

Marcus's laughter filled the small space.

I laughed as well, silently hugging my ribs against the pain.

Rabi's teeth glowed in the darkness and Cowboy Guy's frame shook next to mine.

It'd make a nice epitaph to say we were at Crawford's

before I knew it. But even with gravity on our side, going down the hill took longer than going up. After the first few minutes, I didn't care if we hit a tree. I stared through drooping eyelids with all the energy of a slug and almost as much ambition.

I remember breathing a sigh of relief when we hit the highway. I closed my eyes, leaned back, and drifted off.

After what seemed like only seconds, a firm hand jostled me awake. I jerked my head up and pried open my eyelids. Past the now empty front seat, I saw a wall of white brick that marked the outside of Crawford's offices. The car doors stood open and the cool evening air rushed in.

Cowboy Guy reached toward me. "You awake?"

I looked at him through a blurry haze. The others stood behind him. Suitcoat was off to one side. I noticed because of the way the streetlights reflected off the gun in his hand as he swung it in my direction.

---

24

15 Down; 10 Letters;
Clue: Refused to pardon or excuse.
Answer: Unforgiven

The sight of Suitcoat's revolver sent a double shot of adrenaline through my veins. The last I knew we'd all been friends.

The sharp click of the hammer being cocked split the night.

"Get her out of there."

Cowboy Guy cast me a warning look as he helped me out of the car then shut the door.

The cool evening breeze rattled the sign outside Crawford's second story office. However, nothing explained why I was at the wrong end of a gun. Again.

Panic filled me as I searched for Marcus.

Kevin and Rabi stood shoulder-to-shoulder a few feet from the car.

The boy's legs shifted behind them. He forced his head out between their stiff bodies. "Leave her alone."

Kevin's focus remained on the revolver, but concern filled his gaze at the boy's belligerent tone. "She's okay, dude."

Fear that my son might put himself in danger shifted my worry to outright fear. "I'm fine, Marcus."

A couple of feet closer, Randy eyed the revolver as well.

Cowboy reached a hand toward the stout man. "Don't do anything stupid, Daniels."

"I've waited long enough." Daniels pointed the gun at my chest. "I want the facts, and she's got them."

I was tempted to check over my shoulder to find the person with the answers. In other circumstances, the thought of Daniels looking to me for a solution would be laughable. "What makes you think I have the scoop?"

Daniels jerked his head at Randy. "Blondie there doesn't have the brains God gave a gnat."

If he hadn't been holding a gun on me, I would have applauded his insight.

"Every time he has a problem, he runs to one of his wives," Daniels continued. "He did it in Vegas fifteen years ago, and he did it last week when you two went for your drive."

"That's ex-wife, fella." As my mouth took off, a light dawned. Daniels thought Randy had clued me in during the funeral parlor trip. He probably would have if I hadn't bolted from the car to avoid that very thing. "Even if I had the thumb drive, it's no good without the file in Crawford's office."

"We almost got killed, and you didn't find what we needed?" Randy asked.

Thank God, I'd hidden it while Marcus and I were in that closet. "You didn't find it either."

"I want Cassie Reed." Daniels stepped closer. "Tell me her identity or else."

I waited for fear to kick in. Evidently, my nerves had gone on holiday. My only thought was why Daniels had traveled from God knew where, shot up a mansion, and helped us escape to find Cassie Reed.

"Let my friends and my son go." I waited until Daniels met my gaze. "Then I'll tell you everything I know."

Which was very little.

"Like they'd leave you." Daniels tightened his grip on the gun. "Start talking."

Cowboy stepped in front of me.

"Move, Joe." Daniels waved his gun to one side.

Joe. It was so much easier to keep the players straight with actual names.

Focusing on irrelevant details also helped distract me from the rising tension in the air. I sought Kevin's eyes, knowing I could count on his cool nerves. With a firm hand on Marcus and a steady eye on Daniels's weapon, Kevin looked ready to spring.

Cowboy Joe remained planted in front of me. "This is wrong, and you know it."

"Listen to the man, Daniels." Crawford's husky voice, scratchy from years of drinking and smoking, spoke from the shadows.

Relief seeped through my bones.

A solid tank of a man stepped away from the building. The light was dim, but I didn't need it. Pale hair shot with gray was combed straight back. The face, like the body, was worn, but the jaw was square and solid.

Crawford's craggy face had never looked better. The Glock he held didn't look too bad either.

"About time you got here," I said in a cross tone.

Though Crawford's attention didn't waver, his lips quirked up. The slight smile faded. "You were supposed to back my people up, not pull a gun on them."

"She has the answers." Daniels' voice shook. "She's in this with him."

"No, she isn't, you brainless fool." Crawford's yell echoed off the brick walls. "Tracy has more self-respect than to hook up with an idiot like McKiernan more than once in a lifetime."

At least *Crawford* gave me some credit.

Daniels eyed me, obviously wondering if Crawford could be believed. With his gun holding steady in my direction, Daniels glanced over his shoulder.

Crawford's hard stare had cowed better men.

Daniels flinched. The barrel of his revolver dropped. "I've waited twenty years."

"We all have." Joe's soft comment hit Daniels hard enough to make him wince.

Freed of the latest threat, I let the wheels in my mind started rolling.

Twenty years ago Cassie Reed would have been in her late teens. What had she done to cause these men to chase her so long and so hard?

Daniels loosened his grip. The weapon rolled on his finger.

Crawford gestured Joe forward.

Joe took the weapon, shaking his head as he did.

Daniels looked at me. "Nothing personal."

I quirked a brow but let it pass.

Crawford holstered his gun. He met Daniels' gaze

with a hard look. "You ever draw a weapon on my people again, and I'll nail you to the wall. You and Joe take McKiernan to the office. We'll be up."

The two men turned toward the flight of stairs with Joe holding the revolver.

Crawford walked past Randy and jerked a thumb over his shoulder. "Move."

Randy looked around as if searching for an escape then he gave up and did as ordered.

Marcus squirmed out from between Rabi and Kevin. Glowering at Daniels, he came over for a quick hug.

Rabi ambled toward the building. "I'll keep an eye on them."

Crawford glanced at him. Their gazes locked for a fraction of a second. In the time it takes to blink, they took each other's measure and exchanged nods.

"Good idea," Crawford said.

I roused myself for introductions. "Rabi, Crawford. Crawford, Rabi."

"Rabi's part of our team," Marcus explained with a touch of pride.

Crawford approved. "We need good recruits."

"Great welcoming committee." Anger edged Kevin's tone as he stepped up to join us.

Crawford pursed his lips. "This goes back a long way."

"You could've clued us in," I said. "You're the one who says not to leave anything out because you don't want to be surprised. Now you send us on a case without the facts. Don't think I'm going to let you forget it either."

"I didn't know they were in town until you described the men who chased you from Randy's suite. They weren't supposed to arrive until tomorrow." Crawford's lips eased into a slow smile. "You managed to muddle things up."

"Answers now would be good." With that demand, my bravado collapsed before a wave of weakness. I leaned on Marcus to avoid a collapse.

Kevin's strong arm encircled my waist.

Crawford's gaze narrowed. "You okay?"

"She hasn't had much practice jumping off balconies," Marcus informed him.

I shuddered, remembering how close I'd come to disaster. "I'm hanging up my wings while I still can."

"Come on." Crawford jerked his head toward the building. "I'll fill you in. Then I'll get answers from McKiernan."

Crawford started toward the door.

Kevin fell into step beside Marcus and me. "This should be interesting."

Twenty-four hours from now, I'd probably have the perfect comeback. At the moment, all I could manage was a nod.

MOMENTS later our mismatched group had settled in Crawford's none too spacious office. He sat behind his dark mahogany desk, facing the door. Marcus and I had opted for the leather love seat opposite.

Crawford had made it a point to sit Daniels and Cowboy Joe on folding chairs on his right. Kevin and Randy had snagged the two straight-backed leather chairs and pulled them to Crawford's left. Rabi, standing behind Daniels and Cowboy Joe, faced the windows.

Personally, I don't think he liked the idea of having anyone at his back. I don't know if it came naturally or from military training or both. I was relieved to have him watching them.

"First things first." Crawford looked from Kevin to me. "The thumb drive?"

Kevin pointed a finger at me as if cocking a gun.

Randy huffed loudly and scowled in my direction, obviously waiting for me to admit failure.

"Almost forgot." I couldn't keep the smug expression off my face. I stuck out my leg and retrieved the key ring from my tiny jean pocket. Then I held it out to Marcus. "Care to make the delivery?"

He didn't need to be asked twice. With a triumphant grin, the boy walked toward the desk and dropped it into Crawford's calloused palm.

Randy stared at me. "You lied."

Kevin shrugged. "She's like that."

Crawford swung the key ring then eyed Marcus. "How about you take this to Frankie? She's not having much luck decrypting the files you copied to that CD."

Marcus took the drive. "Don't say anything good while I'm gone."

"Deal," Crawford said.

Marcus had already slipped out the door when Kevin leaned forward. "How's Jimbo?"

"Safe," Crawford answered. "A couple of uniforms I know are watching him."

Marcus thundered into the room on Crawford's last words. "You talked."

Crawford met the accusing gaze with a bland look. "Kevin sweated it out of me."

"What did I miss?" Marcus crossed the room.

"Jimbo's safe," I said.

"Since we're asking questions." Randy managed to interject the words with an arrogant tone. "How did you know the thumb drive was in that hall closet? After the murder, the police cleared it out."

"You said you'd forgotten about the passageway in the second-floor closet. I assumed Duna's killer didn't know about it at all, which meant Duna went in there for a reason."

"To get the drive," Marcus finished, a smug expression on his face. "Detecting runs in the Belden blood."

After this escapade, I'd never be able to talk sense into the boy. "Whoever accosted her upstairs must have demanded the drive. I think once Duna was in the passageway, she tried to trick her assailant. But when they fought, she lost."

Crawford broke the silence. "Her killer panicked. Dumped the body in the passage, shut the door, then ran off without the goods."

"Orduna Grimley is the victim's name." Kevin turned to Crawford. "The real Cassie Reed—"

"Is still out there." Daniels sat forward with a mulish set to his jaw. He drilled Randy with a gaze hot enough to burn through steel. "And I'm going to find her."

Resentment flashed in Randy's eyes. He raised his chin. "Cassie arranged a new identity years ago. It's pointless to prosecute her for a drug deal after all these years."

Daniels was halfway to Randy's throat before I could blink. The stout man could move.

Randy leaped backward, knocking over his chair.

Joe grabbed Daniels from behind.

Kevin stepped in front of Randy.

Rabi didn't move a muscle.

Though my gaze remained glued to the scene, I shielded Marcus in case chaos erupted.

"Daniels." Crawford's tone echoed off the walls and reverberated through the room. It hadn't lost its effectiveness. The other man froze. Like Rabi, Crawford hadn't moved. He fixed Daniels with a hard stare. "Sit."

Daniels pointed at Randy, his arm shaking with anger. "If you think—"

"I left one case open when I retired," Crawford spoke over the other man's words with no visible effort. "I'm closing it this week. I don't care who I have to bury."

Crawford's tone dropped a couple of decibels on the last bit. His gaze, as sharp as a razor's edge, slid to Randy.

Daniels studied Crawford for a second then nodded.

As Joe righted Daniels' chair, the stout man adjusted his tie and sat. Joe and Kevin took their seats in almost the same motion.

Crawford gave Randy a hard stare. "Keep quiet."

Randy was dumb enough to open his mouth. Then his survival instinct kicked in, and he shut it without saying a word.

I let Marcus wiggle out of my protective clasp. An open case twenty years ago, I'd heard this story. I couldn't think how it connected to here and now. I listened as Crawford's rough voice filled the tense room.

"I was a rookie detective. My partner and I had pulled our first big case in narcotics. We went to Wichita, Kansas and hooked up with the State Patrol to catch a smuggling ring funneling drugs from Mexico. They distributed all through the mid-west. My partner and I worked the case with Daniels and his partner, Joe Burnley."

"My father," Joe said quietly.

"The main drop was an acreage in the country. We got

a tip the Mexicans had come for an unexpected visit. The four of us hot footed it out there. We called for backup, but the Mexicans were packing it in. We couldn't wait." Crawford stared straight ahead and met my gaze.

I remembered how the story ended, but my stomach still clenched with dread.

"Daniels and Burnley took the rear. My partner and I had the front. We waited for them to get in place then kicked in the door."

I bit my lip, unable to tear my gaze from Crawford. I didn't see any sign of movement in the room. I wasn't sure any one was breathing.

"My partner took a hit in the shoulder. A few minutes later we'd dropped three in the front room."

Daniels took up the story here. "Burnley and I were in the kitchen. He checked the pantry while I stayed by the door and covered his back. He'd just flushed somebody when I got cold-cocked from behind. They must have gone to the car while we were sneaking in. I went out like a light."

Crawford nodded. "My partner and I were pinned. By the time we got clear, he was bleeding all over the hall. He waved me into the kitchen."

Crawford stopped. His eyes glazed over even after twenty years. He swallowed. "I hit the kitchen in time to see Burnley collapse. He'd taken two shots in the back from less than a yard away. He died at my feet."

Marcus leaned against my shoulder.

I clasped his hand.

"A guy with a gun was racing out the door. I was ready to drop him." Crawford's eyes turned cold. "When I yelled at him to halt, he froze. Just then I heard a car pull out of the backyard. By the time Daniels and I got outside, all we saw was a cloud of dust."

He shook his head. "We set up roadblocks, did a house-to-house. Later that day we found the car abandoned. Never located the driver. All we had were a couple of fingerprints on the gun that didn't match anyone else."

Kevin broke the silence that followed. "You got the gunman."

"Guy had no residue on his hands," Daniels said.

"Whoever hit Daniels brought the weapon in, shot Burnley, then dropped it and took off," Crawford said. "His partner picked it up. Despite every deal we offered, the guy never told us the name of the shooter."

"What changed?" I asked.

"He was executed last week. Six months ago we made a deal with the guy in the next cell. If he got us a name, his sentence would be commuted. He didn't get a peep until a couple of weeks ago. The prisoner asked our snitch to send a letter for him."

Crawford paused for a heartbeat.

"When the letter was returned unopened, our mark broke his twenty years of silence. He told our snitch, 'I protected her for twenty years. She could have at least said thank you.'"

Though Crawford was looking at me, I got the feeling his words were aimed at Randy. "The letter came from Cassie Reed in Langsdale, Nevada."

What crime would keep police on the trail for twenty years?

My boss's next words answered that question.

Crawford's eyes slid to Randy. "Cassie Reed is a cop killer."

25

61 Across; 5 Letters;
Clue: Make an innocent person look guilty.
Answer: Frame

The blood drained from Randy's face as if someone had opened a spigot in his chest. "Duna didn't mention the letter until after she returned it unopened. By that time, I figured it was best to say nothing to Cassie."

Hunting a cop killer explained why Crawford had pursued this case on his own dime. That was the reason the lead detective had given him so much latitude. It also explained Daniels and Joe's determination. None of them would stop until they had the real Cassie or her body.

Daniels picked up the thread of the original story. "Once we had a name, we discovered Cassie Reed left Kansas within a day of the shooting. She had a record of dealing drugs. It wasn't hard to track her."

"Only to learn she'd just been killed," I said. "Sounds like her buddy put a hit on her from death row. Duna was killed by mistake. The real Cassie Reed was the intended victim."

Crawford expression could have been in the dictionary under determined. "She disappeared the day I heard from Daniels and Joe. I figured she took off, and hubby planned to join her, so I had him watched. Then you found the corpse, which turned out to be the wrong woman. Whether she's a mark or not, the real Cassie Reed is still out there."

Crawford's gaze, like mine and everyone else's, turned to Randy. He was already shaking his head.

"I—I didn't know," he stuttered. "She never said anything about a cop getting killed."

"Then you help us find her." Crawford's deceptively calm voice did nothing to hide a strong undercurrent of threat. "Or you'll fry in her place."

Randy blanched. "I'll tell you everythin—"

"Gun!" Rabi pointed to the balcony window.

A buzzing registered the same instant Randy's body arched forward. Blood and tissue erupted into the air.

I threw myself over Marcus and tried to bury us both in the cushions.

"Down." Crawford's gun appeared in his hand.

Daniels and Cowboy held weapons as well. All three leaped to their feet.

The reverberations from two more shots set my ears ringing. The acrid smell of gunpowder filled the room.

Kevin, bent over Randy's supine form, reached toward Marcus and me. "Stay down."

"He's over the railing," Daniels's shout rose above the echoes of gunfire.

Crawford bolted for the side door. Joe and Daniels raced after him without a backward glance.

I tightened my hold around Marcus.

"You two okay?" At my nod, Kevin turned Randy over and pressed both hands against the wound. Blood seeped between his fingers to form an ever-widening stain.

Rabi holstered his weapon and knelt. "Call 9-1-1."

I grabbed my cell phone, but the battery was still dead. Hurrying to the desk, I hit the buttons with trembling fingers.

Marcus eyed the scene with wide eyes.

"Marcus." Rabi's commanding tone caught the boy's attention. "Go to the bathroom. Bring towels. Washcloths. Anything."

"9-1-1, what's your emergency?" A businesslike voice sounded in my ear as Marcus ran toward the hall.

"There's been a shooting." My voice sounded amazingly calm considering the fact that my lungs refused to work. After I gave the address, I waited on the line. I used the moment to try to calm my nerves.

Marcus returned with an armload of towels.

I answered the dispatcher's questions without thinking. All I registered was Marcus handing towels to Rabi.

"Okay. Sure." I held the receiver in a death-like grip. What had I agreed to? Had the operator hung up?

Her soft, steady tone returned. The police and ambulance were on the way. She'd stay on the line until they arrived.

Sirens wailed in the distance.

My gaze slid to Randy's pale face. The blood seemed to have stopped. I wasn't sure if that was a good thing or not.

Kevin's gaze met mine for a heartbeat. Behind the

mute shock, I could see the same calm-under-fire that had gotten us out of jams in the past.

I wondered if I was holding up as well. I doubted it.

The discordant wail of sirens filled the air seconds before I caught sight of the emergency lights through the open window. Two cop cars roared down the street. Then came the ambulance with another police car trailing it at breakneck speed.

I had an overwhelming urge to wave my arm. Fortunately, I resisted.

"They're here," I interrupted the operator's calming words.

Ten breathless minutes later, I leaned against Rabi's tan Jeep with my arms wrapped around Marcus. I gulped in the cool evening air to rid myself of the smell of gunpowder in my nose.

The paramedics finally lifted Randy into the ambulance. They'd spent precious minutes stabilizing him. A morbid corner of my mind wondered if they were waiting to see if he died before they messed up their ambulance. Brennan watched the proceedings from a distance, while speaking with Crawford, Daniels, and Joe.

"You're choking me," Marcus said.

I loosened my arms. Perhaps I wasn't as collected as I'd thought. "Sorry."

Kevin walked toward us, wiping his hands on his jeans. He followed the direction of my gaze. "No dry towels."

I made a face, then eyed Rabi who was right behind him. "You think he has a chance?"

Rabi's head swiveled at the sound of the ambulance doors slamming shut. "Depends if he fights or gives up."

I grunted. Randy's arrogance might come in handy after all. "He thinks too much of himself to give in."

"Damn it!" Daniels stomped toward us with his fists clenched and a mulish set to his jaw. Venom filled the curse, but a heavy dose of defeat laced through it as well.

Joe had a more thoughtful air. As he got closer, he raised his chin and smiled at Marcus. "You guys did good up there. Probably saved his life."

Marcus smiled at the praise, then sobered quickly. "I never knew people had that much blood. When guys got shot in the street, we ran. Rabi knew what to do, though."

"Military drills it into you, so you never forget," Rabi said quietly. "But the man's right, I had good help."

Joe looked at me with a raised brow. "You okay?"

"A little worn around the edges."

I felt Kevin's warmth at my side suddenly. I hadn't even seen him move.

An awkward silence descended. I didn't mind Joe, but I'd had enough of Daniels. Unfortunately, they evidently came as a pair. Not that I didn't feel for them. "The guy got away?"

Joe's frown deepened. "He jumped the railing and drove off. By the time we got to the lot the car was at the corner."

Daniels looked toward the street. "Guy drove without lights. We never stood a chance. You see anything?"

He directed the question at Rabi, who shrugged. "Looked like Marcus' ninja. Tall, black clothes, ski mask. Ran as soon as I yelled."

"Damn." Daniels curse had lost its fire, leaving only a weary emptiness. His shoulders slumped, and the bags under his eyes drooped to his chin.

"I really believed it might finally end." Joe's hopeless tone tugged at my heartstrings.

I couldn't imagine what it would be like to lose your father so young then spend twenty years chasing a will-o-the-wisp. I felt sorry for Daniels as well, despite the fact that I still nursed a kernel of resentment.

"Randy's the only one who knew Cassie Reed's new identity," Daniels said. "Now we have to start over again."

"What's the point?" Joe threw up his hands. "If she were smart, she'd have left the country long ago."

Daniels shook his head. "Crawford thinks she's involved in the Tang Chi smuggling. It makes sense—"

"Which means she's living in Tokyo," Joe said with an air of defeat.

"No, she's not." My observation slipped in between their arguments. They stilled instantly.

"How can you be so sure?" Crawford's gravelly voice seemed to come out of thin air, no small feat for a man his size. However, as usual, he'd managed to come within arm's reach without anyone noticing. Brennan was still directing the other officers in the search.

Daniels reared up like a grizzly ready to attack. "You said you didn't know."

"I didn't." I met his gaze. I was tired of being a target for his temper. "The background you three filled in plus Randy's comment put it all together."

"What comment?" Kevin's reasoned tone worked to diffuse some of the tension. He shifted to position himself between Daniels and me.

Suddenly spoiling for a fight, I was disappointed at the intervention. "Randy said when Duna returned the letter, he decided not to tell Cassie. He made it sound like no big deal, as if they were in constant touch."

"He could have contacted her by e-mail. She could still be living abroad." Though Joe's tone was cautious, he had a gleam in his eyes as if he wanted me to prove him wrong.

"She's been in town the whole time," I said, surprised by my own certainty. "Cassie Reed is Lydia Storm."

"The craps dealer?" Daniels looked as if I'd just announced the world was flat.

Now I knew how Hercule Poirot feels at the end of an Agatha Christie novel.

Crawford, standing on the fringe of the circle, shook his head. "Lydia checked out. Her mother's alive. She'd know her own daughter."

His words didn't dissuade me. "I'll bet you a dime she hasn't been home for years."

"Not since a car accident fifteen years ago. A female passenger was killed. The victim was never identified." Crawford's eyes narrowed. "After the accident, Lydia quit her job in Vegas and moved to Langsdale."

"I think the real Lydia got killed. Cassie Reed, the hitch-hiker, grabbed the woman's ID and adopted a new name and a new life."

"That's not much to go on." Joe's tone was frankly curious.

"Daniels mentioned Randy ran to type." I looked at the stout man. "My ex likes tall, intelligent brunettes."

"I love your modesty." Kevin's murmur tickled my ear.

I smiled. "When you got it, you got it."

"Lydia's blond," Crawford said.

I faced Crawford. "With dark roots. The bartender at the Blue Bayou mentioned them and Marcus told me later her movements and voice reminded him of me."

Kevin smacked his forehead. "I'd forgotten that."

"I didn't think anything of it until everything else started adding up. Remember when Randy told us he got word on the Tang Chi stock deal from a craps dealer?"

Kevin shook his head in disbelief. "Cassie Reed."

"Randy referred to the dealer as a he, but Cassie knew him well enough to trust him with insider information. And with her history of drug dealing, it wouldn't have taken her long to make connections in Vegas."

"That must be when she got in with the Tang Chi." Daniels finished the thought without hesitation, "which is how she learned about the stock deal in the first place."

I nodded. "A quick-thinking woman with a head for figures could rise pretty fast. When the Tang Chi needed a front in this country, she handed them Randy."

"And the rest is history," Joe finished. "Duna was in the picture by then. Cassie would have jumped at the chance to have another woman take her identity."

"The dates all work," Crawford confirmed.

I noticed Kevin had a puzzled frown. "What?"

"All this talk about the kind of women Randy picks for wives," Kevin looked at me. "Duna was an embezzler. Lydia's a cop killer. I'm beginning to wonder if I should worry about you."

Marcus turned to Kevin with a raised brow. "You're just *beginning* to wonder?"

I frowned at them in mock anger. "Be glad I'm on your side."

"We are," Kevin said a shade too quickly.

"Any idea where Ms. Storm is?" I asked Crawford. I knew the answer. Nobody cared about her. Nobody had even known she had existed before Marcus and Steven pulled her into the picture. "I don't suppose anybody was tailing her?"

Crawford snorted. "The last person who followed her is Jimbo, and he's in jail."

"Where was she when he caught up with her?" Daniels pivoted on the balls of his feet suddenly on the hunt.

"Mayor's house," Crawford said. "Then he hid in a cemetery."

"I'd almost forgotten," I admitted. "He drove to Prospect Hill, didn't he?"

Kevin raised his brows. "That makes no sense."

Marcus quivered with excitement. "Maybe he was trying to give us a clue."

"I don't see how, but it was a good idea." When I patted him on the head, he frowned at me. I put my hand on his shoulder, properly rebuked. Real detectives don't get their hair ruffled. "At least I'm not a suspect anymore."

Crawford eyed me with a narrowed gaze.

I wondered if I had blood on my top. "What's up?"

"I spoke to Detective Brennan after we lost the shooter. You can go home," Crawford said. "But don't leave town."

The line came straight out of the police handbook.

"What are you saying?" I pushed away from the car and pointed toward the main drag. "Cassie's ex-friend put out a hit on her before he was executed. The ninja killed Duna in a murder-for-hire gone wrong."

No one said a word.

I didn't like the lengthy silence. "Why's everyone looking at me?"

Crawford shook his head. His sigh had a mournful sound to it. "Why would Cassie's dead friend put a hit on Randy?"

I glanced at the circle of faces, while frantically

grasping at straws. "Maybe the ninja gave the dead guy a two-for-one discount."

I nudged Kevin, looking for support from my own personal Rock of Gibraltar.

"Absolutely." His agreement carried more conviction than even I could have mustered.

God love him.

"That doesn't make sense." Marcus shook his head in an unabashed display of logic over loyalty. "T.R., you're the only one who gets any money if Randy dies."

I patted my honest Abe on the shoulder. "Thanks for pointing that out."

"Good thing you don't have any money to pay a hitman." Marcus's tone ended on up note.

I wasn't sure pointing out my lack of income was helping.

My son continued. "Besides you already saved Randy from the ninja once tonight."

I confess, I clapped like a five-year-old.

"That's right. I did." I hugged Marcus and shot a relieved smile at Kevin. "In the hotel room at the Blue Bayou I kicked the door to distract the ninja when he had a gun aimed at Randy's head."

"Did anyone see this happen?" Daniels asked in a skeptical tone.

"I did." Marcus threw his hand in the air. "It was cool. The ninja shot through the glass door. But we were crouched to one side."

There went my foster-mother-of-the-year award.

"When we were getting away, he shot again." Marcus raised his hands in imitation of a weapon. "Boom. Boom. While we ran for the elevator."

"They get the idea, Marcus." Hopefully his social

worker would never hear my son's version of our escape. The cops and former cops didn't look as relieved as I thought they should. "What? Marcus saw me save Randy."

Daniels leaned closer to Marcus. "You love your mother right? You'd lie to save her life, wouldn't you?"

"Sure," Marcus agreed. "But I'm not. Not this time."

I glanced heavenward. I was beginning to see how this might sound.

Kevin rubbed his forehead. "We going to need a stronger defense before going into court."

Joe eyed Kevin. "Did you see this guy at the hotel?"

Kevin shook his head. "I was driving the getaway car. All I saw were you and Daniels chasing them."

The reminder prompted another possibility. I pointed at Joe. "You and Daniels were the ones pounding on the door after Randy knocked the guy out. You two must have seen the ninja in the suite."

"I saw a dark figure running away," Daniels admitted. "It could have been you or your ex. We ducked when he fired at us. By the time we got around the final corner, the elevator was closed, bullet holes and all. We took the other elevator to the dock and saw you, Marcus, and Randy jump into the white Caddy. Nice car."

The admiring comment was directed at Kevin, who nodded in appreciation.

Men and their cars. "Could we focus? I'm being railroaded, here."

"Don't leave town," Crawford reminded me, an evil glint shown in his eyes.

With no further comeback at hand, I settled for glaring at him.

"The Tang Chi make better suspects than Belden."

Kevin's calm, reasoned tone relieved my anxiety. "It's only Randy's word that they forgave him for Duna's theft. They may be trying to cut their losses."

I jumped on the theory. "That's a distinct possibility."

Crawford unbent enough to nod. "Brennan's considering that theory, which is why you aren't under arrest... yet."

"Lydia could fill in the blanks." I was willing to throw anyone under the bus. "She was at the center of the local smuggling scheme. And don't forget, the last person she visited was the mayor. He might be able to find her."

Daniels balanced on the balls of his feet. "Any chance we can roust the man?"

"Eleven o'clock on a Sunday night?" Crawford flashed a grin the devil would have envied. "Let's see if we've got any leverage from that encrypted file."

The two older men turned and walked away. Cowboy Joe moved to follow then looked at me. "What about you?"

I was too tired and bruised to appreciate Joe's sympathetic smile. "I'm going to sleep for a week."

He sighed. "Maybe by then this will all be over."

I didn't hold much hope. From the wistful note in his voice, he didn't either. Having waited so long and come so far, what would he do if Cassie Reed slipped away again?

After he walked away, I watched Brennan. She gave me a careful glance and a slow nod as she surveyed the scene. Though my puzzle for this case still had a lot of empty squares, I stiffened each time she made a move, wondering if this might be the time she changed her mind and ordered my arrest.

26

11 Down; 10 Letters;
Clue: A relation between people or events.
Answer: Connection

Fifteen minutes later I was still a free woman. Possibly because the police had their own problems.

"The Ransom of Red Chief" had nothing on us. Marcus's unending questions and his attempts to infiltrate the cop cars wore down the uniformed officers in short order.

I didn't even try to save them. After the past forty-eight hours, I didn't have the energy to corral him even if I'd had the inclination.

"Ma'am." A pleading voice snapped me out of a light dose.

When I jerked awake, the young officer in front of me

had one hand on his holster and the other on Marcus's arm.

The uniform cop pushed my son toward me as if delivering a prisoner. "Detective Brennan agreed you can all come in the morning and give your statements."

"I said you'd be willing to stay all night to see justice done," Marcus said.

I compared his hopeful expression to the cop's desperation. A couple of other uniformed officer stood close by, poised to prevent any escape if the prisoner... er, Marcus bolted.

I met his gaze. "We have to go home. It's past my bedtime."

Marcus grimaced.

The cop's shoulders relaxed. "First thing in the morning, ma'am. Ask for Detective Brennan."

Marcus snapped his fingers. "Crawford could bring me home later."

"Get in the car, Red Chief." Five minutes later, I sat in the back seat with a sigh. All I wanted was a long hot soak followed by twenty hours of sleep. I could already smell the lavender scented bath oil Jimbo brought over last week after a runaway scooter at the department store damaged several boxes.

"They were deciphering the disk," Marcus pointed out. "After Crawford explained what we knew, Brennan called somebody. I couldn't hear what she said."

"Oh, darn," I muttered in mock sympathy. A moment of blessed silence greeted my response.

"Rabi, we should drop Kevin off first." Marcus's voice intruded as I started to nod off.

I jerked upright. "Our place is on the way."

Marcus eyed me with an innocent look. "Poor Kevin looks beat."

"I have eight years, two cracked ribs, and multiple bruises on Kevin." I closed my eyes. "Besides, you have to go to school in the morning."

"I have to be at the police station to give my statement," Marcus said.

I eyed him through my drooping lids. "Rabi is still dropping us off first. I have an overdue appointment with my bed."

Marcus grimaced and slumped in the seat.

I was about to settle again when I realized what was behind the boy's scheming. "You don't care about Kevin. You want to drive by the cemetery where they caught Jimbo."

"Good idea, T.R." Marcus whirled to face me. "We need to find a clue to clear you."

I refused to let him make this wild diversion my idea. "There's nothing in that cemetery that will help me. Jimbo drove there to hide."

"Then why did he drive out the other side a minute later?" Marcus asked.

I kept my mouth shut this time. He had a point. From Mrs. C's account, Jimbo hadn't stayed in Prospect Hill Cemetery long enough to ditch his pursuers.

Marcus jumped on my hesitation like a cat on a half dead mouse. "Jimbo went there on purpose. Prospect Hill isn't on the way from the mayor's house to Kevin's."

Marcus's eyes shifted toward the front seat. "Right?"

My synapses weren't firing at full capacity, and I wasn't sure where the mayor lived, but I had a feeling Marcus was onto something.

Rabi nodded slowly. "It's a good six blocks out of his way."

"That's it then." Marcus bounced on the seat. "We gotta go."

"Rabi and Kevin have had a long day."

"They don't care." Marcus swept away my protest with a wave of his hand. "We have to see justice triumph. Don't you want Joe's father to rest in peace?"

"I should have given myself up so I could get some sleep." The boy would resurrect everyone until we did a drive by. "Check out a cemetery at midnight, just let me rest in peace."

Kevin's shoulders shook with laughter.

The rearview mirror showed Rabi's face split in a grin.

"Too bad we don't know where he went into or came out of the cemetery," Marcus muttered.

"Nobody knows except the police," I said with a petty flash of satisfaction.

"And Jimbo," Marcus reminded me.

"Nobody's talked to him," I said.

Kevin hooked an arm over the front seat. "Mrs. C did."

The more we talked, the more I realized how crazy this whole plan was. Soon they'd realize it too, until then I could keep dreaming about my bed. "I'm not going to call her at eleven o'clock at night."

"That's because you don't have a phone." Kevin pulled his cell phone out.

"She'll be asleep by now." I couldn't believe Kevin was letting himself get swept up in Marcus's wild adventure.

"She wouldn't want to miss the end," Marcus said.

Kevin agreed. "She'll be watching the news."

I turned to Marcus. "You've infected him."

Marcus just chuckled.

Kevin pressed the phone to his ear. "How's my favorite Brit?"

Great, now I'd be listening to that British accent for the rest of my days. "Don't encourage her."

Kevin paid me no heed. "We must have been out of range. Did you talk to Jimbo?"

Marcus nudged my arm. "She tried to call us."

"Did he mention the cemetery?" Kevin asked.

While Kevin listened, I looked out my window and watched the turn to my apartment go by. I sighed mournfully, resigned to another sleepless hour.

Marcus patted my shoulder. "It's for a good cause."

Kevin cast a narrowed glance my way. "He did?"

Marcus leaned up, practically in Kevin's face. "What?"

"Marcus, sit," I said.

Kevin covered the mouthpiece of the phone. "Jimbo was glad to hear from his relatives. Family's important. That's why he went to visit the family mausoleum yesterday."

Since none of Jimbo's relatives had ever set foot in this town, I had a sinking feeling this might lead somewhere.

Marcus grinned. "It's a clue."

I slumped in the seat. The last thing I wanted was to find a connection that might lead to something or worse, someone. Why did this information keep landing in our laps? We had no business chasing smugglers.

Not to worry. My usual bad luck would kick in, and our string of hits would end. Maybe this was that time. I perked up at the thought. Surely this would be a dead end. After all, what did we have?

Even if Mrs. C knew the name of the mausoleum, it's not like we could find it amid the graves. Marcus couldn't expect us to search the entire cemetery in the dead of night. Relief swept through me. The others would admit defeat soon.

Kevin pulled the cell phone aside and spoke to Rabi. "The Baltimore entrance."

Rabi nodded silently.

Alert for any sign of success, I jumped on Kevin's words. "What are you doing?"

Kevin covered the mouthpiece again and turned to us. "Jimbo gave Mrs. C the name on the mausoleum. She happens to have an acquaintance who works with an undertaker."

"Cool." Marcus bounced on the seat.

I stared at Kevin, not liking this at all. "You can't be serious."

Kevin smiled. "It's on-line. She contacted a friend earlier, and the guy looked up the location from home."

"That's just wrong." I heard the whiny tone in my voice, but I couldn't stop it. "Yesterday she happened to have an acquaintance at the police station. Now she has one at the cemetery? Nobody knows people who actually work at cemeteries."

Marcus looked at me. "Somebody must know them."

The darkness robbed my grimace of any real force. I didn't mind when Mrs. Colchester came up with a British accent out of nowhere. I didn't object when she hired herself as my maid and started letting herself in. But this business with having more connections than MI-6 had to stop.

I was more interested in hunting up her history than I was in finding mausoleums at midnight. Unfortunately, Rabi turned onto Baltimore and started toward Thirty-fifth Street.

I saw a cemetery in my future.

"Mrs. C, you do good work." Kevin signed off and pocketed the phone. "Take the first fork to the right then go past a high row of hedges. Follow the path to a hill. The mausoleum is at the bottom."

Rabi nodded.

I sought furiously for roadblocks. "Cemeteries are locked. How do you plan to get in?"

Kevin shrugged. "Play it by ear. If the gate is locked and nobody's around, we'll know it's a wild-goose chase."

I liked the sound of that. Lydia, alias the real Cassie Reed, had fled the country. The ninja was chasing her. Nobody would be at the cemetery.

"I didn't tell you the best part," Kevin said.

Wary, I met his gaze. "I don't want to know."

"What's the best part?" Marcus asked.

"The family name on the plot." A touch of humor underlined Kevin's tone. "It's SheYan."

I raised a brow. "Blond-haired, blue-eyed Jimbo is Chinese?"

"You wouldn't know it to look at him, would you?" Kevin grinned. "Guess what the name means?"

The sinking sensation in my stomach had reached my toes.

"I don't want to know," I repeated.

Kevin told me anyway. "It's Chinese for snake eyes."

"Like in craps." Marcus breathed the words, barely containing his excitement. "This all ties in."

I searched for a denial and came up empty. As much as I hated to admit it, even to myself, it made sense. Nobody knew how long Jimbo had been on the mayor's terrace or how much he'd heard before security chased him off. Evidently, he'd heard enough.

"Snake Eyes." Kevin's brow furrowed. "I've heard that phrase recently."

Nobody said anything.

I couldn't believe they didn't remember. Numbers and equations, I can't forget them. "It was on the mayor's file that Marcus hacked into. Buffy equals Cassie. Jade Garden equals Lydia Storm. Great game equals Snake Eyes."

"I knew you'd help, T.R." Marcus exclaimed.

"Steve said the right side of the equation was the real thing. That's how he found Lydia." I tried to stop talking, but my mouth refused to listen. "According to that logic Snake Eyes must stand for something real."

"The mausoleum." Marcus grabbed my arm. "We're onto something."

I shook my head. "Even if someone did head here, they're long gone by now. We should call the cops. They need to investigate this, not us."

"What would we say?" Kevin asked. "Forget about a cop killer, drug smuggling, and dirty politicians. We want you to meet us at the cemetery."

The streets whizzed by. We'd be at the cemetery in minutes. This might be my last chance to put an end to this escapade. But what would I say? "If you put it that way, it sounds a little silly. So tell me again why *we're* going."

"Because we're the intrepid adventurers who uncover unknown secrets while the cops chase false leads." Marcus finished the flowery statement with a flourish.

I frowned at him, wondering what novel he'd pulled that line out of. "No more reading for you."

His laugh told me how seriously he took my threat. "You bought all the books for me."

"On second thought give me the phone." I held out my hand. "I'll leave the information on Crawford's answering service; then he'll know where we went if we get shanghaied."

Minutes later, I clicked off. If I'd thought our reasoning sounded farfetched before, it sounded inane when talking to an answering machine. Halfway through, I wished I'd never started.

As I handed the phone to Kevin, Rabi turned the corner. Of course, the entrance we wanted had to be on the hinter side of the cemetery.

The bumpy road, barren of light, reminded me of where we'd found Duna's body. I shivered.

Fortunately, the headlights vanished and gave me something new to worry about.

I jerked upright. "What happened?"

Rabi didn't look in the least upset at being plunged into darkness. "I turned the lights off. If anyone's in there, they'll see headlights a mile away."

I bit back a comment about driving into a ditch. There's a fine line between commenting on obstacles and being a whiner, and I wasn't about to cross it. Instead, I decided I might as well be supportive. We wouldn't be able to get into the cemetery anyway. "Good idea. Nobody would expect a car to drive on this road in the dark."

Kevin greeted my hearty enthusiasm with a wry grin.

I ignored him.

Marcus snaked his arm over the front seat. "There's the gate."

Sure enough, massive iron gates supported on either side by solid stone columns guarded a sweeping drive. Rabi slowed to a stop. Loops of chain and a solid padlock stared at us.

I forced myself to refrain from clapping. It was a no-go. Even Marcus would have to admit defeat.

"Too bad." I couldn't keep the perky tone from my voice.

Kevin rolled his eyes.

So I wasn't Oscar material. At least I didn't cheer.

Kevin reached for the handle. "I'll check it out."

"Wait." Rabi disabled the interior light. "Go."

Kevin eased the door open and stepped out. Gravel crunched beneath his shoes.

I watched through the windshield. In a minute, we'd be headed home. I felt a twinge of regret at not having all the answers to my puzzle, but there was always tomorrow. As for tonight, maybe I'd sleep first and save the hot bath for morning.

At the gate, Kevin reached for the padlock. The next instant his whole body tensed. He stepped to one side. In each hand, he held one end of the chain. A link in the middle had been severed.

27

24 Across; 9 Letters;
Clue: Draw attention to; create a _____
Answer: Diversion

"They're he-ere." Marcus's breath skittered over the hairs on my arm.

His eerie tone grated on my exhausted nerve. My heart shot into overdrive.

"This isn't happening." Fighting for composure, I chided myself for being sucked into this crazy escapade. "No one is in the cemetery."

"The. Chain. Is. Cut." Marcus spaced out the words as if I'd slept through the latest melodrama.

"This end of the park is hardly ever used," I shot back. "That chain could've been cut weeks ago."

"And someone rewound it?" he asked.

"It's possible."

Marcus didn't dignify my comment with a rebuttal.

"It doesn't mean anything." I watched Kevin unwind the chain. "Snake Eyes might be a common Chinese name."

Marcus put his head in his hands. "Give it up, T.R."

I hunted for a way to paint a strategic retreat as a viable alternative to traipsing around a cemetery. I could appeal to Kevin's protective nature. Neither he nor Rabi would put Marcus in danger.

"What if they're already gone?" Marcus whispered.

"Then there's no point going in," I said.

Kevin swung one gate to the side of the drive.

Marcus shot me a determined look. "We have to check the mausoleum."

I frowned in the darkness. "If someone's in there it would be dangerous. Right, Rabi?"

Without taking his eyes off Kevin, the man shifted his head in our direction. A muscle in his cheek jumped as if he were fighting a grin, but he gave a nod. "It's never good to go into a situation without all the facts."

Though not the whole-hearted support I'd hoped for, I jumped on the response. "See? It's not a good idea."

"I thought you said no one was in there." Marcus parroted my words to me. "Then there's no danger."

"Then why go in?" I asked.

"To check for evidence." His smart-aleck tone sounded a lot like mine. "To see if anyone's been here."

I was trapped. I was too tired for these games.

Kevin's return saved me from conceding defeat. Once inside, he hooked his arm over the seat and addressed us all. "No headlights in sight."

A ghost of a grin lingered on Rabi's lips.

Kevin looked around. "What did I miss?"

Marcus leaned forward with an eager expression. "We have to go in."

"No, we don't." I knew it was pointless, but my ribs would never forgive me if I didn't try one last time.

Kevin twisted his head. "We've come this far, but we have to be careful. The edges on that link are sharp. They look fresh."

I shook my head. "Why would anybody be here?"

He shrugged. "You're the brains of the outfit."

My eyelids weighed a hundred pounds each and my brain had the consistency of chocolate pudding. "If I'm our ace in the hole, you people are in trouble."

"You don't think it's odd that the mayor's file led us here and the chain is cut?" Kevin refused to let it drop.

A slow sigh escaped between my clenched teeth. If I hadn't had it up to my eyeballs with crimes and violence, I might have agreed. However, right now I just wanted to go home, ignore the puzzle poking at my brain, and pull the covers over my head.

I was prepared to lie to Kevin and Rabi. Then I glanced at Marcus, who studied me with a watchful gaze. I sighed in defeat. The boy is a bad influence on me. "Check out your grave. See if I care."

Marcus clenched a fist and smiled broadly. "I knew you'd come through."

Enthusiasm must be contagious. A few fizzles of energy lit my brain and I found myself smiling.

Kevin slapped my knee. "Glad to have you on board, champ."

Rabi smiled quietly and put the car in gear.

"This is still crazy," I reminded them. "Even if somebody had been here, what could they be after?"

"Don't ask me, lady." Kevin shook his head. "I'm the muscle, and Rabi's here for his looks."

That drew a chuckle out of all of us, including Rabi.

"We're here to find the answers," Marcus said.

As the car crept down the drive, my brain fought to complete the puzzle. "Why would the Tang Chi need a mausoleum in Langsdale?"

Rabi eased the car around a turn.

Outside the car, pale moonlight illuminated a lurid landscape of headstones and shadowy trees.

Kevin scanned the dark lane. Evidently satisfied we were alone he shifted to face the backseat. "The mausoleum could be a drop for the drugs and money the Tang Chi smuggle into the country."

I scoffed. "I wouldn't hide illegal drugs and cash in a grave."

"Where would you hide them?" he asked.

By the time I realized I didn't have an answer, he was talking again.

"Cemeteries are open to the public." He pointed out. "People come and go all the time. No cameras. No surveillance."

"A few loose bricks to hide the stuff behind." Marcus bought into the theory with no problem. "No one would know."

I had to admit it sounded plausible, in a made-for-TV-movie kind of way.

"A cache of drugs doesn't explain why anyone would be here *tonight*," Kevin admitted. "Whoever snuck in tried to hide the fact. They cut the chain, not the padlock."

The car slowed to a stop, and Rabi put it in park.

Kevin and Marcus's expressions mirrored my surprise.

"It's never good to go into a situation without all the facts," Rabi repeated his earlier statement with a note of finality.

Marcus made a mew of frustration, but there was no arguing with Rabi's stern profile and set jaw.

An unexpected wave of disappointment came over me, belying my opposition. The puzzle hadn't been completed. I can't leave empty squares, but the fact that Rabi's protective nature had kicked in chilled me.

Kevin nodded. "If there's any chance it's the Tang Chi, we'd best leave now."

"It's not the Tang Chi," I spoke without thinking.

"How can you be sure?" Marcus asked.

"They could wait until daylight." I hated to encourage this escapade, but the puzzle would not be denied. "The only reason for someone to sneak in after dark would be to get whatever's stashed without being discovered."

Kevin's eyes narrowed. "Lydia might be looking for a big strike to start a new life."

"It's possible," I agreed.

"Why would she run now? She doesn't know anyone suspects she's the real Cassie Reed." Marcus asked.

"She might not be the real Cassie." Even though it was my theory, it was all supposition.

"Don't try modesty now. It doesn't suit you." Kevin teasing tone eased my tension. "Marcus' note spooked Lydia. But once she was alone, she must have realized she overreacted. A few calls would have told her she was in the clear. So she left the hotel, but Jimbo saw her."

"And followed her to the mayor," I said, connecting more of the dots. "Randy's contributions to the man's re-election campaign could have come from the Tang Chi. His secret files led us here."

"Lydia had all day to come here." Marcus pointed out.

"The police arrested Jimbo outside this cemetery." I gestured at the surrounding area. "The mayor's body-guards were here as well. Lydia couldn't risk being seen."

"So she laid low until the coast cleared then snuck in to get the stuff," Marcus said.

"Which she probably did hours ago." I studied what I could see of their expressions. "She's long gone, right?"

"Absolutely." Kevin sounded certain, but guys always do.

"We should call the cops," I suggested.

Kevin glanced down the road ahead of us, straining to check out the mausoleum. "Remember how this story sounded when you called Crawford?"

I winced at the memory.

"For all they know, *we* cut the chain," Kevin went on. "Besides, there are... "

"Four of us." Marcus broke in when Kevin's gaze lingered on the boy.

"I don't like going in blind," I said. "Not with Marcus in the car."

"She's right." Rabi popped his door open. "I'll scout it out. If it's clear, I'll call."

His words floated on the night air. Rabi was gone.

"Good thinking." Marcus patted me on the shoulder.

"I meant we should turn around." I searched for Rabi amid the headstones. "Where did he go?"

"He did this all the time in Special Ops," Marcus said. "We'll never find him."

Kevin slid into the driver's seat.

I rolled my eyes. "Now we have to go after him."

"We'll wait for his signal," Kevin said.

"I'll time him." Marcus hit a button on his watch. The illuminated dial lit up his wrist.

I sat on the edge of my seat biting my nail. Would this night never end?

Marcus clicked a button on his watch. "It's been—"

A high-pitched scream split the night.

28

Across; 6 Letters;
Clue: To make a mistake or an error;
Answer: Miscue

A scream in a cemetery is never good. The ear-splitting wail that cut through the darkness skittered along my nerves like a knife's edge.

Kevin dropped the car into drive and hit the gas.

The headlights popped on. The car flew over the low hill. I went airborne for a heartbeat. When the wheels hit the ground, Marcus and I bounced off the ceiling.

When we landed, the headlights illuminated two shadowy figures silhouetted in front of a small mausoleum. One, clad in a familiar ski mask, black jeans, and loose sweatshirt, had his hands in the air. I barely caught sight of the other form when the car screeched to a halt a bare ten feet from the retreating figure.

"The ninja." Marcus slid over and opened his door.

I reached over and grabbed him. "Wait."

Kevin got out of the car. "Looks like the gang's all here."

His stunned tone pulled my attention. I swiveled toward the front to see what he meant. My jaw dropped. My hold on my son went slack, and he slipped out of the car on Kevin's side.

Marcus rushed toward Ninja. "We were right."

Kevin caught his arm in a deft move.

I opened my door and stepped outside. "Mrs. Colchester?"

Her pink slippers looked like muddy remnants of their former glory. A tattered blue robe peeked out beneath her coat, and her sleep bandana was askew. But it was the automatic pistol in her hand that drew my attention. She jiggled the gun at the man.

"Do back up a bit." The polite British accent seemed more incongruous than ever floating through the dark cemetery. "Lock your fingers on your head, ducky."

"Wha–what are you doing here?" I held onto the open door for support. I had to be dreaming.

"Well, luv." Her voice sounded strained. She paused to clear her throat. "I'm a bit out of practice. Though my scream did startle your thief into dropping the gun."

"That was you?" The screech must've echoed for blocks.

"Oh, yes. I knew you were inside the gates and your culprit was getting away."

"How did you know we were inside?" I asked.

"I brought my binoculars." She patted her coat pocket with her free hand. "They're wonderful for long range."

How could I have forgotten? The woman fills her days

scoping out the neighborhood. She can make out a license plate at four blocks.

"If you stand next to the fence you have an excellent view of the road leading up to the gate." She added. "I recognized Rabi's Jeep as it drove into the cemetery."

I exchanged a glance with Kevin. He looked as dumb-struck as I felt, so I repeated my question. "What are you doing here?"

She hesitated for a heartbeat. "I never doubted your ability to cope, but I did get the impression this might be a touch more complicated than anticipated."

I stifled an unladylike snort. If she called a morass of crime involving politicians, smugglers, and a twenty-year-old cop killing slightly complicated, how did she define real trouble?

Kevin closed his car door and took a quick survey of the area. "This the only guy?"

"I've seen no one else," she said. "The getaway car is parked behind that hedge. It's loaded and the loose bricks in the mausoleum are in place, but he's not a—"

"I want to see the stuff." Marcus wiggled but couldn't break free.

Kevin held fast. "Later."

Could the end to this brouhaha be in sight? Hot bath. Bed. Right now, their siren call drowned out unanswered questions in my puzzle.

The cops could look for Duna's murderer. Crawford and his guys would hunt the real Cassie Reed. I was done. "Can I go home now?"

"First the police." Kevin pulled his cell phone out and flipped it open. "Uh-oh."

"What now?" Couldn't anything be easy?

"No juice." Kevin thumbed a couple of buttons. "I'll have to plug it into the dash to dial."

"You needn't bother." A man spoke from behind me.

The voice sounded familiar. I shifted my weight to check the latest visitor out.

"Don't move."

Dread settled in the pit of my stomach. I gripped the still open door and steeled my nerves for another round. Would this case never end?

"Put the gun down," the mystery man commanded.

Mrs. C released her grip and let the gun dangle from her finger. She looked at me with a mixture of apology and puzzlement. Her assurance that the ninja was alone had barely left her lips.

Despite the fact that she liked to do laundry, I gave her sneaking skills higher marks than her work as a maid. She'd seen no one else around. So where had the new player from? And what was this place—the Grand Central Station of cemeteries? I've attended funerals with fewer people.

"Get the gun." The words had barely left the other man's lips before the ninja moved forward.

Mrs. C surrendered the weapon then strolled toward me as if she were unconcerned about the armed man.

I met her gaze and shifted my eyes to Marcus's side of the car. She changed direction smoothly toward the driver's side. If the situation went south and Kevin had to act, I wanted someone in position to keep Marcus safe.

"Is this all of them?" the man spoke again.

His voice tickled my memory. I pursed my lips in frustration. The cultured tone sounded so familiar.

The ninja, facing me with a gun in hand, nodded.

"Is the money in the vehicle?" The inflection of the man's voice caught my attention.

Something in the cadence of his words sounded familiar. Cadence? Rhythm? Music! The bulb went off. Opera. Funeral Guy. I closed my eyes and pictured him behind his desk. I heard his measured tone as he spoke of his love of opera.

I'd felt happy for him when he relived his audition at the Met. Now he was holding a weapon on me. Rude!

Although, it made sense. Who had easier access to a cemetery than a director of a funeral home? A hearse with a casket would be a perfect cover for smuggling. He'd probably been at the main building and come running when he heard the scream.

I opened my eyes. Just when I thought I had some of the clues filled in on my crossword puzzle for this case, the universe threw in a twist. Now I had new, unfilled squares to torment me.

The ninja nodded again.

Speaking of voices, why didn't this one talk? I shoved the thought aside. Best to concentrate on getting us out of here. Rabi was out there somewhere. I had to buy him time. "I know it's cliché, but you won't get away with this."

"Keep quiet." Funeral Guy's tone wavered.

"Nobody's been hurt." Unless these two had killed Duna. I didn't want to consider that possibility. "If you talk to the police, you'll get a lenient sentence."

That's my motto, bargain basement crime deals.

A snort sounded behind me. "There's no one left to blame."

"You know the Tang Chi routes and delivery system." Kevin managed to interject a note of helpfulness into his comment. "That's a high dollar bargaining chip with the police."

I latched onto his opening with both hands. Sowing chaos and mistrust could only help our side. "It's either deal with the police or go down for murder with your buddy."

"What? Is that true?" Accusation filled Funeral Guy's tone.

The ninja pointed the gun at him. "Shhhh."

"Don't shhhh me," Funeral Guy said. "I can't be implicated in murder."

"Why do you think your friend is taking off?" Nothing like adding fuel to the fire. "He shot Randy McKiernan in front of witnesses. He probably murdered Randy's wife."

I had no qualms about making stuff up as I went along. I was on a roll. "When the Tang Chi find out their drugs and money are missing, you'll be the only one to blame."

From the gasp behind me, I figured I had his attention. "If you talk to the police now—"

The ninja crossed the distance between us in two swift strides. He pointed the gun right between my eyes. "Shut up."

The low guttural tone couldn't mask the sounds of a scuffle on the far side of the car.

"No, dude." Kevin's whispered voice carried to me.

Talk about thudding hearts. I could barely hear over mine. I swallowed hard and tried to look harmless.

The ninja's gun didn't waver.

I'd like to say I looked down the barrel with a calm, deliberate stare. If my mind hadn't blanked out and my lungs hadn't seized up, I might remember enough to tell the lie well. As it was, my fingers gripped the car door so tight they lost feeling.

Keeping the weapon at eye level, the ninja maneuvered around me. The grass rustled as he walked to join Funeral Guy.

Once he passed out of sight, I forced a breath through my clenched teeth and talked my lungs into working again. I glanced sideways.

Kevin gaze met mine. Concern burned in his eyes but his nod sent a wave reassurance in my direction.

Mrs. C had her arms around Marcus who looked ready to climb over the car.

I put my hand up, palm out, hoping it wouldn't tremble. If Marcus thought I had a plan maybe he wouldn't do something stupid. I mouthed Rabi's name. With Funeral Guy and the ninja together, Rabi might get the drop on them.

Furious whispers filled the air behind me. Now would be a perfect time to drive the wedge between them deeper. But my toes were cold with fear, and the middle of my back itched as if it had a bull's eye stitched on it. With the image of the gun fresh in my mind, I told myself to say something, do something.

Funeral Guy had been wavering, but the ninja was solid as stone. What lever could I use? I searched for a detail I may have overlooked. Who was the ninja? How had he found Randy? I'd found my ex based on my experience with him. Cowboy Joe and Daniels had admitted following me.

Despite the danger, the guns, the imminent possibility of death—the puzzle commanded my attention. If I was going to get shot, I wanted to have the solution.

"Go to the office." The ninja's whisper carried on the night air. "You won't be implicated."

I broke out in a cold sweat. Shoving aside thoughts of hidden identities, I strained to hear Funeral Guy's response. All I heard was heavy breathing.

Wait, that was me.

Finally, the funeral director answered. "What about when their... bodies are found?"

Uh-oh. I counted the thuds of my heart and searched for something to say. Nothing came.

Kevin's expression was a mask of concentration, probably searching for a way out. I sought for a cavalier response to imminent death and managed to produce a strangled squeak.

"Keep quiet." Funeral Guy had evidently opted for repetition to cover up his indecision. "Put your hands where I can see them."

I raised my hands. I had to do something. No way would Funeral Guy stand up to the ninja.

"I'll leave them to you," Funeral Guy said. "Wait until I'm clear."

"You're making a mistake if you leave." Kevin turned and stepped toward the two figures, with the sublime confidence of a con artist playing a mark. "Think about it, if your partner kills us, you're the only loose end left."

His calm certainty cut through my panic. Gathering up my courage, I spun to face the guns as well.

The ski-masked figure had the gun aimed at my chest from less than a yard away.

I usually admire someone who does their own dirty work. I just hadn't expected such quick action.

Funeral Guy stood behind his accomplice and to the left. Dressed in a classic gray pinstripe, he readjusted his grip on the revolver as if it were slipping out of his hand. His Adam's apple bobbed. At this rate, he'd shoot one of us accidentally.

Focusing on random details helped contain my fear enough to look at the ninja rather than the gun pointed at my heart. The eyes in the mask were as blue as a Kansas summer sky. But cold, so cold. Though the sweatshirt added some mass, up close, the dark clad form was no bulkier than me.

I picked up my earlier train of thought, trying to fill in the empty squares of the puzzle. Something in the back of my brain screamed for attention. Memories flipped through my mind—Randy's scuffle with the ninja. My ex's cavalier dismissal of his attacker. The black form framed in the headlights. The low voice, filled with anger. Finally Mrs. C's words. "But he's not a—"

Surprise smacked me upside the head. I wasn't sure if my eyes bulged out, but they may have, because that's when a hazy answer appeared on the edge of my mind.

I'd lost a runaway craps dealer.

Crawford was hunting a cop killer.

The police wanted the woman who matched dental x-rays from Kansas.

Everyone was looking for a missing female. Could all those missing people be standing in front of me?

A cloud chose that moment to slip in front of the moon and cast the cemetery into even darker shadows. Telling my wilting nerves the darkness was not an omen, I took a deep breath.

"The police are going to find you." My voice sounded casual. "You know that as well as I do, Cassie."

29

20 Across; 11 Letters;
Clue: Deserved retribution; Just deserts.
Answer: Comeuppance

"Who are you talking to?" Funeral Guy spun to search the trees behind him.

Kevin's gaze darted my way. His flicker of surprise was so fast anyone else would have missed it. But his quick mind caught on like quicksilver.

"Appears you don't know your partner very well," Kevin broke into the conversation. "Cassie, or should I say Lydia, has a history of leaving her buddies to take the fall."

A quick peek across the car showed no sign of either Mrs. C or Marcus. I hoped they were cowering in front of the car.

What was I thinking? I was talking about an eleven-year-old out to prove he was a detective and a woman who'd come to a cemetery in a robe and slippers. The odds of those two being sensible were non-existent.

"What's he talking about?" Funeral Guy pulled me back to the immediate crisis.

"Cassie is her real name." When a branch twitched behind the funeral home director, I put it down to the wind. Until I realized there was no breeze. "Behind the masks and aliases, she's just a small-town girl from Kansas."

With a gun, I added silently. "Oh, and she's a cop killer."

The woman's whole bearing tensed.

"Shooting us won't help you." Best to reinforce that as often as possible. "They found fingerprints on the gun. It's only a matter of time before they make a match."

"I'm not worried." Her voice, low and husky, actually sounded unconcerned. She still made no move to take off the ski mask. Had she hidden behind a false identity for so long she couldn't face being robbed of the safety net?

"As a cop killer she has nothing to lose, but you do." Kevin sounded like he was Funeral Guy's best friend. No one would have guessed he had a gun pointed at him. "Save yourself. She did. Her buddy was executed for killing that cop."

"Shut up." Lydia jabbed her gun at Kevin.

Fear consumed me with such a rush that I almost missed her next words.

"There was nothing I could do. Going back would have gotten us both killed."

For a moment I caught a glimpse of the scared nine-teen-year-old who'd fled in a moment of panic. The one who'd probably steeled herself with that rationalization for decades. Then her gaze turned cold and the moment was gone. Or maybe I'd imagined it.

This was the woman who'd hooked up with Randy in a rundown RV after I left him. The woman who'd worked with the Tang Chi. She'd survived by looking out for herself.

Her gaze narrowed on me. "You've been nothing but trouble with your bumbling around."

I couldn't deny the bumbling, but... "Thanks, but I can't take credit for everything. It's not my fault Duna stole the money and set the ball rolling."

"Randy said you were smart." Her voice held a note of grudging respect. "Smarter than I gave you credit for."

"She surprises a lot of people that way." Kevin's flippant words diverted the woman for a second.

I couldn't let Lydia's comment pass. "Why were you and Randy discussing me?"

"Randy had some hair-brained idea you could find a solution to this mess." Lydia snorted. "He was going to lay it out like a puzzle, with a different twist of course."

After our visit to the funeral home, when I'd bolted from the car.

"He might have been right." She raised the gun higher. "Because you sure don't know when to quit."

Not the first time that comment has been tossed my way.

The darkness behind Funeral Guy moved. Rabi? Whatever was going to happen, it had better be before Mrs. C and Marcus carried out whatever hair-brained scheme they'd cooked up.

Definitely before I got shot.

My peripheral vision caught sight of a shadow as it rose out of the ground six inches behind Funeral Guy.

Kevin stepped forward, his gaze riveted on Funeral Guy. "Think of yourself."

Lydia stepped away. "Shut up."

I inched to within an arm's length of the woman, forcing her attention to me.

"He's right." Funeral Guy gripped the gun with a decidedly shaky hand. "I want no part of murder."

Kevin focused on his pigeon as if Rabi wasn't standing behind the man ready to pounce. "You made the right decision. There's no need for more deaths."

Funeral Guy couldn't answer. One of Rabi's hands was clasped over the guy's mouth and nostrils. His other hand grabbed the gun out of suddenly slack fingers.

"Why don't you leave?" I gestured toward her car. "Take whatever money or drugs you've got and go. We won't stop you. You can't get us all, not with your buddy switching sides."

"Don't worry about me." Lydia's voice hardened as she spoke. "I'll manage just fine."

I was more concerned about my friends and me. Though, now that Rabi's hand encircled the Funeral Guy's throat, I breathed a little easier.

In only seconds, Funeral Guy went limp. Rabi lowered him to the ground.

Kevin looked at Lydia with a steady gaze. "If you kill us, you'll have to get rid of him, too."

"You and I are partners." Though Lydia kept her gaze on me, her comment was obviously aimed at the now unconscious Funeral Guy. "Have I ever let you down?"

Panic filled me as I realized she'd expect an answer. "If you're going to kill me, grant me a request."

I brought my hands in front of my chest, palms together, hoping I remembered the self-defense move correctly. Now I wish I'd paid more attention to the teacher's instructions than his looks.

She gave a short laugh. "One final prayer?"

"No." I thrust my hands between her arms then flung them up and apart.

Her gun hand sailed wide.

I ducked as a deafening shot exploded by my ear.

Rabi sprung up behind her like a silent movie come to life. He locked his forearm around her neck. His other hand trapped her wrist and twisted.

Kevin slid across the trunk and landed in front of me. "You okay?"

After checking all my body parts for blood and finding none, I managed a nod.

The eerie wail of sirens sounded from the top of the hill. Red and blue lights sped down the twisting drive like a multi-colored centipede.

"Now the cops show up," I muttered. "Isn't the cavalry supposed to rush in *before* the crisis?"

Kevin offered a cheeky smile and put a strong arm around my waist. "Better late than never."

I didn't intend to take this situation nearly that well. But for the moment, I hid my shaking hands by holding them against my ribs. "I'm putting in for hazard pay."

"OOOhhh me slippers. Me poor slippers." A mournful wail in a British accent came from the front of the car.

Marcus careened toward me; arms open wide. "I knew you could do it."

I braced my ribs for the impact, but he stopped inches short and gave me a cheeky grin. "Mrs. Colchester and I were going to help. But you and Kevin had her all the way."

I wondered what their 'help' would have been, then decided I didn't want to know.

Mrs. C only had eyes for her slippers. The pink balls of fluff were speckled with grass and matted with dew and dirt.

"We can put into Crawford for a replacement pair." The look on my boss's face when he saw that on the expense account would be worth it.

Dark forms flowed out of the shadows and coalesced into five bulky figures in riot gear with SWAT emblazoned on their chest. The first figure pointed his weapon at Funeral Guy while two team members stopped to check the still form.

I was in no mood to be grateful as I realized they'd been hiding in the bushes while I sweated bullets. "What took you so long?"

The leader gestured to Lydia/Cassie, and two squad members took her from Rabi and cuffed her.

"Everyone okay?" The leader did a double take when he saw Mrs. C, but he shifted his gaze to Rabi without waiting for an answer. "We got into position as you made your move. You had things under control so we waited."

Rabi nodded.

"Whose dumb idea was that?" As far as I was concerned, they could've gotten involved a whole lot sooner.

"You were in no danger," the leader assured me.

It hadn't felt like "no danger". I opened my mouth, but by the time I sucked in a lung full of air, I was too late.

"T.R. had it under control," Marcus told the guy blithely, shifting to face them.

Gathering my strength, I rolled my eyes and stepped out of Kevin's warm arms.

The SWAT guy finished reading Lydia her rights. They'd pulled off the ski mask. A lock of pale blond hair with dark roots curled along the side of her face. Sweat plastered it to her cheek.

Now that the crisis was over, weariness sapped my animosity. However, from the glare in Lydia's eyes, she was still spoiling for a fight.

"The cops would never have found the body if you hadn't gone looking for it," Lydia spat the words at me.

"You're giving me way too much credit." I didn't want to argue. I wanted to go home and spend some quality time with my bed.

"Our team had you nailed." Marcus jabbed a finger at the woman. "My buddy and I did the legwork. Kevin and Rabi were the muscle, and Jimbo and Mrs. C were the runners."

Marcus generously included everyone. "T.R. was the brains the whole way."

Next thing you know he'd crown me queen of the detectives.

The cops were staring at me as if they were taking him seriously. This was getting out of hand, not to mention embarrassing.

"Marcus, enough." I put all the force I could muster into the words. On my best days, it's all I can do to rein in the boy, and this wasn't one of my best days. He carried on as if he hadn't heard me.

"Once T.R. knew the dead lady wasn't Cassie Reed, she figured Randy was in deep. We already knew about the mayor's files, and they linked him to Randy." Thankfully, he paused for breath.

I straightened and shook my head. I didn't need the

cops getting annoyed. "The lead detective and her team had those angles covered."

"You were the one who found Randy's hiding place." Marcus refused to let the matter drop.

"A lucky guess. I grew up with him," I said.

"You saved his life when she tried to kill him." Marcus pointed an accusing finger at Lydia.

"I almost had him, too," she forced the words through gritted teeth.

I was tempted to point out how tacky it was to argue with an eleven-year-old, but her comment reminded me of an unanswered question in my puzzle. Besides if Lydia Storm started talking, Marcus might settle. "Why *were* you after Randy? You had to know he wouldn't turn on you."

Lydia looked down her nose at me. "You don't know anything, do you?"

Marcus leaped forward and jabbed a finger at her. "She knew enough to catch you."

The woman kicked at him. "Shut up, you slanty-eyed runt."

Marcus danced out of reach.

Fury overwhelmed my aches and pains. I grabbed her shirt and pulled her to me. "Don't talk to him like that."

Bodies surged forward. Hands pried at my grip.

I held on and shook her until her head snapped back and forth. "Don't you ever talk to him like that."

The cops finally forced my fingers apart.

Kevin held me while the police pulled her out of my reach. Rabi hadn't interfered.

Shaking off Kevin's hands, I fisted my hands on my hips. "That boy put everyone on your trail by uncovering the file with your identity on it."

If I hadn't been so furious, I'd have stopped, but I was hot. "Because of him, you're going to spend the rest of your days in a cell."

The only change in her expression was a narrowing of her eyes. Not a shred of remorse shown in her gaze.

I put an arm around Marcus's shoulders. Rage must have cleared my mind. I saw the answer.

"You didn't kill Duna to get back the stolen thumb drive." I pointed at her. "You went after the McKiernans because they knew your secret."

Her jaw tightened.

I stopped to let my brain catch up. "The one thing Duna and Randy knew was your real identity. What they didn't know was that you'd left a dead cop in Kansas."

She drew away as if unwilling to hear more.

Busy unraveling the story, I thought out loud. "Why kill them after all these years? Why would they unmask you now?"

I couldn't lock onto a reason. When no one else spoke, the whisper of the leaves filled the silence.

Though desperate for an answer, I was stumped. Then Kevin spoke.

"It's harder than most people realize to cut all ties to the past, to know you can never go home."

The emotion in his tone drew me. He'd split from his family he was a teenager, I hadn't realized it still bothered him.

He met my gaze with a calm expression. "It's different if you find a new family. A home where you were meant to be. Most people aren't that lucky. Duna wanted to go home."

Relieved by the contentment in his eyes, I faced Lydia again. "Duna was tired of being you. Randy mentioned that her former boss died recently. Free of his vendetta, she could reclaim her identity. I'll bet Randy offered to clear your record as well. But for you, there was no going back. You weren't about to trust them with your last secret."

Lydia stared at me for a long minute. The scene could have been frozen in time. Even the cops, who should have led her away long ago, seemed too caught up to interrupt. A glint of emotion surfaced in her eyes.

Remorse? Anger? Maybe she finally realized there was nowhere else to run. She shook her head ever so slightly.

"Duna's embezzlement ruined her former boss. Though he was able to start again, he swore to see her in jail. He kept tabs on her family." A short hiss of air escaped between Lydia's lips. "When he died last month, Randy told me they planned to start the process to clear Duna and me."

"Good old Randy." I knew how stubborn he could be when he thought he was helping. "He was ready to buy everybody off."

Lydia shook her head. "I couldn't let them dig up the past. I snuck in to the gala as one of the hired help. I was hiding in their bedroom, waiting for the guests to leave. Duna came out of nowhere. She assumed the Tang Chi sent me to recover the drive."

That reasoning made no sense, but guilt can mess with a person's mind, and Duna wouldn't have had much time to think it through.

"When we got to the hall closet, she got suspicious. She opened the secret passage and tried to push *me* in." A burst of outrage hardened Lydia's voice. "We fought. Her neck snapped and I shoved her in the passage. When

Randy called her, I shut the panel and ran down the stairs to the kitchen."

"You were gone before the cops were called," I interjected.

"I returned and moved her body to the construction site." Her lips curled up in a cold smile. "The cement would cover the body, and Cassie Reed would disappear. When you led the police to her before that could happen, I figured Randy would ID the body. Cassie Reed would still be dead. That didn't work either. That's when I decided to give the police someone to blame."

I frowned. She'd lost me.

"I found an old yearbook with a note you'd written Randy in high school. So I wrote Duna a letter, signed your name, and left it where Randy would find it," she said smugly.

I'd almost forgotten about the letter that had kept me on the run. "That was you?"

Lydia simply shrugged.

"Enough talk." A plainclothes detective took the other woman by the arm and turned her toward the police cars. "Lydia Storm, alias Cassie Reed, you are under arrest for the murder of Orduna Grimley."

"Also known as Cassie Reed," Kevin muttered in a wry tone.

I had a sudden picture of the media trying to explain how Cassie Reed killed Cassie Reed.

As if a spell had been broken, the cops broke into a flurry of activity. A detective barked orders. "Set the perimeter and secure the scene. Check the mausoleum."

"What about the cop twenty years ago?" Marcus watched them lead Lydia away. "Why didn't they charge her with his murder?"

"They'll wait until they confirm her fingerprints," I said. "They may leave the official arrest for Daniels."

The detective who'd been issuing orders walked up to us and flashed his badge. "I'm Detective Davis. Crawford vouched for you. Leave your names and addresses. You can come to the station in the morning and give your statements."

In my mind, my head was already sinking into a pillow.

Moments later we piled into Rabi's vehicle. I reclaimed my seat in the back with Marcus and Kevin beside me. Mrs. C settled herself in the front.

"Mrs. C, how did you get here at this time of night anyway?" I asked.

"I have an acquaintance who drives a taxi," she said. "I rang him up and he dropped me off."

I shook my head. I should have known. Leaning back, I closed my eyes. Mysterious maids with British accents would have to wait. I'd unraveled enough puzzles for one night.

30

6 Across; 9 Letters;
Clue: Inactivity after exertion.
Answer: Restbreak

Monday morning dawned without a corpse in sight. Just me at my kitchen table with a cup of hazelnut roast, a half-finished crossword puzzle, and a pile of bills I was ready to let slide for another day.

I scribbled in the answer to twenty-five across when the return address of the top envelope caught my eye. It was from the on-line shopping company that accounted for most of my income. I took another sip of coffee as I pulled out the letter.

The front door banged open. I didn't bother looking up. "Marcus, don't throw open the door."

"Sorry." He ran to the table and plopped down. "Kevin sprang Jimbo from jail."

"Hello, ducks." Mrs. C breezed into the kitchen. Blue muffs adorned her feet. The pink ones had been bagged and tagged for Crawford's bookkeeper. "I'm a bit late. I'll make up the time after I've talked to the bobbies."

Wonderful, I still had a maid who did nothing but take up space and drink my coffee. Okay, she does fold and iron clothes, but only when she feels like it. Which, I have to admit, is more than I do. I figure that's why God invented hangers.

I set my cup down with a thud. "The shopping company sent me a check."

"Payday?" Marcus asked.

"I have direct deposit." I bit my lip as I read the letter. "This says 'Please accept these funds for your loyal service.' Hmmmm."

Marcus's expression lit up. "Free money?"

Mrs. C pressed her lips together. Lines furrowed her brow. She looked as worried as I felt.

"There's no such thing as free money." I fingered the check. I had a bad feeling. "Why use snail mail? They're an Internet company."

I was debating whether to go with the 'glass-half-empty' or 'glass-half-full' when I saw a second letter from the company.

Marcus knelt on his chair and stretched his body over the table. "Is that another check? We're rich."

At least one of us was an optimist.

Mrs. C's smile appeared forced.

I ripped open the second envelope. No check fell out of this one.

After waiting a full millisecond, Marcus inched farther over the table. "More money?"

My hands fell to my lap. "I've been replaced by a machine."

Talk about a gut punch.

Mrs. C's frown cleared to a resigned expression. She gave my arm a pat. "I'm sorry, ducks."

Marcus's face scrunched up.

I tried to muster my reserves to put on a brave face when a grin split his face.

"That's great."

"Excuse me?" I eyed my miscreant, wondering if the shock had unhinged him. "Have you decided to give up eating?"

"Now you can follow your dream and be a full-time detective."

"That was never my dream." I pointed out. "That's your dream."

The wattage fueling his smile didn't waver. "This is so cool."

Raps on the open door saved me from responding.

Kevin sauntered in, followed by Jimbo.

My buddy headed for the cupboard and grabbed two mugs. "We brought your car back."

"Thanks." I flicked the letter aside and eyed Jimbo who quietly accepted a cup of coffee. "How are you doing?"

He shrugged. "I knew you guys wouldn't let me down."

"You're one of the team," Marcus assured him. "Now, you can be part of our new detective agency."

Kevin snagged a chair and flipped it backward, before sitting and facing me. "Going into business for yourself?"

I fanned the check and both letters, explaining my upcoming free time.

His response was a smile that equaled my son's. "That's perfect."

I tossed the letters in the air, careful to note where the check landed. "Am I the only one who sees imminent poverty as a bad thing?"

"This couldn't have worked out better if I'd planned it." Kevin inched his chair closer to the table. "I've been developing plans for a partnership. This time my proposition is one you can't refuse."

He paused, obviously for effect.

I crossed my legs, folded my arms over my chest, and waited.

Kevin shot Marcus a conspiratorial look before aiming his smile at me. "Have you forgotten the woman at the Blue Bayou? Twenty-four-hundred dollars?"

I gasped, stunned to admit even to myself that I *had* forgotten.

"Oh, good show," Mrs. C said as she applauded.

I put my hand over my open mouth. "We're splitting it?"

"What about me?" Marcus fisted his hands on his hips.

"We're all in this together." Kevin held out his fist for Marcus to knock knuckles. "That's where the partnership comes into play."

"We could open the Belden Detective Agency," Marcus said.

"I'd hate to take business away from Crawford." Kevin's solemn expression gave every indication of considering the idea. "Especially when it's easier to grab a piece of his action. We already have an 'in' with his latest operative."

He jerked his head in my direction.

Marcus stroked his chin.

He looked so serious I had to bite my lip to keep from laughing.

"I didn't think of that," my son said. "What's your plan?"

"I'd like to know, too." I chimed in. "Explain this partnership."

I narrowed my gaze in silent warning that it had better not involve any hint of a romantic proposal.

From the twinkle in his eye, Kevin had evidently read my mind again. He took another sip of coffee, dragging out the moment. "This is about a handyman and house painting company of our very own."

"That's a great idea." For once I didn't mind that my mouth by-passed my brain. His plan dovetailed with on and off imaginings we'd discussed for years. Proposals to be our own bosses. To do more than scrape by. To build Marcus a secure future. "The windfall is a perfect opportunity to make our dreams reality."

Marcus raised his glass of orange juice in my direction as if in salute. "And you can still be a PI. We'll need the money."

I wasn't sure I liked the sound of that. However, he had a point. It would take time for a small business to pull in enough cash to survive on. Reluctantly, I gave in. "At least surveillance mostly involves sitting on my butt."

"Wait until Rabi hears the news." Marcus's grin couldn't have gotten any wider.

As if on cue another knock sounded. A chorus of "Come in" echoed before I could open my mouth. I smiled into my cup. Who needs money? I had family and friends.

Rabi ambled in and accepted a cup of coffee from Kevin.

Marcus picked up his glass and smiled. "Rabi, guess what?"

And he was off. Marcus announced the news in a rapid-fire delivery that required only a slight clarification. Just when I thought he'd wound down, he took another breath. "Now that everybody's here we need a report."

"Good idea." Kevin shot him a nod of approval that set the boy beaming. "Let's start with Randy. Status?"

"He'll live," I said, setting aside my list of items required for opening a business. "The gaming commission and the Feds are both in line to question him. He'll have to come clean on his business associates if he wants to avoid hard time. He'll probably have to go into witness protection. Maybe even get a real job since his fortune was due to insider trading and money laundering."

All the money in the world wouldn't buy him out of his troubles. I almost felt sorry for him.

Almost.

"Are we going rich when he dies?" Marcus asked.

I shook my head. My pot of gold had vanished as quickly as it had formed. "He doesn't have the money for the payments. With Duna dead, he also has no reason for the policy. He's letting it lapse."

An unexpected knock on the door sounded above Marcus's disappointed groan.

I looked around. "Who's left?"

"Can't be Randy this time," Kevin quipped.

I shot him a withering look and started to stand, halfway up I decided it wasn't worth the effort. I plopped into my chair. "Come in."

When Joe strode in I almost dropped my teeth.

Caught in the act of removing a bona fide cowboy hat, his liquid brown eyes lit with a slow smile. "Mornin'."

Busy debating whether or not he had a dimple in his right cheek, a moment passed before my brain focused. "Good morning. Would you like some coffee?"

"If you have enough," he said. "Sure smells good."

"There's always plenty." I tried to act casual in the face of six pairs of eyes studying my every move. "You know everybody?"

"I don't think so," he admitted.

After introductions were made and coffee poured, he lowered his cup. "Crawford sent me over to give you the latest updates."

Marcus scooched up his chair. "More updates."

I was going to have to talk to that boy. I diverted my gaze to Cowboy Joe. "Lydia?"

He nodded. "They matched her fingerprints with the murder weapon. Daniels officially charged Lydia, aka Cassie Reed, with killing my father. He's headed home with the news."

"Must be a big relief to have it over," I said.

"It is," he said with a nod.

"You said Daniels is leaving. What about you?" I asked.

He shook his head. "I didn't run for sheriff last month. I'd already decided no matter what happened it was time to move on. I'll be working for Crawford for a while."

Caught by surprise, I noticed a tightening of Kevin's expression.

"This case closed a lot of old files," I said.

"When are we were going to the police station?" Marcus interjected.

"We can leave now." I happily focused on the present. "Rabi, can you go with us?"

He agreed. "My boss said I could make up the time."

"Think they'll fingerprint us?" Marcus asked.

"Been there. Done that," Jimbo answered. "I'm going home."

"That ink is hard to get off," Mrs. Colchester assured him.

Over the past few days, the woman had shown a definite familiarity with the wrong side of the law. I opened my mouth to broach the subject.

"I have the Caddy for anyone who wants to visit the cops in style," Kevin said.

I shook my head. "Jimbo'll have to bail you out when the police run a check and realize that thing's hot."

"Oh, ye of little faith." Kevin graced me with a compassionate look. "Juan assured me the car is legit."

"Tell it to the cops."

Kevin's gaze flicked to Joe. "Not all of us will fit in the Caddy."

"Someone can drive with me," Cowboy Joe offered.

Kevin's carefully neutral tone didn't escape me. Nor did his glance in my direction.

I didn't hesitate. It would be wrong not to close the case in the big white elephant, not to mention with my business partner and best friend. After all, he'd gone body hunting with me.

Marcus jumped out of his chair. "I'm driving with Kevin."

"Me, too," I said. "No telling where you two will land without my supervision."

Kevin's expression softened. He pushed back his chair and put a hand on Marcus's shoulder.

Mrs. C, Rabi, and Jimbo opted to drive with Cowboy Joe.

"That'd be fine," he said with one of his slow smiles.

Marcus looked around with a hopeful expression. "Think they'll show us jail cells?"

"Marcus." I put a warning note in my voice, but nothing could dampen his spirits.

"I can't promise anything," Cowboy Joe said. "But I know a few detectives."

"All right." Marcus shared a grin with the others. His energy was contagious. "I can't wait to tell everybody we solved the case of the missing wife."

I rolled my eyes. "That sounds like an episode of Perry Mason."

"We're better than him." Kevin grinned. Like me, he loved nothing more than watching old detective reruns on Friday night. "They never had to find *two* missing wives."

"That's right." Marcus jabbed a finger at Kevin. "We found them both, wifey-number-two and Cassie Reed."

I put a hand on my hip. "Do you have to encourage him?"

Kevin looked far too pleased with himself. He didn't even respond to my mock outrage.

Marcus thrust a fist into the air. "The Belden Detective Agency has solved its first case."

I took a sip from my mug. "What is it with you and this Belden Detective Agency business?"

He fiddled with his glass of orange juice, looking suddenly shy. "No one ever breaks up a successful team."

My heart melted at the determined set to his chin. As if I'd ever let anyone take him away.

"No one's going to break us up. We're family." I met

his gaze then scanned the circle of faces. "Even I have to admit we make a good team."

Marcus grinned and raised his glass. "The Belden Detective Agency."

I gave in and clinked my mug to his glass. The others raised their cups as well. Even Cowboy Joe joined the circle. After the clinking of glasses was complete, we filed out the door. When the others clattered down the stairs, Kevin and Marcus stayed while I locked the door.

"You realize my first case may be my last," I said.

Marcus eyed me as if I'd just canceled Christmas. "No way. We're just beginning."

"This case was a fluke." I didn't want him wandering the streets looking for crimes to solve. "No one's going to break us up. Ever. But depending on Crawford's caseload, I may go back to filing or research."

Kevin frowned as we walked down the narrow wooden stairs. "What's the fun in that?"

I shot him a look over my shoulder. "My bruised ribs like being on the sidelines. No more balcony leaping. No more bodies."

Marcus gave an exaggerated sigh. "Those were the best parts."

"I'm telling Crawford to go easy on me. No more murders."

Marcus ran ahead and opened the door. Sunlight bounced off his black hair and golden-hued skin. "You're a natural."

"It's a gift." Kevin joined Marcus at the door. "My mother always said everyone is born with a talent for something. I think we found yours, Belden."

Just my luck. "How did my talent for solving puzzles get tied up with dead bodies?"

I gave a fatalistic sigh then brightened at the familiar ding-ding of an ice-cream truck. Murder and mayhem could wait. "Anyone up for ice cream before we head to the police station?"

After all, a girl's gotta have priorities. With all the answers to the murder puzzle filled in, I could finally focus on more important things. Cookie dough ice cream? Or praline pecan?

NEXT IN THE SERIES

Read Two Down in Tahoe book two in the series now:
    https://www.amazon.com/Two-Down-Tahoe-Cross-word-Mystery-ebook/dp/B0996C8ZBY/ref

TWO DOWN IN TAHOE

9 Down; 4 Letters;
Clue: To discover by chance.
Answer: Find

"We need an electric drill." Marcus Belden, my eleven-year-old foster son, stared at the yellow, plastic box on the kitchen table with a laser-like intensity. His eyes narrowed in determination as he flipped a pancake onto the serving dish.

His golden-hued skin and straight, silky black hair marked his Korean ancestry, but the mischievous gleam in his dark eyes was all him. He's my ray of sunshine. Even if he does eat me out of house and home, and even if he is the reason I was in the Emergency Room of Langsdale, Nevada, until midnight last night.

Which is where I got the mysterious box.

Relishing the smell of bacon hanging in the air, I

sipped my hazelnut-flavored coffee. A rush of affection overwhelmed me at the sight of the boy-child who had stolen my heart and turned my life upside down several years ago. In the next heartbeat, a dose of reality brought me back to the moment. "We don't have a drill."

The box looked like a small self-contained toolbox, about the size of a paperback. Hard molded plastic, five-by-seven inches, then two-inches deep. The latch was a simple tab. It should have opened with the flip of a thumb.

It didn't. Someone had glued it shut.

I frowned at Marcus's head, which had inserted itself into my line of vision. Putting my finger on his straight, black hair, I gently pushed him away. "You need to stop messing with that box."

"We have to get it open."

"No, we don't." A lack of caffeine after a late night had dampened both my curiosity and my trepidation. "Whatever is in here will keep. It obviously wasn't meant to be opened easily."

The unsettling thought sent a shiver up my spine. Questions and possibilities pulled at me, but I squashed them. I did not need trouble.

"What if Rickson needs help?" Marcus asked. "The guy who chased him through the ER had a gun."

"Rickson knows where to find me," I said. "Which is more than I can say about him. Besides, the cops arrested the other guy."

Welcome to my life. Tracy Rae Belden. Thirty-five-years-old. Five-nine. Spiky brown hair that goes in and out of style. Slim.

Moderately slim. Okay, not as slim as I used to be, but who steps on the scale more than once every three years?

"Cook or eat." I pointed to the stove then a chair. "I'm done discussing this box."

Marcus shot me a frown. "This isn't over."

"I didn't think it was." I gave him a mock glare. As expected, my stern words did no apparent damage to his psyche. After being abandoned at a young age, he'd lived on the streets for several years. He was tough. At least on the outside.

I met him years ago when he tried to steal my wallet. Instead, he stole my heart. We bonded over mystery stories in the local library. Including, yes, the Trixie Belden Young Adult mysteries from decades ago, my supposed 'cousin'.

Yes, I'm shameless. It's best to know that up front.

I needed an 'in'" to get the boy off the streets. It worked. He's been living with me ever since as a ward of the state. I'm trying to make the arrangement permanent, but a tsunami of bureaucratic regulations has the matter tied up in a thousand knots.

Unlike my foster son, I don't look for trouble. I don't have to, it finds me. Like yesterday. At nine o'clock in the morning, a pipe burst in my bathroom. At ten last night, Marcus cut his hand on a broken car window. In between, B & T Inc., the fledgling handyman business my best friend and I recently started, lost two jobs.

Big jobs, with paychecks that would have paid the rent for months. Now my only guaranteed income was my part-time gig as a private detective. That's the one that pays the bills.

Well, most of the bills. Most of the time.

That's also the one that gets me in trouble with my boy-child. My goal as a PI is to cash the paycheck. Period.

His goal is to live up to our family heritage and solve the case, whether we get paid or not.

That's just crazy talk.

The job I enjoy the most, pays the least. It's a work-for-hire gig creating crossword puzzles. The money barely keeps me in flavored coffee, but puzzles are my addiction. Once I start one, I have to solve it to the very last square or it haunts me. Besides, creating clues and answers that I have total control over keeps me on the right side of sane.

I picked up my cup of coffee. The aroma alone woke up the blood vessels in my brain, ambrosia with a touch of hazelnut. "If Rickson doesn't get in touch this morning, I'll contact Crawford and see what's going on."

"Bossman left for his Canada fishing trip yesterday." Marcus, who wanted nothing more than to be a PI, made it sound like we both worked for Crawford Investigations.

"Oh, I forgot." Typical male. Never around when you need him. I pulled my rattled thoughts together. "That area doesn't have cell service."

Marcus punched me lightly in the shoulder. "Until he returns, you're in charge."

Unlike my crossword puzzles, I couldn't solve this puzzle by switching out the clues and answers. The yellow box sat there taunting me. What could it contain?

My first guess? A seven-letter word for agitate or harass.

Answer: trouble.

"We have to investigate." My son waved the box in front of my face.

I refused to take the bait. Keeping food on the table fed the body. Creating crossword puzzles fed the soul. Being in charge brought only trouble.

"Getting up to speed on Rickson's case is your duty." An overly somber note deepened Marcus's tone, in contrast to his slim, undersized frame. "This is a piece of a puzzle."

The boy knew my weakness.

"Rickson is your co-worker. Your friend. Your buddy." His tone rose as my bored expression remained unchanged. "How can you leave him out in the cold?"

Drama never takes a day off in this house.

"Langsdale is three hours north of Las Vegas. It's never cold here." I can state the obvious, too. It's also best to take every chance I can to ground the boy in reality, rather than feed his flights of fantasy.

"I was speaking metaphorically." Marcus scrunched up his nose, evidently looking for another argument. "You won't be able to live with yourself if you do nothing."

"I'll be fine," I assured him. "I'm good at doing nothing. Besides, Rickson hasn't asked for my help and I doubt he needs it."

"He hunted you down in the ER." Marcus pointed the pancake flipper at me. "He passed you the box while staring down the barrel of a police gun."

Good grief. "I was there. Remember? The cops never drew their guns."

Marcus threw his hands up in the air. "Rickson was chased by a vicious assailant. Did you miss that?"

"Rickson is six-foot-nine in his stocking feet. He's over three-hundred pounds of solid muscle. David Ferguson, the skinny, redheaded guy who chased him and claimed Rickson stole that box, was maybe five-seven."

My son drew his undersized frame up to full height. "Vicious can come in small packages."

I had no comeback. Fighting a smile, I raised my coffee in salute and took a long sip. Ferguson's claim had started me wondering what Rickson had gotten himself into with his latest case. Unfortunately, Crawford, my boss of seven years, my friend for fifteen, wasn't around to ask.

Though Rickson and I both worked for Crawford Investigations, the big guy is a retired homicide detective, twenty-five years on the force. I'm a newbie with less than a year under my belt as a solo investigator in the field.

Langsdale has a relatively small population of twenty-two thousand, but the city has transformed itself from a once thriving town of wealthy silver mines into a high-end resort. The pricey boutiques, eclectic gourmet eateries, and high-priced galleries offering exclusive auctions, attract both national and international tourists. All awash with disposable income. A specialist was even brought in to design a world-class golf course. The constant flow of tourists, residents, and cash keep Crawford Investigations plenty busy.

Unfortunately, my income barely makes it from one month to the next. My second-floor apartment sits in a so-so neighborhood in a faded, three-story brick building. My main floor is a large, open room. A kitchenette in the front corner overlooks the street. My bedroom is in the back corner. Marcus's bedroom is up a small flight of stairs on the second level.

"Oh, come on, T.R." The boy dropped his actor's mask, replacing it with a thirty-year-old attitude in an eleven-year-old body. "I won't survive not knowing what's inside or who sent it."

"Frustration is good for the soul." I didn't even flinch

at hearing my grandmother's words coming out of my mouth. "It builds character."

"I have enough character," he assured me with aplomb. "What I need, after my tortured, deprived childhood, is instant gratification."

"If you're done cooking, turn off the burners." I pushed myself to my feet. "I'll put this somewhere safe and we'll deal with it later."

When a stubborn gleam shown in his eyes, I braced myself for battle. Instead, he heaved a sigh. "Don't do anything with it behind my back."

"Don't worry," I assured him as I headed into the other room. "I have no intention of messing with this thing."

I stepped out of his line of sight. Feeling like a child playing hide-and-seek, I checked over my shoulder before hiding the package.

As I returned to the kitchen, Marcus flipped the last pancake from the grill to the platter. "What if we x-ray the box?"

Same song, second verse. Luckily, a drumbeat on the door saved me. "Come in."

Kevin Tanner, twenty-eight-years-old, longtime friend, current business partner, and recently minted boyfriend opened the door. He strode across the large, open living room like a man on a mission.

My heart did a little skip at the sight of him. I couldn't stop the smile that touched my lips. I've known him for ten years. He was eighteen when we met, so our instant chemistry settled into the best-friends category. As the years flew by, he started to push for more, but I resisted.

My luck with love makes my shaky bank account look good. I hated the thought of risking our friendship.

However, having fought against my attraction and affection for several years, all the walls I'd built crumbled a few weeks ago.

Maybe because one of my last investigations brought me up close and personal with my ex. At some point during that case, I realized how much I'd grown up since I'd made the mistake of marrying an arrogant, self-absorbed man-child.

I knew I would never have cause to doubt Kevin's character, loyalty, or love.

My call to action came when Marcus told me about the blind date Kevin's work buddies had set him up on. Hurt and fury erupted in me like a volcano. I was ready to find him and the unknown woman and do... I don't know what.

That's when my son shrugged and said, "Why do you care? It's not like you and Kevin are dating."

I should have smelled a Marcus-sized setup that instant, but I had boiling lava in my veins. When I calmed down, I realized that due to my reluctance to commit, I might lose Kevin entirely. The very thought opened a void in my heart.

Still, I hesitated. Though I trust him with my heart and my son, part of me wondered if, after the newness of romance wore off, he'd wake up one day and change his mind.

But I screwed up my courage to the sticking point and decided to move forward. Two days later I ambushed Kevin and asked him out on an official date. I later learned that the alleged blind date had been a work party.

Since our 'getting to know you' stage has been the longest one in history, we've leaped into the relationship with both feet. Though finding time alone isn't easy, thanks to my inquisitive son, I love the feeling of being in love.

The memories and conversations flashed through my mind as my boyfriend walked across the room. The fact that his T-shirt didn't have a wrinkle on it and his khaki pants were perfectly pleated didn't surprise me. I just don't know how he manages it. My clothes don't leave the store looking that good.

Kevin stands six-foot-two and has a body hardened by years of working construction. Add to that the fact that he's been graced with wavy black hair and blue eyes to die for and it's hard to make him look bad.

"Little early to be spacing out, Belden." He pulled out a chair and shot me a distracted look that seemed at odds with his teasing words. Leaning over, he brushed a kiss across my lips.

I blamed my woolgathering on last night's ER adventure and a dangerously low caffeine level. Okay, blame it on love. Ignoring the uncertainty coiling in my gut, I went on the offense. "You look worried. Does Juan want the Great White Beast back?"

Kevin froze in the act of grabbing a mug off the shelf and shot me a look of recrimination. "Don't even joke about that."

He's currently making payments to his mechanic on a 1967 pearly white Cadillac, otherwise known as the Great White Beast.

I smiled. "Someday the rightful owners will find out where their Caddy is and you'll be out the money you've spent."

When he didn't leap to the defense of his beloved vehicle, I knew something had him worried.

"What's up?" I asked, all too willing to forget my own troubles.

Marcus leaned over the table. "What's the prob, man? Spit it out."

Kevin's smile didn't quite reach his eyes. He raked a hand through his hair. "I'm not sure where to begin."

The scent of fresh warm pancakes hit me. "A full stomach always helps me think."

Kevin's expression lightened and he sniffed. "Smells good."

"Thank you," I said with pride of ownership.

Hesitation, or perhaps fear, flashed in his eyes. "You made the pancakes?"

"I could have." None of my past attempts had ever looked this good, but I *could* have.

Marcus set the platter of hotcakes on the table next to a plate of bacon. His expression never wavered. Cooking isn't his only talent. He's a great little con artist.

Kevin studied the stove. "No smoke. No scorched grill. I'm betting on the kid."

So, I'm not Betty Crocker. "It's not my fault the batter got in the burners. The stove top moved when I wasn't looking."

Kevin speared a couple of hotcakes. "Happens to a lot of people."

"I helped." I pointed at the plastic bottle of syrup. "I nuked it with my own little hands. See? The label reads Hot."

"I'm impressed," Kevin assured me.

For the next minutes, we occupied ourselves with smearing butter and pouring syrup until I broke the silence. "Tell me what's got you worried."

Kevin took a bite. "Godert has been named as Murph's replacement."

"Your old boss?" I don't know why I asked. I mean, how many Murphs could a guy know? I blame Rickson's package for my confusion. "You were happy when Murph retired. I was there when we waved him and his wife off for their RV tour of America."

"What's bad is that his replacement has it in for me." Kevin bit off the words. "I've had run-ins with Godert in the past. Now, he's changed my schedule and I'm on the list for reduced hours."

I grimaced in sympathy. "That's not going to pay the rent."

"Let's get back to the box," Marcus said.

I sighed. That's my boy—never say die. I set my mug down and met his gaze. "Kevin and I are talking."

"You and I were talking about the box before he came." Marcus's innocent stare was amazingly believable.

"Forget the box," I said, wishing I could.

Kevin didn't even ask. He mopped up his syrup with a bite of pancakes and bacon and lifted his gaze to Marcus. "What happened to your hand?"

Marcus wiggled his fingers to show the bandage to better advantage. "Cut it on Mr. Rheault's broken windshield last night at ten o'clock. We were in the ER until after midnight."

Kevin shifted his gaze to me as I picked up my mug. "What was he doing in the street at that time of night?"

"Do you know, you're the first person who asked me that?" Gratified someone else showed an interest in my son's welfare, I never dreamt of taking offense. During the years Marcus has been in my life, Kevin has spent as much time raising the boy as I have.

"After Mrs. Colchester woke us up for the street fight, I saved the kitten from the fire." Having given his version, Marcus, took a bite of pancake.

Kevin favored me with a raised brow.

"It sounds so much worse in the light of day." I took a breath then decided we didn't have time for the gory details. "A few facts are missing, but the players are there."

"Uh-huh." Kevin sipped his coffee. He knew Mrs. C, my seventy-plus landlady, well enough not to be surprised at her role in the latest Belden crisis. "And in gratitude for his rescue, the kitten gave you this mysterious box we're going to drill open?"

Marcus laughed. "Rickson slipped the box to T.R. after a gunfight in the Emergency Room."

Kevin froze, then looked at me for a reality check. A rattling windowpane filled the silence.

Marcus's explanation sounded like a TV blurb for an adventure show. I raised my mug to my lips. "I hate to admit it, but that's pretty much what happened."

Kevin cocked his head. "Hear that?"

The window rattled louder this time. It sounded like it was coming from upstairs.

"It's in the bathroom." Marcus bolted out of his chair.

I caught him on the fly without spilling a drop of coffee.

It's taken some time, but I'm definitely getting the hang of this parenting biz. I put aside my cup. "Stay here."

Turning toward the stairs, I grabbed the wooden bat leaning against the railing. I may not be an Iron Chef, but a tomboy past has left me with a swing that can clear the bases. It's come in handy during some of my stints for

Crawford. I told myself the noise was nothing but the wind or perhaps an errant squirrel dropping by for breakfast.

Halfway up the steps, I felt, more than saw, Kevin behind me.

"Hey, sport," Kevin spoke over his shoulder to my son. "How about you lock the door so nobody sneaks up behind us?"

Marcus nodded and ran toward the door.

Kevin has a knack with the boy.

I favored my buddy with a raised brow. "You know something I don't?"

"I've learned to cover all exits when I'm with you." He came even with me and reached for the bat as we walked into Marcus's bedroom. "I'll go first."

I pulled the bat out of his reach. I was in the mood to bash somebody. "You might be too nice."

Kevin wisely didn't comment.

I stepped over an electronic robot then did a two-step to avoid a remote-control truck.

"Maybe we should let them come in and take their chances with the obstacle course," Kevin whispered.

I swallowed a nervous laugh.

A tapping sounded from behind the bathroom door. I stepped to one side, gripping the bat firmly.

Kevin twisted the knob and flung the door open.

I jumped into the room, bat poised for a home run. The room and the lone window were empty. Some of the tension drained away. "Nobody's here."

As my shoulders relaxed, a dark-haired form popped up outside the window. The man's shoulders were wide enough for an elephant, and the face would have looked at home in a police line-up.

My heart leaped into my throat. The bat was already in motion. I swung for the outfield with the guy's head as the ball. Then my brain recognized the face. "Rickson!"

I almost pulled a muscle trying not to break my bathroom window. Catching my balance, I watched as Kevin flipped the lock and opened the pane.

Anxious to vent my pent-up nerves, I fixed Rickson with a glare. "You're a detective. You can't find the front door?"

Minutes later, Rickson finished squirming through the window and stretched to his full height. In these close quarters, he made Kevin look like a child.

"When did you start double locking the window?" Rickson asked in an aggrieved tone.

"Since people started using it as a separate entrance."

"Hey, Kev." Rickson's smile brought to life a puckered scar that ran across his right cheek. "How you doing?"

Kevin leaned against the bathroom door, twirling the bat. "Not bad. You?"

Rickson shrugged. "Can't complain."

"If you two are done with the social niceties, how about we get some breathing space?" I gestured toward the door.

Kevin spun around, hoisted the bat on his shoulder, and led the way through Marcus's bedroom.

The boy-child peered at us from the top stair. His face lit with a smile. "Hey, Chichi."

"Rickshaw boy, you got the goods?" Rickson asked.

Rickson's Chinese mother endowed him with his golden-hued skin, his nickname, and the right to make Asian jokes. His English father accounted for his size, his police career, and a love of soccer, all of which had contributed to his bashed-in face and assorted scars. "Do I smell the Korean pancake special?"

Moments later the three of us watched Rickson plow through the remainder of the pancakes and bacon.

"You do the best flapjacks I ever ate, kid."

What was it with men and food? I'd waited long enough for an explanation, time for the thumbscrews. "Today, you crawl in my window. Last night, you hunted me down and passed me a box full of incriminating evidence. What gives?"

Rickson's face lost all expression. Eyes wide, face pale, he grabbed my shoulders with a tight grip. "What evidence? Not the box? Tell me you didn't open it."

I stared at him, stunned by the raw fear that roughened his tone.

The crossword puzzle related to this book (w/ the solution) can be solved online at http://crossword.info/ Paws42/mystery_puzzle_1

MEET THE AUTHOR

I didn't pursue a writing career until I was well out of college. However, a lifelong love of reading and solving puzzles proved to be good training when the writing bug bit. While I enjoy reading many different types of books, from thrillers to fantasy to science fiction, mysteries have always intrigued me.

Working on jigsaw puzzles as well as crossword puzzles with my family has also been a constant part of my life. A habit that carries through to today.

In the Crossword Puzzle Mystery Series, my love of writing and solving puzzles came together. I hope you love the quirky characters and their high-spirited adventures as much I enjoy writing them.

To learn more about the Crossword Puzzle Cozy Mystery series, visit my website www.louisefoster.com and sign up for my newsletter. You can also solve a crossword puzzle related to each of the books as they're released, either on-line or by downloading it.

Find me on Facebook: Louise Foster, Author

I love to hear from readers: email me

Thank you for giving me your time to read this book and your support by buying it. I don't take either for granted.

Louise Foster

DEAR READERS

Welcome to the adventures of Tracy Belden and her son, Marcus, along w/ their adopted family: Kevin Tanner, Mrs. Colchester, and Jack Rabi as they are drawn into Tracy's PI cases. While Tracy would prefer to drink her flavored coffee and create crossword puzzles, like most of us, she has to pay the bills and keep food on the table. So, she puts her puzzle solving talents to good use as she dives into her cases.

While most of her cases are non-violent, the murder cases are often so complicated she despairs of solving them. However, Marcus, with the confidence of youth and his pride in the detecting heritage of the Belden family, never wavers in his belief that the Belden Agency can solve any case as long as they work together.

Among the many books I read while growing up was the YA mystery series involving Trixie Belden and her group of young friends. While no part of this book is based on those stories, Tracy did tell Marcus that she was a distant cousin of Trixie's. Her good intentions were based on her efforts to get him off the streets, but her alleged relationship with Trixie is a claim Tracy is never allowed to forget.

I hope you enjoy your time in Langsdale, Nevada, and the stories of Tracy and her adopted family. If you like the story, please leave a review at your favorite bookseller or at Goodreads.

If you'd like to learn more about the other books in the Crossword Puzzle Cozy Mystery series, please visit my website www.louisefoster.com or my author page on Facebook www.facebook.com/Louise-Foster-Author-107517717508196/

Thank you for buying this book and giving me your time. I don't take either for granted.

Louise Foster

DEAR READERS

Welcome to the adventures of Tracy Belden and her son, Marcus, along w/ their adopted family: Kevin Tanner, Mrs. Colchester, and Jack Rabi as they are drawn into Tracy's PI cases. While Tracy would prefer to drink her flavored coffee and create crossword puzzles, like most of us, she has to pay the bills and keep food on the table. So, she puts her puzzle solving talents to good use as she dives into her cases.

While most of her cases are non-violent, the murder cases are often so complicated she despairs of solving them. However, Marcus, with the confidence of youth and his pride in the detecting heritage of the Belden family, never wavers in his belief that the Belden Agency can solve any case as long as they work together.

Among the many books I read while growing up was the YA mystery series involving Trixie Belden and her group of young friends. While no part of this book is based on those stories, Tracy did tell Marcus that she was a distant cousin of Trixie's. Her good intentions were based on her efforts to get him off the streets, but her alleged relationship with Trixie is a claim Tracy is never allowed to forget.

I hope you enjoy your time in Langsdale, Nevada, and the stories of Tracy and her adopted family. If you like the story, please leave a review at your favorite bookseller or at Goodreads.

If you'd like to learn more about the other books in the Crossword Puzzle Cozy Mystery series, please visit my website www.louisefoster.com or my author page on Facebook www.facebook.com/Louise-Foster-Author-107517717508196/

Thank you for buying this book and giving me your time. I don't take either for granted.

Louise Foster

CROSSWORD PUZZLE COZY MYSTERY SERIES

An Ex in the Puzzle

Tracy Belden's first solo case in the field lands her in the middle of a murder when her ex-husband's second wife disappears and Tracy becomes a suspect.

Two Down in Tahoe

When a PI friend asks for help, Tracy and her trusty gang head to Tahoe, but things go from bad to worse when her friend goes missing and the client dies with Tracy on the scene.

Adventures in Vegas

A getaway weekend in Vegas turns dangerous when Tracy's whistleblowing client is murdered and both the secret files and a priceless golden artifact go missing.

A Question of Murder

Tracy is drawn into the world of fine art and a possible forged masterpiece when a friend's involvement in a present-day murder uncovers a hidden past and a connection to a 50-year-old murder.

Five Clues to a Killer

Tracy Belden and Kevin Tanner's trip to the altar turns deadly when a dead man is discovered at their reception and their best friend is suspected of murder.

Six Across is Murder

Tracy's investigation of a philandering husband is cut short when her client is suspected of murdering the man. As the evidence against her client mounts, Tracy must cut through a tangled trail of money and betrayal to discover the killer.

Glue Guns for Christmas (Novella)

When Tracy Belden is called to the principal's office, she never expects to be handed a case of extortion with a three day deadline to track down a murderer so eight teachers can have a Merry Christmas.

Made in United States
Orlando, FL
01 June 2023

33702614R00224